WHEN THE
MOUNTAINS
DANCE

Also by Christine Toomey

The Saffron Road: A Journey with Buddha's Daughters

WHEN THE MOUNTAINS DANCE

Love, loss and hope in the heart of Italy

CHRISTINE TOOMEY

WEIDENFELD & NICOLSON

First published in Great Britain in 2023 by Weidenfeld & Nicolson
This paperback edition published in 2024 by Weidenfeld & Nicolson,
an imprint of The Orion Publishing Group Ltd
Carmelite House, 50 Victoria Embankment
London EC4Y 0DZ

An Hachette UK Company

1 3 5 7 9 10 8 6 4 2

All internal images courtesy of the author

A CIP catalogue record for this book is
available from the British Library.

ISBN (Mass Market Paperback) 978 1 4746 1465 8
ISBN (eBook) 978 1 4746 1466 5
ISBN (Audio) 978 1 4746 1467 2

Typeset by Born Group
Printed and bound in Great Britain by Clays Ltd, Elcograf S.p.A.

www.weidenfeldandnicolson.co.uk
www.orionbooks.co.uk

For Inés

'A bad earthquake at once destroys our oldest associations: the earth, the very emblem of solidity, has moved beneath our feet like a thin crust over a fluid; one second of time has created in the mind a strange idea of insecurity, which hours of reflection would never have produced.'

Charles Darwin, *Voyage of the Beagle* (1839)

Contents

Prologue

'*Si abita un suolo chiamato per errore terraferma.*'
'We live on land mistakenly called terra firma.'

Erri De Luca, *Naufragio in terra* (2016)

Since ancient times, there have been tales of strange behaviour in the animal kingdom before a major earthquake: birds taking to the wing and bees leaving their hives in unusual numbers, dogs whining for no apparent reason, snakes emerging from their burrows and going suddenly rigid, deep-sea fish rising to the surface.

But the only fleeting warning most humans may have of what is about to overwhelm them are the sounds the earth emits when about to unleash forces capable, quite literally, of moving mountains.

In imperial China, the people of Hebei Province likened the sound they heard before one strong quake in the mid-nineteenth century to the hooves of tens of thousands of galloping horses in retreat as defeated troops took flight. In San Francisco, those who survived the 1906 earthquake say it was preceded by what sounded like a convoy of ore cars rumbling underground. Ahead of Japan's 2011 magnitude 9 Tōhoku earthquake and tsunami, underwater microphones positioned nine hundred miles away, off the Aleutian Islands of Alaska, captured sounds emanating from the earth's crust similar to a rocket launching into space. While in Nepal at the time of the 2015 quake, trekkers in the Himalayas say they heard a noise like jet engines powering overhead moments before it struck.

But for those whose lives and family histories have been rooted for centuries in the Apennine mountains of central Italy, the sound the earth made before it began to shake, violently, on 30 October 2016, was like a great howl, an *urlo* or a *boato* – a ferocious roar. It was, they say, as if the mountains were crying out. As if the very earth were in labour.

In a way, it was.

For as the giant jigsaw puzzle of fault lines threaded throughout the Apennines ruptured, and the central section of this cordillera that forms the spine of Italy convulsed in the country's strongest earthquake for nearly forty years, a geological chain reaction was triggered that changed forever the lay of the land and the lives, including mine, of those above.

The clocks had gone back in the early hours of that Sunday morning. It was the end of daylight-saving time, and many took the opportunity to rest longer in bed. But not Antonio. Those who work the land had been awake since before sunrise and were already outdoors. Sundays are days for tending to chores neglected during the week, and that Sunday Antonio rose as usual at 5.30 a.m. By 7.30 he was preparing the tractor he would need to reach overhanging branches of laurel and lilac to be pruned along the driveway to his farm.

Antonio's farm sits on the outskirts of Amandola, a small medieval town just within the boundaries of the Monti Sibillini national park, a wild and spectacular section of the central Apennines where wolves, bears and wildcats roam and golden eagles soar above forested slopes. Antonio's family have worked this land for generations, originally as sharecroppers under Italy's *mezzadria* system, prevalent until the 1970s, which saw *mezzadri* surrender half of any produce or profit from the land to the *padrone* who owned it. But after decades of back-breaking labour, while also working as a voluntary driver for the Red Cross, Antonio finally bought the farm and raised his family there.

That morning of 30 October, his eleven-year-old grandson Alessandro was by his side. Ever since he was a small boy, Alessandro had been eager to help his grandfather whenever he could and dreamt of one day becoming a farmer just like the *nonno* he adored. They had not yet started the tractor engine, so all was silent but for birdsong and Antonio's patient voice explaining the task at hand.

The sky in those early hours was the colour of Venetian glass tinted turquoise blue, holding promise of a perfect autumn day. There was nothing to suggest a storm was brewing. But above the murmur of Antonio's calm instructions, as if far in the distance, a low rumble could be heard that quickened at lightning speed to the roar of an approaching gale. A sound like a high wind tearing through mountain passes that transformed within seconds to an onslaught coming not from above but deep below, where the earth had begun to tremble. It was a sound that all who live close to the Apennines of central Italy have come to dread.

For months, hundreds of communities in and around this stretch of mountains had been braced for turmoil after a summer of being battered by a series of seemingly never-ending strong tremors and aftershocks – a sequence of such severe and enduring seismic activity as has rarely been experienced in these parts.

When the earth gave its first great heave in the early hours of 24 August it buried nearly three hundred men, women and children beneath the rubble of the medieval town of Amatrice and other towns and villages on the southern edge of the Sibillini and neighbouring mountainous Gran Sasso national park. The discovery of two little sisters locked in an embrace under the wreckage of their home for sixteen hours, the elder shielding her four-year-old sibling until only she could be rescued, was heralded as a defining moment of both sorrow and hope. Tens of thousands were made homeless and countless medieval churches and rare works of art were reduced to dust.

In the wake of the many aftershocks that followed, Italians began speaking of the earth beneath their feet as *la terra ballerina*, the dancing earth. The dance they spoke of was unrelenting. It shredded nerves. But Antonio was not alone in believing the worst to be over.

The first shudders on that October morning were slight. A vibration of the sort you might feel as an express train speeds by a platform. But these quickly grew in intensity to a violent agitation that triggered powerful lateral jolts, as if this central section of the Apennines were being shunted from one set of terrestrial train tracks to another. A manoeuvre that in places tore the sides of mountains apart, leaving dark gashes of freshly exposed rock which stretched for miles.

When the mountains began to howl, Antonio understood immediately what was happening. He had lived through earthquakes before.

But nothing like this.

As man and boy looked towards the fields, they saw the earth moving as if morphing from solid to liquid form. It was as if this span of pastures that stretched away into the mountains had been seized by an apprentice god intent on reshaping it with a cosmic hammer.

Long before the advent of the scientific revolution brought more rational explanations for such shattering shifts in the lay of the land, ancient civilisations did indeed attribute the shaking of the ground to the movement of gods, demons and mythical creatures. The ancient Greeks believed it was Poseidon, god of the sea, striking out in anger with his trident. The Japanese thought that a giant catfish called Namazu was thrashing about in underground mud. For Mexico's Aztecs it was caused by a jaguar leaping towards the sun, and Native Americans in the Pacific Northwest believed that it resulted from fights between a thunderbird and a whale.

Regardless of the cause, Antonio's only thoughts were for the safety of his family. With his grandson Alessandro clutching his waist, he urgently instructed the boy to look at the ground, as if blocking his sight might lessen the anguish of what was unfolding. But neither covered their ears, and the sound of timber groaning, of buildings splitting and collapsing, was impossible to block out.

In those moments, Antonio heard his wife screaming and, looking towards the old farmhouse, saw her scrambling from the front door behind Alessandro's mother, father and younger brother. They escaped the building just as one of its far walls collapsed and part of an old chapel that had stood within the boundaries of the farm since 1611 crumbled to the ground.

Many of the inhabitants of towns like Amandola were still in bed or just beginning their morning routine. Brushing hair, getting dressed, making coffee, they froze where they sat or stood, some crying out 'terremoto!' – earthquake! – less warning than terrified confirmation.

Unable to make their way down swaying stairwells and hallways to flee outdoors, they remained trapped within walls they feared would turn their homes into tombs. Encased by shuddering ceilings and floors, rattling windows and doors, they were wrenched up, slammed down, flung back and forth, again and again and again. The smell and taste of crumbling plaster and brickwork choked them as the ferocity of the shaking gradually juddered to what many feared would be but a temporary lull.

From a distance, clouds of dust billowing from the rubble made it look like the medieval towns and villages that cling to the mountainsides, or perch on hilltops, or nestle in valleys below, had been set on fire.

In all, the earthquake that Sunday morning lasted thirty seconds. But in those thirty seconds, the history of this land that gave birth to much of Western culture and civilisation was being rewritten.

Fault Lines and Fragility

'Human life has always been lived on the edge of a precipice.'
C.S. Lewis, *The Weight of Glory* (1941)

Chapter 1

The first time I saw mention of Amandola was in a copy of *Italy* magazine, bought hurriedly at King's Cross station on my way to Edinburgh, where I was taking my daughter and a schoolfriend for a half-term break. It was a bitter February day and a blur of mist-shrouded trees and sodden fields glided by the train's rain-flecked windows. As the girls chatted, I leafed through the pages of the magazine and sank into an account of how a Canadian architect had converted two cobblers' cottages into a spacious home with spectacular views of the Sibillini mountains in a region of Italy I knew little about – Le Marche. The photographs were inviting, and I promised myself I would visit one day.

For years, when taking my daughter to visit her Italian grandparents in Umbria, on the other side of the Apennines, I had trekked along dirt tracks throughout central Italy, often looking at little more than piles of stones, with dreams of how I might reconfigure them into a haven of rest from my busy London working life. A place where I could find stillness in a life of perpetual movement.

More than two decades of working as a foreign correspondent and feature writer for the *Sunday Times*, bearing witness to the darker side of humanity and reporting from over sixty countries around the globe, had taken its toll. Much of my time was spent in parts of the world riven by conflict, confusion and crises of one kind or another. From the Amazon to the Arctic Circle, Guatemala City to the Gaza Strip, Kosovo to Colombia, to Cuba and Kathmandu, more often than not I was writing about those whose lives were marked by suffering. People caught in the crossfire of civil wars and drug wars, or discarded and killed by society because of their gender, or lied to and locked up by authoritarian regimes. Their stories of sorrow and struggle stayed with me.

Raising my daughter alone also had its challenges. While my relationship with her father had failed to weather the storms of a life far removed from either of our families, in Mexico, where we first met, fell in love and where he continues to work as a doctor, my love affair with the country of his birth endured.

Although I knew Umbria well, I had never ventured across the mountains to Le Marche – partly because of the family pull to the west, but also because Le Marche's charms are less obvious than those of Umbria and its alluring north-western neighbour, Tuscany. Lodged between the Apennines and the blue waters of the Adriatic, it has long sat askew to the rest of Italy. Even its name, 'the borderlands', signals the fierce sense of independence which has run through its veins since time immemorial.

But over the last twenty years, growing numbers of foreign visitors seeking out quieter corners of Italy have discovered the region's mellow appeal. Much of it is given over to farmland, state forests and national parks, and significant art treasures are hidden away in small country churches with no queues. One of the most important industrial activities here is shoemaking, a cottage industry of thousands of small workshops and factories supplying behemoths like Tod's, Prada and Versace.

Seduced by the region's restful charm, growing numbers of those who have come from abroad to visit have chosen to settle here permanently, most electing to renovate tumbledown farmhouses and other rural places fallen into neglect. At first, I too dreamt of a secluded home in the countryside surrounded by rolling fields and woodland. But after one excursion to the remains of a remote lodge with a half-collapsed chapel, gold-painted stars on its cupola, I struggled to navigate the hire car back along miles of winding mud paths. It was then that my oldest and dearest friend from university, Emma, who had patiently accompanied me on my search, suggested I might want to consider restoring a townhouse instead.

Since I would be overseeing works from London, during snatched weekends and holidays between reporting assignments in trouble-torn corners of the world, I realised she was right. It was the gentler pace of Italian life and its sense of continuity I wanted to savour when I could, and what better way to do this than in the heart of a small community?

While taking on the restoration of an abandoned dwelling within the medieval walls of a hilltop town like Amandola was more unusual, I could see the advantages, the lure of freshly baked bread and a strong morning espresso or *aperitivo* in the late afternoon just a short stroll away.

At its height, in the late Middle Ages, Amandola was a thriving woollen milling centre with a population of more than eighteen thousand. Such was its prominence that it features on the walls of the Vatican's opulent sixteenth-century Gallery of Maps. There was a time too, when the town and its surrounding hamlets supported more than ninety churches and small chapels, some of which formed a corona – a protective circle beyond the town walls – to ward off demons and ill spirits.

Today, despite the survival of a number of grand buildings, including a jewel-box theatre, a cinema and hospital, Amandola might be considered more of a village than a town. Named after a legendary almond tree, a *mandorla*, which once stood here on high ground, fewer than four thousand souls have resided here in recent years, though this number traditionally swells in summer as Italy's city dwellers seek escape from the lowland heat to the cooler air of the Apennines, which offers welcome respite.

Many of those who come here in the summer months are also returning to visit relatives: those like Antonio, deeply rooted in this land farmed by his family for more than a century, and others who preferred to stay close to their provincial roots or lacked the opportunity to leave. Many come from Rome, which lies less than ninety miles away to the south-west as the crow flies. Yet a journey here from the Eternal City is not straightforward.

The Apennines, though often thought of as a single range, cleave into multiple parallel chains. These stretch for nearly a thousand miles from Liguria in the north to Calabria at the tip of the Italian boot. Beyond the Straits of Messina, a granite outcrop extends the cordillera further still, into northern Sicily. Here it is dominated by the brooding presence of Mount Etna, before finally bowing beneath the waters of the Mediterranean off the western shores of the Aegadian Islands.

Once believed to have been an extension of the Alps, the Apennines are now known to have been formed aeons later, roughly twenty million years ago – young in geological terms, and still evolving. Fossils of ancient sea creatures found at high altitudes offer a glimpse into such chasms of time. These petrified forms attest to their once having lain beneath primordial oceans until heat rising from the earth's core caused our planet's crust to rupture and migrate.

While the Apennines' western flanks tend to more gentle inclines, created by the spreading tilt of the earth's crust under the Tyrrhenian Sea, many east-facing escarpments are more precipitous. They were formed, and continue to be formed, by this section of the earth's crust compressing beneath the waters of the Adriatic, causing it to buckle and fracture. Cycles of storms, ice and gushing rivers cutting into these strata over millennia have further sculpted the landscape into jagged peaks and gorges which make traversing the mountains a meandering affair.

Those in a hurry to reach destinations such as Amandola on the east circumvent the Monti Sibillini at the heart of the central Apennines by following ancient Roman roads. To the north these roads pass in the direction of Foligno along the Flaminian Way. To the south, they trace the old via Salaria, the ancient salt road that cuts through where they narrow. Both journeys from the capital take around three hours.

Others with more time navigate switchback roads that snake between 7,000-foot and 8,000-foot snaggletooth pinnacles and deep ravines with names such as *Pizzo del Diavolo* (Devil's Peak), *Passo Cattivo* (Evil Pass) and *Gole dell'Infernaccio* (Hell's Gorge). In winter these routes are snowbound. But in spring and summer they pass through high meadows painted with a patchwork of blue gentians, cornflowers, white buttercups, alpine edelweiss and wild orchids.

There are times when small towns and villages like Amandola are shrouded in the mist that envelops the Sibillini mountains; looking on from a distance they seem to almost float in the clouds rather than be tethered to the earth below. A supernal sense further deepened by the abundance of superstitions and ancient myths that envelop the Sibillini themselves. Though I knew nothing of such myths at the time, there was something that exerted a stronger pull than pure romance when I first visited Amandola in the spring of 2004.

The moment I pushed open the flaking wooden shutters on the top floor of the house in the *centro storico* – the historic centre of the town – I was captivated. Looking out over terracotta rooftops towards the octagonal spire of the church of Saint Augustine, I saw swifts dipping and soaring around its campanile, their high-pitched chorus accompanying a graceful aerial ballet.

Leaning out of the window, I saw the mountains stretch across the horizon, from Monte Sassotetto in the north to Monte Vettore, known as 'the cloud maker', in the south. At that time of year their crests were still capped with snow, and below these white capes, a mosaic of woods and mountain pastures were threaded with small hamlets and twisting white roads.

One of Italy's most celebrated poets, Giacomo Leopardi, a native son of Le Marche, named the Sibillini the *Monti Azzurri*, or Blue Mountains. Look at them long enough as the light and weather shifts and you see their slopes and valleys washed with every shade from celeste in the morning to deep indigo as daylight fades.

In his poem, '*Le Ricordanze*', Leopardi wrote that it was these *Monti Azzurri* that inspired him to *pensieri immensi* and *dolci sogni* – expansive thoughts and sweet dreams. And long before I read these words in his collected works, *Canti*, I admit I cherished hopes that they might awake the same in me.

I had never before considered myself a 'mountain person'. I was born within the sound of the 'fishingboat-bobbing sea' of Dylan Thomas's *Under Milk Wood*, in a small Welsh village called Mumbles on the Gower Peninsula, across Swansea Bay from the former mining valleys and mountains of South Wales. In keeping with a popular belief that babies are born on the flood, I took my first breaths to the soft lapping of waves against a sea wall less than twenty paces from the front door of my first home; I have always been drawn to water, be it a river or a lake or stretch of coastline.

Looking out at the Sibillini that day, however, I was spellbound. Although the house itself had stood virtually abandoned for a hundred years and was in a state of severe neglect, I bought it early that summer.

Perhaps it was the prospect of bringing the old shell of a place back to life that seemed to offer solace. Six months before, a call had come in the early hours telling me a close member of my family had died that night. The shock of a life of someone so young cut suddenly short was a warning of how quickly things can fall apart. Imagining how this wreck of stones and mortar could be revived was something that felt within reach at a time when healing broken hearts seemed impossible.

But there was something too in the way Amandola is bonded to the land that enchanted me from the start. Even though it lies within the boundaries of a mountain national park and its municipal borders rise in places to heights of more than six thousand feet, the part of the historic centre where the house stands feels somehow nestled in a hollow. Of the four roads that lead into the *centro storico* from opposite directions, those that come from the north-west and south-east rise steeply to the brow of surrounding foothills before dipping down to cradle it in a sheltered spot.

As for the house itself, quite apart from the stunning view of the mountains from the top-floor windows, I felt it had an almost palpable sense of calm.

The last permanent resident in the house, I soon discovered, had been a priest at the turn of the last century. This detail had been offered grudgingly, in an airless notary office, during the time it took to exchange contracts with the cleric's distant relatives, a mother and her policeman son, into whose hands the deeds had eventually passed. The duo had long since moved some distance away and appeared in no mood to elaborate.

I could see that, from their point of view, the place was unmanageable. It rambled over different levels, rising one storey higher at the front than at the back due to its position on the slope of one of the three hills around which the gathering of ancient settlements that became Amandola were situated. The thickness of some walls at its base dated the footprint of the house to sometime in the Middle Ages. One wall was still embedded with heavy metal rings where animals had been tethered and watered before trudging up to the town's original market square.

But over the years, new floors and extensions had been added, and as the shell of the house expanded, old windows that would once have faced outwards were bricked up to form internal alcoves. The only traces of these were the remnants of heavy wooden architraves. In one corner of the basement there was the shaft of an old stone well that would also once have sat outside.

Some ceilings on the first floor had wooden beams so thick it was hard to imagine how they had been hauled into place. Others were concealed under wattle and daub panels that had begun to rot. On the top floor, at the front of the house, were two rooms with graceful domed and vaulted ceilings. But the balance of the building had been marred where rooms had been subdivided, turning it into an awkward maze.

There were no bathrooms to speak of. The kitchen countertop consisted of two stone slabs, one with a slight indent serving as a basin beneath a cold-water spigot. The roof leaked and damp and mould crept across the walls. Soot spilt out of several small fireplaces that must have fought to keep the place warm in winter. I was surprised to find light fittings that worked.

One of the greatest delights of the property, however, was its secluded garden, a rare privilege for a dwelling close to the main square. This overgrown oasis of fruit trees and unruly vines had a tall palm improbably planted in the middle and two mature walnut trees standing sentinel at the far end. Sheltered from the bustle, it had become an avian playground. Blackbird song filled the air, and small birds, searching for insects, fluttered close to crannies in its old stone walls.

The place was too large for me to take on alone, so I reached an agreement with Claudio, a local builder, and his girlfriend Alessandra from Rome, to divide it into two. With more time to tend it, Claudio took a larger share of the garden and a smaller portion of the dwelling, leaving me with the palm, vines, walnut trees and the front of the house with its vaulted rooms and windows overlooking the Sibillini.

Even before the purchase papers were drawn up, I pictured a space filled with light, calm white walls, wooden floors and stairways of locally quarried, pale travertine stone. By knocking down as many partition walls as the integrity of the building would allow, I would banish its labyrinthine feel, restore a sense of flow and create a place that unfurled, not inwards but outwards, towards the tranquillity of the garden to the south and the beauty of the mountains to the west.

During the early years, while this remodelling was being carried out, I often took a room in the grandly named Hotel Paradiso which stood at the top of a long flight of stone steps that wound around the back of Claudio and Alessandra's share of our newly divided garden. The Paradiso, though also in the old town centre, on the crest of the hill behind my house, was an incongruously 1950s-style building with more than two dozen rooms shielded from view by a thick stand of pine trees.

Over time I developed a friendly rivalry with another regular guest – an English novelist based in Shanghai who was restoring an old house some distance away – for a corner room we both loved overlooking the mountains. For in those years the Paradiso was something of an oasis for travellers from different corners of the world wanting to set up home in this quiet corner of Italy. Of an evening we would sit for hours on the outside terrace, drinking wine and exchanging tales of our travels and experiences and the latest hurdles we faced in achieving our dream, not least the welter of bureaucracy involved.

More often, however, talk turned to hidden gems we were discovering: secluded trails through the Sibillini, small rural churches adorned with rare art, a particular restaurant or colourful festival celebrating traditional skills such as the making of hats, shoes and lace, or seasonal produce such as artichokes, chestnuts, truffles, even the humble potato, pea and fava bean.

But one of the greatest joys of being a regular guest at the Paradiso was getting to know the family to whom it belonged. Above all the great-nephew of the original owner, Oreste, a tall, amiable figure with a shock of thick salt and pepper hair, a gentle nature and quick wit who always took time to stop and chat. At first I only caught glimpses of the other members of the family when the kitchen door swung open, and I saw Oreste's mother and wife-to-be Manuela toiling over steaming pots and pans with the hotel cook.

As time passed, however, Oreste, his mother and Manuela treated me less as a guest and more as one of the family, inviting me, in the quiet winter months, to share meals with them in front of the glowing hearth in their private quarters behind the kitchen. As we sat warming ourselves by the fire, the sound of builders working on my house drifting up from below, I loved listening to the stories Oreste and his mother told about characters who once lived in the town. One of the most colourful Oreste remembered as a boy lived in the house next to mine.

Her name was Ninetta and she was, he said, 'a kind of fortune teller'. According to Oreste, Ninetta would lean out of her window, cigarette in mouth, and beckon in, one by one, those who stood in a huddle in the lane outside. 'She read cards and interpreted people's dreams. Sometimes you would hear people whispering about it when they came out of the house afterwards,' he said with a smile, cupping his hand to his mouth. 'We used to talk about her as children. For us it was very exciting.'

Before my house was complete, I made a start on its unruly garden. It was then that I first met Antonio, the farmer, by then in his late sixties, when he appeared at the front door of my house late one afternoon in blue overalls, cap pulled low, spade and hoe in hand. He had heard from a local shopkeeper that I needed help and wanted to offer his services. He knew the plot had been abandoned for many years and was happy someone was willing to care for it again.

Together with his nephew Luigi, a friendly road sweeper with a penchant for singing opera when in a good mood, we gradually cleared the ground of discarded bottles and crockery, transformed the weed-ridden slopes into grassy terraces connected by rough wooden steps, and planted roses, scented jasmine, geraniums and a Virginia creeper on the far wall. Antonio's sometimes brutal pruning methods left me fearing some of his targets would never regrow. But working alongside him became one of the great pleasures of time spent in my Italian home. As we worked, I listened to his stories, many told with infectious laughter, of how Amandola had once been.

As I listened, sometimes interrupting him for explanations of the local dialect, I found myself delving into the complicated history of Italy and this region at its heart. I came to understand that Le Marche's fierce sense of independence dated back to the Iron Age, when these lands were home to an Italic tribe, the Piceni, whose totem, the woodpecker, *picus*, was the sacred bird of the war god Mars. It was during such times, when Le Marche's lengthy coastline was subject to attack by foreign invaders, that the mountains in the interior offered relative safety and the rugged, down-to-earth character of the Marchigiani is said to have been born. After the fall of the Roman Empire, however, Le Marche was sacked by Goths, Vandals and Lombards before coming under the direct sovereign rule of the Pope. It then remained a Papal State until 1861, long after many territories on the Italian peninsula were released from Vatican control.

But it was the latter years of the Second World War that Antonio reminisced about most often, when the mountains of central Italy were the scene of heavy partisan resistance, and many suffered for it. Amandola sat close to Germany's last major line of defence before Nazi troops were routed from Italy and the town found itself occupied by a nest of *Wehrmacht* intelligence officers and soldiers from the autumn of 1943 until the following summer.

There was a large prisoner of war camp in nearby Servigliano where many British and American POWs were held by German soldiers under orders to shoot anyone found helping escapees. But Antonio remembered making his way through the fields at dusk as a small

boy, carrying food to a British medical officer whom his family hid
for weeks on their farm. One afternoon as we sat on the stump of
an old tree in the shade, Antonio pulled a bundle of photographs
and greetings cards from the nylon sack in which he kept his tools –
cards written at Christmas over many years by the officer's daughters,
thanking the family for saving their father's life.

Of all Antonio's stories, among those I most loved to hear were
the tales of the old ways of working the land. Especially those that
touched upon the influence of the Moon and the way farmers would
track its progress across the night sky to guide their tasks at hand.
When I struggled to understand the term *gobba*, hump, Antonio
arched his frame over his spade to mimic the arc of a crescent Moon.
When the hump faced east, this meant the Moon was waxing and
it was not a good time to plant seeds. But when it faced west, this
signalled it had become a *luna buona*, a good Moon, which made
it a good time to kill a pig, plant seeds – especially onions – and
cut wood less prone to woodworm and therefore ideal for making
furniture. Potatoes, on the other hand, he said, could be planted at
any time since they grew underground, in the dark.

Such rituals were *credenze campagnole*, country beliefs, passed
down from father to son around the fire on winter nights when
'respecting the land and the rhythm of nature was sacrosanct, a matter
of survival,' Antonio explained. 'But now technology has overridden
nature and the old ways are forgotten,' he said as he struck down
hard on his spade and carried on digging, momentarily lost in thought.

When I bought my home, I had given little thought to the fact
that it was inaccessible by car, and after hauling bags of garden
rubbish to a skip beyond the main square with Antonio, my legs
like dead weights, I sometimes regretted it. The lane leading to the
house lay in a narrow pedestrian pathway that twisted around the
back of a series of old stone and brick dwellings which look out over
Amandola's main piazza.

Many who lived along this path were elderly, two of them sisters
who lived just a few doors apart in the tall narrow houses overlooking
the square. Neither had gardens but spent hours on their doorstep,
tending to a profusion of plants potted in rusty tins balanced on
bricks and planks to compensate for the steep incline. Though I
often struggled to understand what they said, since they too quickly
lapsed into dialect, I grew especially fond of the elder sister Delia,

by then in her eighties, who every morning would take her small dog for a walk up the lane past my house. When I heard the heels of her heavy leather shoes clicking on the cobbles, I would throw open my window and we would exchange greetings. Sometimes I left roses from my garden by her front door.

On warm evenings Delia, her sister and the other women in the lane, would while away their time hunched on stools or plastic benches, cotton housecoats eased open at the waist, airing their memories and concerns among themselves. Catching a few phrases as I passed by, I would hear talk of food or friends and family, some of whom might perhaps have preferred their affairs to remain private. But in the heart of a small community like this there are few secrets. And, during my first year in Amandola, I provided plenty for my Italian neighbours to talk about when the local newspaper ran an article about a near disaster on their doorstep involving an unnamed *signora inglese*.

Chapter 2

The stark headline the *Corriere Adriatico* ran on 15 September 2004 informed its readers that a 'rocket bomb . . . ready to explode' had been found in a long-abandoned house in Amandola's *centro storico*.

'A very dangerous discovery that would, at the very least, have caused the house itself to collapse had the bomb detonated,' the story beneath continued. A catastrophe only narrowly averted due to the *accortezza*, vigilance, of the anonymous *signora inglese*. 'But, above all, thanks to the quick thinking and professionalism of the police and other law enforcement agencies.'

I have never ventured a different version of events in my discussions with the old ladies who live along the lane leading to my Amandola home. For the truth of what happened that first summer only deepened my affection for this place.

At first, I had paid little attention to the odd assortment of belongings scattered about my old house: odd cooking utensils, cloudy demijohns, a broken wooden wine press and a strange array of scraps of metal, one of which caught my attention. It was a peculiar object, over a foot long, with a smooth, dark tip and base perforated like a giant salt cellar. I found it perched upright on a shelf in one of the upstairs rooms. It looked like a rusty old shell. But, judging by its weight, it didn't feel spent, so I was hesitant about tossing it in a skip.

From an upstairs window, I could see my neighbour Claudio in the garden, hauling bricks for the wall he was building to mark our boundary line. I knocked on the glass and held up the shell. He put down his load, strained his eyes, then signalled he was coming to take a closer look.

'*Mannaggia!*' – damn! – he said, as he bounced the ordnance gently in his hands as if measuring it in a scales, before propping it back on the shelf. 'I'm not sure what you should do with this. But I have a friend in the police I can ask.'

Later that day, a good humoured *poliziotto* called by to inspect the find. It was a hot afternoon and he showed only mild interest. Striking a pose in his knee-high black boots, tight trousers and shiny white belt, he held it up in one hand for me to photograph before nonchalantly tucking it under his arm and taking it away for disposal.

Within the hour, he was back, looking flustered and cradling the weapon a great deal more cautiously. '*Scusi, signora*, but we can't allow this to be taken out of your house . . . *È troppo pericoloso.* It's too dangerous,' he said, before hotfooting it back upstairs and gingerly placing it back on the shelf, prone this time, and in a box.

A few minutes later, the wail of a police siren could be heard approaching the main square at speed. Leaning out of a top-floor window I saw two more policemen in even more dashing uniforms, one with the epaulettes and braided cap of a chief inspector, hurrying up the lane.

'This matter requires the attention of experts, *signora*,' the *ispettore capo* said, before ushering me politely out of my front door and motioning to his subordinate to seal it off. This left my house looking like a crime scene with red-and-white-striped incident tape wound around the brass door handles and secured to an adjacent drainpipe.

Front door sealed off by police after discovery of unexploded ordnance

Later that day, the chief inspector contacted regional police headquarters in Ascoli Piceno and passed me a copy of the fax he sent. Marked '*URGENTISSIMO*', in it he reassured his superiors that, following the discovery of *materiale esplosivo*, 'all access to the property has been blocked pending further arrangements.'

There was talk of evacuating residents close by. Instead, a *carabiniere*, a member of Italy's paramilitary police force, was posted to keep a nightly vigil and a request was sent for an army bomb-disposal squad to be dispatched from Rome. Urgency notwithstanding, I was warned it could be some time before they were able to attend.

With the chief inspector assuring me he would keep me updated, there was little for it but for me to return to London. Weeks of waiting turned into two months. In that time the chief inspector, with whom I was by then on first name terms, called with some regularity, though I got the impression it was sometimes less to inform me of progress than to while away the time.

I was not surprised therefore that I received little notice of the day the bomb disposal team would arrive and by then was five thousand miles away, on assignment in Money, Mississippi. As I drove through the cotton fields and sat listening to Black residents talk about one of the great travesties of justice that helped spark America's civil rights movement – the 1955 acquittal of the murderers of Emmett Till – events unfolding in Amandola felt far-removed.

As reported in the *Corriere Adriatico*, what had seemed like an 'innocent discovery' was later found to be of 'utmost danger'. Identified as a German 'rocket' left over from the Second World War, it was found to contain half a kilo of TNT and had a range of more than half a mile. It also had a double-trigger mechanism, which made it doubly unstable as it deteriorated with age and would almost certainly have exploded had it rolled off the shelf or been dropped.

On the day the bomb disposal squad from the Italian army's sixth regiment of *Genio Pionieri* swept into Amandola, an ambulance was placed on standby in the main square, together with officers from Italy's three main police forces; the *Carabinieri*, *Polizia di Stato* and *Polizia Municipale*. Cutting the security tape on my front door and marching up to the top floor, the army crew confirmed the ordnance was still live and were less than reassured seeing it resting on a rough plank held up by two nails.

When it was removed from my house for the second time, the engineers placed the device in a metal case lined with sand and drove it to a remote field where it could be detonated remotely. The controlled explosion gouged a deep crater in the ground and sent earth flying nearly thirty feet into the air.

A few weeks later, as I sat in the chief inspector's office, he eased himself back behind his desk, festooned with several revolving wheels of rubber stamps, and asked if I had by any chance taken any photographs of the 'bomb' while it was still in my house. I took out my digital camera and pulled up the image of the *poliziotto* who first came to inspect it.

'I thought so,' he said, slapping his hands on the desk and throwing his head back with a deep laugh. '*Ecco le prove.*' Here's the evidence!

It seems the dashing young officer may have implied to his superiors he had never touched the device, let alone removed it from my house. I was afraid I might have compromised the unfortunate's career. But the chief inspector waved his hand and carried on laughing.

Over time the saga passed into local lore and I was sometimes jokingly referred to as '*la signora della bomba*', as if hiding an underworld connection. It was a story I enjoyed retelling.

With hindsight, however, the discovery of this explosive device feels more like a premonition of grave events that were to follow.

But in these early years, my Italian home yielded yet more surprises. Just a few months after the 'bomb' incident, I heard one of the workmen helping me clear the house call out as I unwound vine stalks from what was left of a crumbling arbour in the garden.

'*Vieni qui, signora!*' Come! There was a note of urgency in his voice.

Pulling gloves stiff with dirt from my fingers, I climbed the stairs to the top floor to see his head poking through a small door that led to the attic. Closer inspection of the roof had revealed it was rotting in places and most of it would have to be replaced. Two labourers were making sure the space beneath it was clear for the work to begin. To do this one had to crawl up into a loft space little more than waist-high where it passed above the vaulted ceilings.

Judging from the accumulated dust and cobwebs, the attic had remained undisturbed for decades. Parts of it were largely hidden from view by thick wooden arches holding the vaults aloft. But when the elder of the two men crawled under the rafters and shone his torch, he saw an assortment of mysterious items in a far corner. Edging closer, he found a wooden crate covered with cloth, a large box and an oddly shaped bundle, the length of his arm, stacked in a far corner.

It took some manoeuvring to get the box out of the attic. When we opened the lid, we found two statues inside. One small, the size of a loaf of bread, of a reclining saint in painted red robes, metal halo askew, with a bouquet of drooping silk flowers in her hand. One larger, around two feet tall in off-white ceramic, was of an imposing, portly figure wearing a cassock and skull cap seated on a throne with the lettering '*Pio IX*' embossed at its base.

'*Pio Nono!*' said the older man, a stocky figure with stooped shoulders, as he lifted out the statue.

At first, I thought he was saying *nonno*, grandpa, rather than *nono*, ninth, and assumed he must have felt some special affinity for the former pontiff. Only later did I discover that Pius IX, an authoritarian figure who ruled the Holy See for thirty-two years from the middle of the nineteenth century, making him the longest-reigning pope, was a native son of Le Marche and revered in these parts.

After the older workman clambered back into the attic, he handed down first the wooden crate and then the bundle. As he did so, the cloth around the bundle loosened and slipped to reveal two rolls of stiff fabric. As one of these started to unfurl, I caught a glimpse of colour and the outline of a woman's face. When his younger companion helped me set them down on the floor, they unravelled further and he let out a low whistle and whispered expletive. Though grimy with dirt, we could see they were large oval canvases. Each measuring around three feet tall by two feet across. Oil paintings that had remained hidden away, for who knows how long. One of them, worn thin in places, had a series of fraying holes around its edges showing where it had been unpinned from a frame. The back of each was discoloured with watermarks. But otherwise they were remarkably intact.

As I carefully smoothed away their coating of dust, delicate portrayals of angels and saints emerged. The darker of the two appeared to be a pregnant Madonna, swathed in a pink dress and blue cloak with one bare foot precariously balanced on a crescent Moon and the other pressed against the neck of a coiled serpent. The second, more damaged canvas, depicted a scene of greater tenderness and had been painted as if framed by the folds of a heavy curtain with angels looking down on the figure of a brown-robed friar, an open book on a table by his side. As the angels looked down at him, he in turn was gazing down at an infant, clutching a lily, cradled in his arms.

'San Antonio!' whispered the older man as he swept his cap from his head, traced the sign of a cross with his fingers and brought his calloused palms together.

I smiled. But my ignorance must have shown in my face.

'*Il santo di quello che è perso*,' he said, closing his eyes briefly before glancing up to see if I understood. The saint of that which is lost.

Content with these impressive finds, the workmen showed little interest in the crate lowered from the attic. Disappearing back under the rafters they left me alone to examine it further and I sat on the floor, unpacking its contents and laying them out on the speckled tiles.

On top was an assortment of books and papers, most of which looked like clerical records. Some were handwritten in immaculate script, partially in Latin, and embellished here and there with floral flourishes. One of these was a small journal bearing the words '*Diarium Missarum*' and was bound with embossed black crêpe paper. The name Federico Bellesi was written in the same careful script on the inside cover. Was this, I wondered, the priest to whom this house had once belonged?

As I leafed through the journal, looking for clues, I saw its pages were full of columns marked with dates and names alongside small sums of money. Stipends petitioners must have paid for the priest to say mass on their behalf. The first handwritten entry in this account of sorrows, hopes and joys was for 24 October 1909, the last for 6 May 1912.

Next, I unearthed a sheaf of etched prints: lithographs of stern-looking men, some with elaborate whiskers, some dressed in sombre morning coats with knotted kerchiefs and wire-framed spectacles. There was a missionary almanac too, dated 1910, and a local magazine from the same year. There were several musty books, one intriguingly entitled *I Limiti della Morale Sessuale*, The Limits of Sexual Morality, I assumed to be a guide to the sort of behaviour a priest from a bygone age might expect of his flock.

The most intimate discovery of all, however, was a shoebox full of postcards and letters dating from 1899 through to 1918. The majority were addressed either to *Distinguibilisimo Giovane*, most distinguished young man, or *Pregiatisimo Signore*, most precious sir, before the name of the addressee Federico Bellesi, the same name as inscribed in the diary of stipends. Some of the earliest letters had been sent to a seminary in Fermo, a city with ancient roots less than thirty miles from Amandola near the Adriatic coast. Those of a later date were addressed to the same Federico Bellesi, by then an *Egregio Sacerdote*, esteemed priest, at a number of different churches close to both places.

Some letters were smudged and damaged and had corners nibbled away by mice. All were written in elaborate looping script that was hard to read. But as I sat listening to the thudding sounds of the workmen above my head, I carefully prised open one delicate page after another and saw some letters signed *Papa*, others, *Nonno*, Grandpa, or *Zia* and *Zio* – aunt and uncle. One of the most intriguing was a letter postmarked Boston, Massachusetts and dated 1 January 1906.

Though I longed to know more about the lives of those behind this intimate correspondence and why it, together with the paintings and other personal belongings, had lain hidden for so long, I simply did not have the time to investigate. With the house a building site and nowhere safe to store them, I had little choice but to bring the trove back to London in the hope that I might return to study it more carefully one day.

Some months later, on the advice of an artist friend, I took the canvases to be cleaned by someone she knew with experience in working with delicate works of art. With what I imagined to be a patina of smoke that had once circled up from liturgical candles carefully swabbed from their surface, the vibrant colours and finer details of the images were revealed.

In the more elaborate composition, the one I thought of as the pregnant Madonna or the Madonna and the Moon, a halo of twelve stars emerged around her against a sunlit background. The scarf covering her head and trailing behind her appeared made of fine golden gossamer caught by a breeze. The folds of her indigo cloak and pink gown were billowing too, their surface gleaming as if made of sumptuous satin. Her hands were lightly clasped in prayer, but her gaze was distracted by what lay below: the slender crescent Moon on which one foot was balanced, now brought into sharp focus and looking more like a rounded blade, a scythe, than a softly luminous arc. The coiled serpent with pinprick white eyes under her other foot near a dark-robed figure I had not noticed before. Half-hidden in the shadows, looking up at her in veneration, he had one hand outstretched and the other clutching a wooden staff. Beside him was a winged cherub with fair curls, apple cheeks and a wisp of scarlet cloth over a bare torso, hovering in mid-air and offering up to the Madonna a flaming crimson heart bearing the word '*CHARITAS*' in golden letters.

At the time it felt somehow sacrilegious to stow both paintings away again. But I was so busy with my work and my daughter I had little opportunity to do anything else. So, carefully rolling the canvases inside a sturdy cylinder, I propped them behind the door of my study in London. From time to time, in the years that followed, the cylinder sometimes toppled to the floor, as if nudging me for attention.

Chapter 3

The restoration of my Amandola home took nearly five years and was not without its difficulties. Not least, the discovery that the temperamental plumber I used briefly had once worked as a barman, a position for which he was, hopefully, better suited. For he seemed to know little about laying pipes, as became evident when steam circled up from toilets on the top floor after flushing produced hot water.

There were surprises too in the weather. Having viewed the house in spring and sealed the purchase just a few months later, I knew little of the sudden onset of heavy snow that can envelope the Sibillini mountains within a matter of hours once winter sets in. Had I paid more attention to the presence of ski lifts snaking up into the mountains from the neighbouring town of Sarnano I might have been better prepared. I soon learnt my lesson when I failed to attach snow chains to the tyres of my car in my first winter and skidded off the road into a deep drift some way out of Amandola.

As I opened the door and sank up to my thighs, a passing car stopped; its driver offered to give me a lift into town and send someone to pick up my stranded vehicle. Seeing I was both cold and shaken, as we drew into the piazza he invited me to have lunch with him and his wife Luisa at their home nearby to warm up. It was only then that we realised we lived just a few doors apart and over the years that followed we became firm friends.

Domenico, a busy accountant with a shock of thick grey hair, ready smile and a restless air spent much of his time on the go, visiting clients in surrounding towns and villages, sometimes returning with trays of their home-grown produce – sweet red apples, fresh vegetables, jars of honey, freshly laid eggs – which the couple were quick to share. Ever since the day of our first meeting, Dom, I discovered, had my number registered on his mobile phone under the name *Biancaneve*, Snow White.

Luisa, a retired schoolteacher with a slight frame, delicate features and kind, patient manner was more often at home. So, on market days, I would often knock on her door as I passed, and after weaving our way through the small cluster of stalls in the piazza, picking out fruit and vegetables, we would sit chatting over coffee outside one of the cafés set back from the square under a shaded colonnade.

Market days were often the only time when some in the Sibillini's more remote villages and hamlets ventured in to buy supplies. Then every café would fill with men who stood around drinking espressos, often laced with something stronger, while wives with weathered faces and stout shoes filled their baskets. For besides the cluster of battered vans selling fresh produce were others catering to a range of needs from kitchenware to ladies' underwear, aprons and other items of clothing that swung from hangers in the breeze.

When the lengthy renovation of my house was finally complete, I called it *Casa Luna* in recognition of the means by which I had first been able to put down a deposit on its purchase: a book I wrote in collaboration with one of only twelve men to have set foot on the surface of the Moon, American astronaut and *Apollo 15* commander David Scott, and his Russian counterpart, cosmonaut Alexei Leonov, the first man to walk in space.

Returning to Amandola and the comfort of my now light and airy Italian home from assignments on troubled streets in far-flung places I soaked in the pleasures of life in this quiet mountain community and the sense of grounding it gave me. Some years later I would choose to step back from the turmoil of reporting from such places, prompted in part by the sudden death of both of my parents. Though they had not lived together for many years, they died within a few months of each other, and after so long spent writing about the suffering of others, I realised I was struggling to handle my own.

Around the same time, while on a trip to the foothills of the Indian Himalayas to interview the exiled prime minister of Tibet, I had a brief encounter with a Tibetan Buddhist nun forced to flee her homeland after enduring years of persecution and torture. This left a deep impression on me and sparked what would become a 60,000-mile global journey to write a book about the lives of women who choose to become Buddhist nuns in order to dedicate their lives to cultivating a sense of peace, both within themselves and in those whose lives they touch. On completion of the book, I did not feel ready to return to the fray of breaking news. I wanted to turn away from darkness.

Whenever I could, I had always tried to find a glimmer of light and hope in the desperate situations in which many of those I wrote about found themselves. The precious thread that pulled them through the darkest nights and helped them carry on with their lives. Most often it lay in the love they felt for those they had lost or saw suffering. But as years of reporting on the devastation caused by those with little regard for human life or dignity passed, I began to lose heart.

With my daughter Inés by then away at university, I took to spending more time in Amandola, soothed by the mellow rhythm of its daily routines. Together with family and friends who came to visit, I enjoyed long walks in the mountains, swims on summer mornings in the Adriatic, less than an hour's drive away, and on winter nights warming ourselves beside an open log fire. Over the years, the house that had stood silent for so long filled with laughter and music. One trip to the world capital of accordion manufacturing, the small town of Castelfidardo further north in Le Marche, saw a shiny red instrument take up temporary residence in my home until some gentle pleading succeeded in persuading its new owner to revert to the more melodic playing of his guitar.

At times throughout the year Amandola too came alive with music during its own succession of festivals, fairs and feasts. The festival of *Befana*, the giving of gifts to children on the eve of Epiphany. The pre-Lenten *Carnival de li Paniccià*, named after the wool-makers and dyers of Amandola's once thriving wool industry. The *Processione delle Canestrelle* which every August saw women in traditional dress of white blouses, long dark skirts and red aprons carry baskets of wheat, *canestrelle*, on their heads through the streets. Often at such *festas* local dancers and musicians in knee breeches carrying tambourines and small button *fisarmonicas* would perform the traditional folk dance of Le Marche, the *saltarello*, a boisterous show of heel clicks and continuous jumps dating back beyond the Middle Ages.

In spring and summer there were sporting festivals, including sailing regattas on San Ruffino lake, and tennis and volleyball tournaments, the latter culminating in the piazza being covered in sand where teams of skimpily dressed girls would compete to the amusement of the boys and older men whose eyes were otherwise firmly fixed on their playing cards at tables under the colonnade.

On warm summer evenings, a giant screen would be unfurled from the facade of Saint Augustine's church and the wide shallow steps leading down to its great wooden doors would double as tiered seating for a makeshift open-air cinema. Other churches would host classical concerts and through July and August a wooden stage would be set up in the piazza for live events – often tribute bands with a particular fondness for painful renditions of 'Stairway to Heaven'.

At the centre of every celebration there was of course food and wine. A succession of regional specialities according to the time of year: the *Sagra della Fregnaccia* in July, at which the traditional farmer's dish of egg pasta with rich meat sauce and black pepper is served; the *Castagnata* in October when the town is strung with colourful pennants and the air fills with the smell of roasting chestnuts from braziers set at intervals in the narrow lanes of the *centro storico* and pungent steam from vats of hot *vino cotto*, the strong sweet wine of pre-Christian origins fermented from the must of local vines.

Higher up in the mountains, in the unlikely setting of a remote mountain village, a small restaurant with bow-tied waiters speaking in hushed tones served more refined delicacies on a tasting menu. Dishes such as *diplomatico* of lamb offal, fatty liver and cherry soup, spaghetti with snail *ragù*, partridge *al Marsala* or, the local speciality, slowly braised pork shank, known simply – and unappetisingly, to English-speakers – as *stinco*.

But the event that has drawn most visitors to Amandola for many years is the *Diamanti a Tavola* truffle festival usually held in the first or second week of November. In some years marquees were erected in the piazza where notable chefs conjured up specialities for diners seated shoulder-to-shoulder at long tables and cheers went up as every new creation was laid on plates before them. The central Apennines are said to be one of few places in the world where fresh truffles can be eaten fresh all year round, making *tagliatelle al tartufo*, with its pencil-like shavings of the marbled tuber on home-made pasta and its rich, earthy flavour, one of my favourite dishes.

During truffle festivals, the cloisters of Saint Francis's church at the far end of town would be lined with trestles on which truffle hunters with leathery skin and rough hands would set up their scales. There, under the flinty gaze of their wives, they would arrange the knobby tuberous lumps like museum specimens under glass cloches and carefully weigh them for customers who often haggled over the high price. In some years the rarest white truffles, *tartufi bianchi*, would sell for prices, ounce-for-ounce, as high as gold.

I knew nothing about truffles before I made my home in the Sibillini. But one winter's evening, after a walk in the mountains with friends, I noticed an elderly man in a battered felt hat sitting in the corner of the simple *osteria* where we had stopped to warm our bones and eat a plate of pasta. He was alone, but for a handsome white pointer with black ticking spots. The man's weathered face told the story of a life exposed to the elements with his beloved dog, which he spoke to in a low voice, feeding it titbits from his plate.

As I returned from the bathroom I smiled at the old man and bent down to admire the dog. Both looked at me with soulful eyes, but the man said nothing and returned to feeding his companion a scrap of cheese.

'He's a *tartufaio* – a truffle hunter,' one of my friends explained. 'They keep themselves to themselves, spend their life in the forests up here in the mountains.'

As he spoke, the door to a secret world opened on a way of life in these parts dating back to Roman times. Both the Greeks and Romans once prized these pungent fungi as the food of the gods, an aphrodisiac and precious source of vitality. In the past *tartufai* would search for truffles with the help of pigs. Now it is specially trained dogs that sniff out these delicacies, concealed beneath the soil at the root of oak trees like buried treasure. Those who seek them rarely speak of the places where they can be found. They forage alone. Sometimes at night. Some for the money, swapping their finds for wads of cash in hastily arranged clandestine meetings. But most *tartufai* do it out of a lifelong passion for the deep immersion it gives them in nature.

Before that evening in the mountains, I had given little thought to the way nature hides her secrets. But as time passed, I became increasingly aware of what lies hidden and how often this can yield unexpected gifts but also, sometimes, harbour a destructive power.

For I also came to realise, too late, how little heed I had paid to a fleeting comment my genial estate agent Gildo made when I first viewed the house that would become my home. When I noticed a couple of zigzag cracks in the brickwork of an imposing palazzo that partially overlooked its garden, with nesting birds swooping in and out of its broken windows, I believe he mentioned the word *terremoto*, literally earth motion; more precisely, earthquake.

But the quake Gildo spoke of had struck seven years earlier, in 1997, and its epicentre lay on the other side of the Apennines, in the ancient Umbrian town of Foligno, thirty miles or so due west of Amandola. That quake killed eleven people, destroyed many homes and severely damaged Assisi's basilica of Saint Francis, partially destroying frescoes by Giotto and Cimabue. On the few occasions I heard Amandolesi speak of it, however, they stressed the generally long-term, cyclical nature of such events. I detected no sense of alarm in their voices. And, as an Oxford graduate with a degree in geography and some knowledge of geology and seismology, I naively assumed a repeat of significant seismic activity in the area was unlikely anytime soon. This, I later learnt, is what behavioural scientists call gambler's fallacy. The belief that if something with low probability has occurred recently it is unlikely to occur again soon afterwards. A belief that often leads to the event being treated as something with a probability of zero.

Besides, by the time I heard the word *terremoto* mentioned I was already beyond dissuasion. My decision to make a home in this small community tucked away in a fold of the Sibillini mountains was a decision of the heart, not the head, and I lost my heart to it from the very first moment.

Chapter 4

On the morning of 30 October 2016 I was asleep in west London and knew little of what was unfolding a thousand miles away. The first I heard of it was the ping of a message flashing up on the screen of my mobile phone:

'7.40 bigger earthquake.' I felt my stomach pitch and jolted upright.

It was 7 a.m. in London. The message was from my Italian friend Simona, with whom I had sat sipping coffee the week before in a café in Amandola's main square. I had just returned from overseeing repairs to small cracks that opened up in my ceilings and walls when the powerful earthquake that struck two months earlier, on 24 August, destroyed Amatrice and its surrounding towns and villages, burying hundreds of poor souls beneath the rubble.

Amatrice lies less than thirty miles to the south of Amandola and, as a result of that quake and the thousands of strong aftershocks that followed, many homes and buildings in Amandola were also damaged, with some left in danger of foundering. But up to now there had been no serious casualties.

'Are you OK?' I tapped the words back quickly, fingers shaking. No reply.

My thoughts began to race. What did Simona mean by *bigger*?

Surely she was not saying the area had been struck now by a quake measuring 7.4 on the Richter scale? That, I knew, would be catastrophic. The magnitude of the first fatal earthquake that August was 6.2 and largely razed communities close to its epicentre. The few houses still partially intact were left gaping open to the elements with intimate scenes of domesticity and ruined lives exposed. In the wake of the many aftershocks, rescue workers searching the rubble first for survivors, then bodies, were forced to halt their efforts again and again for fear they too would be interred.

Most residents of these small communities were evacuated to the coast or sought refuge elsewhere with family and friends. Those who stayed were kept constantly on edge, every tremor triggering a bone-deep dread. A dread I too felt as I worked on repairs to my house in the weeks immediately afterwards. Even when the earth was still, the slam of a door or vibrating machinery would spark a rush of adrenaline, ignite muscle memory, nightmares, snapping you awake at 3 a.m.

I knew the instant terror that comes when everything around begins to shake. I had felt it before, but in destinations far from the Sibillini mountains, when strong earth tremors rocked Los Angeles, Tokyo, San Salvador and Bogotá while I was in each city covering other news. I remembered the panic-stricken faces of those around me. Guests screaming and running along the hotel corridor in El Salvador. The smell of fear in the lift I was trapped in with others in the Colombian capital when a quake hit, jamming its hydraulics. Tarmac rippling like an ocean swell as I drove along a Californian highway. The sudden ping of a government warning message flashing up on my phone in the middle of the night in Japan.

But none of those quakes had been severe enough to make international headlines or warrant my editors diverting me from the task at hand. And I had never before felt the earth beneath my Italian home tremble so fiercely that the effects were felt as far away as Rome where the walls of what remained of the Colosseum, largely destroyed by earthquakes long ago, once again shook. Yet still, that August, most of us thought that the seismic activity rocking central Italy would gradually settle.

Then, just days after I flew back to London, two powerful quakes, one measuring 5.5, the second 6.1, downed power lines and brought already weakened buildings to the ground. Far from diminishing, the quakes seemed once again to be increasing in intensity.

In the months since that August when Amatrice was destroyed, I had come to understand the significance of a single seismic digit, even that of a few decimal points. Earthquakes are measured on logarithmic scales, which means that one with a magnitude of 7 releases a thousand times more destructive force than one with a magnitude of 5.

One account I read of the last earthquake to have hit Italy with a magnitude of more than 7, early on a December day in 1908, spoke of the 'utter horror and desolation' that followed. In less than a minute, the densely populated Sicilian city of Messina and the mainland port of Reggio Calabria were largely destroyed and then deluged by a tidal wave. It was one of the most lethal seismic events in the history of the Western world. The dead, buried or drowned as they slept, were never accurately counted. To this day, some record the toll as 'between one hundred and two hundred thousand'. One survivor likened the noise preceding it to a thousand red hot pokers burning the water.

Urgently scanning news sites on that fateful October morning, I saw footage of nuns and monks with stricken faces hitching up habits and fleeing through rubble-strewn streets. Behind them lay the ruins of one of Italy's most sacred sites: Norcia's Basilica di San Benedetto. This was the birthplace of Saint Benedict, patron saint of Europe, whose teachings laid the foundations for Western monasticism and, more widely, many of the basic tenets for modern democratic government. All that was left of the basilica now was a ghostly facade, enveloped in a cloud of dust.

Italy's state-owned broadcaster RAI was reporting the earthquake that morning as measuring 6.6 – 'the strongest in Italy for nearly forty years'. One headline spoke of 'fears for one hundred thousand displaced'. The epicentre of this latest quake was said to be Norcia. Since seismic fault lines do not travel in the same way humans choose to on the earth's surface, geodesic distance is the real measure of proximity to threat of destruction. And Norcia lay over a mountain crest from Amandola, just nineteen miles away as the crow flies.

The reports confirmed the earthquake had struck at 7.40 a.m. local time. Now I understood Simona's message. Scrolling through more news bulletins I saw panic on the face of the mayor of the small town of Ùssita, a few miles from Norcia. 'It's a disaster,' he moaned. 'A disaster . . . I've seen hell.'

I thought of my friends, my neighbours, the hilltop town where I had made a home.

Fearing the worst, I tried calling Simona. But the phone rang out. I messaged again.

'We're safe,' came her reply, finally. 'What about your house?'

There was relief, and fear, in my neighbour Claudio's voice when he eventually answered the phone. He and Alessandra had managed to run outside when the earth started to churn. Standing at the end of their garden holding on to each other they watched their house, and mine, rock from side to side.

'The trees seemed to be dancing around us. Everything was shaking so violently. We were sure it was the end,' said Claudio. 'But together we prayed "Resist! Resist!"'

When the shaking stopped, both our homes were still standing.

As the hours passed, I managed to speak with more friends in Amandola and beyond and began to understand the enormity of what had happened. An area from the Apennines to the shores of the Adriatic was so violently shaken, and in places ripped apart, that countless more homes and buildings, including schools, hospitals and churches filled with priceless works of art, were brought down, or damaged beyond repair.

There were no immediate reports of casualties, but only because so many had already evacuated the area after the August earthquake. And, because the clocks had changed that Sunday morning, churches were not yet filled with worshippers. Nor had emergency workers, still toiling to shore up buildings left teetering by the earlier quake, started their 8 a.m. shifts.

Like many others whose houses and apartments lie within the boundaries of a *centro storico*, I was advised to stay away from my Italian home until stability tests could be completed. In the aftermath of the quakes, scores of engineers, architects and surveyors volunteered their services to carry out these tests. The scale of their task was daunting. More than a thousand square kilometres, over four hundred square miles, were classified as a disaster zone, designated *Il Cratere* – The Crater – by the *Dipartimento Protezione Civile*, the agency that oversees all earthquake relief work in Italy.

Within this area of The Crater there were one hundred and forty *comuni*, or local administrative districts, encompassing hundreds of towns, villages and small hamlets, all of them set in some of Italy's most spectacular scenery. But why those who lived here now, and had done over centuries, chose to stay in an area so prone to natural disaster was a question that began to play on my mind with increasing urgency. As did my own decision to continue living here, if only for part of the year.

In the weeks that followed, I had plenty of time to reflect on what it means to lose the most fundamental sense of security we take as given. The sense that, whatever else might fall apart in life, the ground beneath us remains solid, steady, unmoving. That we live on *terra firma*.

In my travels as a foreign correspondent, I had been deeply affected by the stories of those whose lives had been torn apart by open conflict or who struggled with the torments of torture, crime and neglect. Most caught up in such turmoil had no control over their fate and their suffering was beyond measure. But few of mankind's or nature's catastrophes strike with so little warning and create such devastation as the sudden rupture of the shell of our fragile planet. We may know when storms will hit, and floods rise. We can track the path of wildfires and forecast drought. We know the signs of approaching war and may instinctively sense when the threat of violence is close, even if we are unable to escape it. But we have yet to discover a way of accurately predicting when the earth below us will convulse and break apart.

So how, I asked myself, had people in such seismically active zones found ways of living with the ever-present threat? Had this contributed to what seemed to me to be the capacity of Italians to live more in the moment than those in countries further north? In the way our own geography as an island nation with a highly changeable climate has tended to make us more insular, reserved and obsessed with the weather. How do encounters with fragility, transience and instability, both in the physical world and in our personal lives, shape us all, I wondered. Such questions, however, were put on hold in the face of more immediate concerns.

Despite assurances from my neighbours, who believed any damage to my house had been relatively light, I knew the fate of my home lay in the hands of those the state had charged with inspecting it. Since tens of thousands of homes and public buildings had been subjected to sustained battering, the scores of engineers, architects and surveyors who volunteered to carry out this work could do little more than carry out cursory inspections and tick boxes according to an arcane coding system that was all but unintelligible to the uninitiated. But it was these swift decrees that determined whether those whose homes had not collapsed entirely were safe to stay or must evacuate. When it came to my own, I did not know which box the engineers would tick.

Then, days before I was due to fly to Italy, an email arrived from Amandola's *comune* with a letter attached. The official document

bore Amandola's elegant coat of arms – an almond tree circled by
two olive branches topped by a crown – and the moniker by which
the town is known: *Città del Tartufo Bianco dei Sibillini* – City
of the Sibillini White Truffle. Beneath these elaborate flourishes
were typed the words 'Order No. 69'. My heart raced as I ploughed
through a flurry of references to legislative decree 267/2000, then
read the following:

> Due to the seismic crisis that began on 24/08/2016 . . . Article 50
> recognises the legitimacy of the mayor to issue orders in cases where
> imminent dangers may arise that are unavoidable . . . and therefore
> to declare, according to Article 54, that the above-named property
> is UNINHABITABLE [written in capital letters] due to earthquake
> damage which makes it urgent to stop its use . . . The building must
> therefore be closed, with immediate effect, and all access must be
> prevented . . . until the revocation of this provision.

The letter went on to inform me that copies of this order were being
sent to two police forces and seven government offices.

I stared at the letter and read it over and over again. My thoughts
flashed briefly back to the months after I bought my house when
incident tape was wound around the handles of my front door and
I was forbidden from entering until the 'bomb' had been safely
removed. Back then I had laughed at the farcical nature of the affair
and never really believed my home to be in any serious danger. But
in the wake of so much destruction, with so many homes lost, I
sank into despair. I not only felt far away and ached to be back in
Amandola and the community I had come to care so much about; I
also saw that the dream I had created, the place in which I sought
refuge, now teetered on the brink of collapse.

There was nothing in the letter that explained why my house was
now deemed uninhabitable. Surely my neighbours would know if the
damage was severe. And if only light, why could I not live there while
I oversaw any necessary repairs as I had in the wake of the earlier
August quake, I reasoned. The letter, however – Francesca, my architect friend explained – was an *ordinanza di sgombero*, a formal eviction order, and so a fait accompli.

*

My return to Italy after the October earthquake was further delayed by bitter weather. As if people had not suffered enough, the amount of snow that fell across the central Apennines that winter brought life to a standstill. In places, it lay over six feet deep. Drifts banked up against honey-coloured stone and brick buildings. A deadening silence descended on narrow walkways and cobbled paths. Some spoke of seeing wolves, unable to find food in the mountains, lurking on the edge of villages and towns.

As strong tremors continued and buildings shook, many who remained found themselves trapped. Windows were encased in ice. Doors opened onto sheer white walls. The weight of snow brought down trees. Power lines were cut. Thousands were plunged into darkness. Many sat by candlelight, nursing limbs that ached from shovelling channels through the downfall.

High in the mountains it was deeper still, gathering in natural folds and canyons that formed conduits which pointed in the direction of dwellings below. As the earth continued to shudder, the consequence of such events at high altitudes was inevitable. Sheets of crusted ice shattered like panes of glass, sending avalanches thundering downhill.

When the region was struck by four strong quakes within a few hours one morning in mid-January 2017, thousands of tonnes of snow and uprooted trees came crashing down a mountainside in Abruzzo. A small spa hotel with forty staff and guests lay in their path.

It was nightfall by the time the alarm was raised. Roads were impassable. A small team, including a surgeon and two veteran alpine guides, set off on skis to battle through the blizzard. When they finally reached the site where the hotel once stood, only the tip of a twisted roof remained visible. There was little they could do until dawn, when more rescue workers, some of whom had dug through the rubble of Amatrice five months before, were flown in by helicopter.

For days, the exhausted workers burrowed down through the snow, searching for survivors. Early mobile phone footage, and, later, news bulletins, followed their progress. As I waited to fly out to Italy, I was awed by their dignity and devotion and hoped the end had been swift for those entombed below.

Then, thirty hours after the search began, a hand was raised to call for silence and the first faint cry was heard. It was the voice of a woman pleading: 'I am Adriana. Please help us. I am with my son. My daughter is inside, in the next room. Please, please help us.'

First the mother was hauled to the surface, followed by her two children, tugged from a jagged belly of ice, broken wood and crushed masonry. Eight more survivors were eventually pulled from the same frozen womb, most after more than fifty hours. Twenty-nine others perished. It was the deadliest avalanche in Italy in more than a hundred years.

Chapter 5

By the time I made my way along my usual route from Ancona airport into the mountains to assess the damage, I dreaded what lay ahead. Seeking to calm jittery nerves with the familiarity of old working habits, I made several detours on my way to Amandola to see how other communities had fared. I told myself I was gathering material for an article I would write about the devastation visited on Le Marche. But I knew it was little more than a delaying tactic.

As I followed a track up the western flank of the Fiastrella valley to the picturesque town of San Ginesio I passed a familiar sign: 'Welcome to the Balcony of the Sibillini'. But it was not the panoramic views of the snowy peaks in the distance that held my attention. As I approached San Ginesio's main square I found my way blocked by a wooden barrier with red mesh fencing and a warning sign strung across the road: 'Zona Rossa', Red Zone, meaning access was forbidden. Beyond it, through a medieval arch, I could see lanes choked with rubble, the walls of houses split apart, and the façade of the town's main church cracked and crumbling. I did not stop to interview soldiers manning the barricade as I would have done had I been on assignment. Any sense of detachment I might have felt as a journalist evaporated. I was no longer reporting the story, I was living it.

I retraced my route and tacked along a road on the opposite side of the valley to Gualdo, another small town I knew. There I found the same barriers, mesh fencing and warning signs. Trailing off in all directions from these were stone walls of buildings that had stood solid for centuries but now tumbled outwards into narrow passageways, leaving eaves hanging with no support. On the outskirts, I passed a heap of rubble with the remains of a tiled roof draped over it like soggy icing. Torn curtains, a crumpled washing machine and slabs of concrete lay tangled between rods of twisted metal. I assumed this to be the place where debris from the town was being dumped. But when I stopped to speak to an old woman in thick woollen stockings, walking with her dog along the verge away from the town, she told me it was once a house.

'Destroyed,' she said, punching her wooden stick into the ground, as if to punish it. 'Everything gone.'

The people in these mountain communities are known for their longevity. Years of walking and working this land of steep inclines, on a diet of largely local produce, extends their lives beyond that of many city-dwellers. From her rugged features and stooped posture, I took the woman to be in her late eighties, possibly nineties. As I drove on, I thought of the troubles of war and destruction her generation had seen.

The road leading on to the Sibillini national park twists through many small villages and towns. But I did not stop again. I wanted to reach Amandola before nightfall. As I passed under the ornate Porta San Giacomo, an imposing archway topped with elaborate ironwork, two bells and a large clock, it seemed as if the town was under siege. The main square was full of military vehicles, fire trucks and *carabinieri* jeeps. Tired-looking men in helmets and heavy uniforms stood huddled in small groups under the colonnade which ran along one side. Some smoked. Others talked urgently on mobile phones, arms gesticulating, fingers pinched in frustration.

Skirting an escarpment, I reached the spur of land at the far end of town where Amandola's hospital looms over the valley. It looked abandoned. Not a single light was on. The car park empty. The emergency department entrance sealed with the now familiar red mesh. Behind this I saw the part of the building that had crumbled onto waiting ambulances during the first August quake. Within hours of its collapse, patients were evacuated and driven in convoy to the coast.

Close to the hospital, a high wooden barrier had been erected to block off the lane that led past a once bustling Benedictine convent. Peering through a crack in the barricade, I could see part of its roof had caved in. And an enclosed elevated walkway of brick and glass that had spanned the width of the lane for centuries, allowing the cloistered nuns to pass quietly above the townspeople's heads to reach their small private chapel on the other side, looked precariously close to doing the same.

Looking back, I saw the top of the spire of the much larger medieval church of Saint Francis was missing. Its conical steeple had been toppled by the quake and lay buried in undergrowth behind the apse like an empty discarded ice cream cone. What was left of the bell tower had been hurriedly sealed with crude wooden boards to protect it from the elements. The church itself was in the process of being barricaded shut by harried engineers in hard hats, allowing only pigeons to flutter in through a gaping hole in its facade.

When I craned my neck to look in through the door, I saw the mess that both pigeons and the latest quake had made. This church, the origins of which date back to the fourteenth century, was built on the site of a primitive settlement of Franciscan friars even further back in time and had been damaged and rebuilt after successive earthquakes in the past. Now bird droppings and feathers flecked piles of bricks and plasterwork shaken loose from the church walls. And, to one side of the church, in the Chapel of the Annunciation, I saw a fifteenth-century cycle of frescos had also partially crumbled, leaving the limbs of the Archangel Gabriel, the Virgin Mary and her attendant saints lying below in the dust.

As the engineers shouted urgent instructions to stand clear I stepped back out into the cobbled lane and saw that some of the old houses near to the church looked, at first glance, as they always had. Some even had freshly tended potted plants outside. But nearly all had piles of bricks and stones neatly stacked against their outer walls; as I wiped dust from windows and peered inside, I could see sections of floors and ceilings had caved in. Further on, rows of tall houses were supported by thick timber braces and steel bands, like giant trusses supporting aged patients.

Doubling back, I took the steep road that led up to the Piazza Alta, Amandola's oldest square, and stood there for some time looking out over the rooftops of houses that descended step-like towards the valley below. There was little of the familiar smell of wood smoke that usually filled the air at that time of year. The town seemed half deserted and disconcertingly quiet. The church bells that have marked the passage of each day here for generations were silent.

Street lights flickered on as I started down the long flight of stone steps leading from the high piazza to my house and passed the tall wrought-iron gate and curving driveway of the Hotel Paradiso. My heart sank as I saw a thick chain and padlock looped through the bars of the main gate and knew the hotel too had been declared *inagibile*, unfit or uninhabitable, robbing the family of their livelihood. In the one brief phone call I had managed to have with Oreste following the quakes he told me that Manuela and the couple's young daughter had gone to stay with her parents in a village in the mountains, while he and his mother had found temporary lodgings with different relatives.

Oreste was so downcast we did not speak for long. But as I continued on down the steps, I felt a growing sense of foreboding. I knew I was lucky that my home was still standing and felt a surge of relief as I rounded the last bend in the pedestrian lane and saw that its tall facade appeared intact. It still felt as if it had been violated by an unknown intruder and I expected to find it in the kind of shambles thieves might leave behind. Yet turning the key in my front door, it was I who felt like the intruder. The eviction order made it clear I could be subjected to heavy fines if found still occupying the property. I knew some were choosing to run the risk of severe financial sanctions and were steadfastly remaining in their damaged homes. But knowing that the police or government inspectors could knock on my front door at any moment only added to my feeling of unease as I stepped across the threshold.

Not sure if the electricity was still connected, I felt my way along the wall to the switch. The floor-level lighting on either side of the wide travertine staircase began to glow. I braced myself for debris and collapse as I climbed, but at first could see little out of place. The wooden-beamed sitting room and galley kitchen leading to the garden appeared unharmed. The only signs of a disturbance were the twisted frames and shattered glass of black and white photographs bought years before in Vietnam, and the thick dust which covered wall hangings and carpets collected from assignments in Turkey and Iran.

It was not until I reached the top floor that I saw any real damage. Since the house stands taller than its neighbours, the effect of the earthquake was amplified here. The repairs to the two vaulted ceilings which I had overseen were now undone, and the cracks had split further apart – finger width in some places, fist width in others.

The wall of the upper landing had a fracture which ran the length of the corridor and chunks of plaster had crumbled to the floor. Some of the plaster bore dusty fragments of the pale red and blue pastel stencils which had lain concealed beneath thick whitewash on one of the vaults when I bought the house – one of the few traces of the modest affluence it once enjoyed. As a tribute to the craftsmen who had once painted the stencils, I had left them partially visible during the original restoration of the house. Seeing them damaged now made me feel I had failed in my duty as temporary caretaker of this dwelling that must have witnessed so many changing fortunes.

As I picked my way through the breakages and opened the windows facing the main piazza, the normally floodlit bell tower and huge stained-glass windows of the church of Saint Augustine that dominate the square were in darkness. The gentle light they cast over the town's sleeping households had always felt to me like a blessing. Its absence made it seem as if those who lived here had somehow fallen from grace.

What was once my sanctuary from a troubled world now stood at the mercy of unpredictable forces and, suddenly, I felt I had lost my footing. Yet I knew others had suffered far greater losses. While Claudio and Alessandra to one side of my house and my other direct neighbour, Elio, remained deeply shaken by the earthquakes, their houses, unlike mine, remained intact. But the home of Elio's elderly parents in the small village of Pretare, which lay close to the epicentre of the August quake, had totally collapsed and they were now living with their son in cramped quarters. As I passed Elio's front door that day, I raised my hand to greet his mother who I saw through a window standing at the kitchen sink, a blank expression in her eyes as if she had forgotten quite how she came to be there.

Many others whose houses were severely damaged had to move in with generous friends. That evening I sat with two friends of mine, an Irish writer and her Dutch husband, whose house in the countryside outside Amandola had been so severely damaged they were told it would have to be demolished entirely and warned it could be years before they received permission and state funding for it to be rebuilt. In the aftermath of the October quake, friends of theirs, whose home survived intact in a hamlet some distance away, had offered them a place to stay until the family returned in the summer, and I found brief refuge there too.

Over the coming years, the couple would have to relocate again and again as they were forced to find new temporary lodgings. But that night, none of us knew what lay ahead. We were grateful for the warmth of a log-burning stove and sat, like dazed evacuees, cupping bowls of soup in our hands. We talked of the farmers up in the mountains who, reluctant to leave their livestock, would be bedding down in old industrial containers hastily shipped in by rescue workers as rudimentary shelters. Isolated and remote, they were seeing out the winter in severe hardship.

We spoke too of the many thousands of families who would be going to sleep surrounded by the few belongings they had managed to salvage stacked in seasonal hotels and apartments requisitioned by the government along the Adriatic coast. Others, able to stay close to their crippled communities, had taken to living in second-hand caravans hastily purchased and parked in the driveways of their ruined homes, or in Portakabin-style containers provided by the state. There was a small straggly encampment of these caravans and containers, huddled like a Wild West wagon train, on common ground on the outskirts of Amandola.

But even more painful for many than the hardship of such living arrangements was the psychological stress of not knowing if or when there might be another major quake. 'Every time there is an after-shock and the furniture rattles, we brace ourselves,' my Irish friend Fiona sighed. 'Our nerves are in shreds. Some people are getting strange ailments, mysterious aches and pains. There's always a long queue now waiting to see Doctor Rossi (a popular local physician) every morning.'

For some, the strain of such uncertainty and distress had already proven too much. In the wake of both the August and October earthquakes, hospitals reported a notable increase in the number of deaths from strokes and heart attacks, particularly among the bewildered elderly.

'Yes, it's true. We've heard this too,' my friend explained. 'Once an illness comes, some let themselves go. They feel there's nothing left for them to live for.'

That night I lay in bed and could not sleep. My thoughts kept returning to a short report I read in a local newspaper about a pensioner from Monte San Giusto who was evacuated to the coast and threw herself in front of a train a few weeks later. A few days later, a local journalist friend from *Corriere Adriatico* said his news-paper had reported at least eight suicides. 'These are the known cases,' Francesco said. 'No one knows how many there really are.'

One elderly farmer from Montappone, rather than be evicted, had dressed himself in his favourite hunting clothes, wandered up into the mountains to sit beneath a chestnut tree and, blinded by despair to the beauty around him, put a shotgun to his head. A livestock breeder from Fiastra hanged himself in his barn. A young entrepreneur from Camerino whose business was destroyed chose a similar fate. While a stonemason from Amatrice who tried twice to take his own life succeeded on the second attempt. Some left notes.

One office worker from Sarnano, a neighbouring town to Amandola, left a letter for his brother saying his damaged home was so full of memories and affection that, when forced to leave it, he could no longer smile. 'All became darkness,' he wrote before returning to the cellar of the condemned building with a rope.

The fate of those who lost all hope haunted me and returned to me in my dreams. It triggered memories of some of the darkest places I had been to on assignment where unspeakable atrocities were committed. Sometimes a sound or smell was enough to evoke such demons and years later they continued to torment my sleeping and occasionally waking hours too. I had tried for a long time to block those memories. But our unconscious is like magma deep below the surface of the earth; it erupts suddenly and without warning, often in the middle of the night. For our lives are laid down like sediment, each layer accruing and compressing the one below until hairline fractures, fault lines form. My own, I realised, were buried deep, and over time I felt them begin to give.

It was then that the sanctuary of my Amandola home had become ever more precious. For on those nights, when beset by bad dreams, I could open my bedroom windows, drink in the cool night air and the stillness of the sleeping town bathed in the soft glow of the lighted bell tower; I could feel the silent theatre of stars above shrink my unease and put earthly cares into perspective. In such moments the presence of the mountains in the distance felt like a colossal steadying hand.

Yet it was little over a year after finishing my book, which chronicled the lives of women on the Buddhist path and had taken me around the world on what became a healing journey, that an apocalypse of sorts enveloped these mountains. And as government promises of solutions to the crisis in central Italy became embroiled in the country's revolving-door politics, it was clear more and more people were beginning to lose hope.

'It's as if in the heart, the precious heart, of Italy there is an almost biological change,' an editorial in one Italian newspaper concluded.

'Distrust, sadness, fear of not making it, is balanced only by stubbornness and deep attachment to this land.'

Unable to stay in my own home, I could do little more than travel back and forth to Italy for short spells in the months that followed to discuss prospects for the repair of my house. Each time I did I noticed more and more 'For Sale' and 'To Rent' signs in shuttered shop windows in Amandola as even those whose homes had not been damaged took the decision to try to build lives elsewhere.

By the end of 2017, more than a quarter of Amandola's population would pack their bags. Who knew how many would return?

It felt as if central Italy was now on life support.

One evening, as I spoke on the phone with Luisa she echoed what many of those who left, whether temporarily or for good, must have felt. For she and Dom had moved into a small apartment they kept on the coast shortly after the first August quake.

'I can't bear to look at the mountains any more,' Luisa told me, as if she held them responsible for the misfortune visited on Le Marche and the rest of central Italy.

Certainly, the forces that formed them were. But it saddened me to hear the Sibillini spoken of as if by a jilted lover, since it was those mountains that had first drawn me to this place.

Chapter 6

The sound of a violin echoed along the valley as summer slipped into autumn that year. Sweet chestnut trees with burnished leaves shimmered in the distance as the young violinist before us swayed to the strains of Coldplay's 'Fix You', his audience seated on white plastic chairs arrayed in a semicircle on the grassy forecourt of an abandoned yeast factory.

The factory lay by the side of a road that led from Amandola into the mountains and had long since ceased production and fallen into disrepair. But it had been in the violinist's family for generations, a woman beside me whispered as the small audience broke into applause.

Few public meeting places had been left untouched by the earthquakes. So, when a group of concerned citizens decided to hold a day of cultural events to try to rally people's spirits, the factory forecourt in the small hamlet of Cremore was offered as a safe place to congregate. Everything that day would take place in the open and the mountains provided a perfect backdrop for what the organisers intended: that the day be a celebration of the *genius loci* of the Sibillini.

In the absence of any real political will by the Italian government to address the crisis unfolding at the heart of the country, those gathered that day were intent on seeking solace in the country's rich cultural past and in a love of the landscape that enfolded us. At the time of the Roman Empire *genius loci* often referred to the deity believed to preside over a particular place. And first to take the microphone, after the applause died down, was a local doctor devoted to the legend that gave these mountains their name. The legend tells that deep in the midst of Mount Sibilla there lies a secret cave, a cave said to be the seat of a divine oracle, one of a clan of female prophets recognised by both the ancient Greeks and Romans. In Virgil's *Aeneid*, the Apennine Sibyl is linked to the Cumaean Sibyl, prophetess of the Nativity and the Apocalypse who, like all the Sibyls, was said to have wandered from place to place, under the influence of a pantheon of deities, uttering predictions.

After Catholicism assimilated the tradition of the Sibyls, the Apennine Sibyl was said to have been banished to a remote grotto as punishment for daring to believe that she, and not the Virgin Mary, was destined to be mother to God's only son. From this mix of pagan and Christian lore, tales of the Apennine Sibyl came to life in medieval chivalric literature. They paint her as a seductress visited by knights, necromancers and wizards drawn from all over Europe by the promise of her prophesies and erotic charm.

Such was the popularity of these tales in the fifteenth century that a papal edict was issued threatening excommunication to anyone making a pilgrimage to her Apennine domain. Centuries later, tunnels leading down to what were believed to have been the Sibyl's cave were dynamited to bar access and prevent the ruinous power of the temptress from escaping.

Yet even today, the myth of the Apennine Sibyl is said to influence many who live here or visit, drawn, some say, by the female power the mountains are thought to emanate. Of this the doctor speaking that day was sure. 'Our Sibylla, these Sibillini, are not just a physical space,' he declared passionately, as we shuffled our chairs to make room for new arrivals. 'These mountains exist in our psyche. They are our inspiration. They have given birth to a land of strong women.'

These beliefs and legends of the Apennine Sibyl have tradition-ally drawn strength from the existence of a rock formation at high altitudes with a strangely feminine silhouette. Some have led to fantastical explanations of the deep rumbling and roaring sounds that foreshadow earthquakes in these parts. One holds that the ancient prophetess surrounds herself with handmaidens with golden, cloven hooves which they tap as they dance to lure in strangers.

I had hiked several times to the 5,500-foot crest of Mount Amandola and, in the company of my lover at the time, a Spanish poet, diplomat and experienced mountain climber, almost reached the 7,600-foot peak of Mount Priora, before the sight of the precipitous drop into the *Gole dell'Infernaccio* – Hell's Gorge – induced a sudden onset of vertigo and cautious descent. But I had never attempted to climb Mount Sibilla, the summit of which stands at just over 7,000 feet and is the central peak framed by my bedroom window.

As the doctor meandered in his epic tale of the Apennine Sibyl and the 'land of strong women', I found myself pondering the ways in which the land where we are born shapes us all, and how this can take years for us to understand. The Welsh village of Mumbles where I was born lies on the westernmost edge of Swansea Bay, where the anthropomorphic shape of two small islands off its headland are said to have led it to be named after a corruption of the French term for breasts, *les mamelles*. Swansea Bay has one of the highest tidal ranges in the world, second only to the Bay of Fundy in Nova Scotia and another further north in the Inuit territory of northern Quebec. When the tide is in, and the sea rough, waves crest the sea wall and flood inland, mocking our attempts to hold it back. But within hours the water retreats far into the distance, exposing a vast expanse of shimmering sand riven by rivulets of brine.

This cosmic sleight of hand remained a mystery to man for millennia. As did the reason the earth shook. For just as the Japanese once believed earthquakes were caused by a giant catfish thrashing about in underground mud, one ancient belief held that the constant ebb and flow was due to the inhalation and exhalation of a great creature beneath the waves. And, a hundred years before Newton's explanation that tides derive from the gravitational pull of the Moon and rotation of the Earth, Galileo thought them due to great volumes of water slopping from side to side in ocean basins.

Looking back, I can't help but wonder if the spectacular tidal flux near to my place of birth instilled a restlessness in me from an early age. As an infant I might have been immune and, by the age of three, had moved away from the sea, relocating several times due to my father's work, before we moved back to Mumbles when I was nine. My mother, who grew up in Cornwall, had, since marrying my father, relocated many more times than that – so often that it made the front page of the local paper for which she wrote a regular column as a freelance journalist. Many years later I found a faded newspaper clipping of this, together with poems she had written, in a folder of personal papers in the bottom drawer of the desk where she kept her old Olivetti typewriter.

Under the headline 'They've moved 13 times already . . . And now they're off again!' was a black and white photograph of me and my sister squeezed onto a small sofa on either side of our parents: my sister in a sixties-style dress with psychedelic swirls, me in a tartan wool kilt I remember scratched my knees. In contrast to my father's handsome tanned face – he took pleasure in his looks being likened to Robert Redford's – my mother, sister and I appeared wan. I was the only one not looking directly at the camera but rather off to the side. Perhaps I was distracted, perhaps nervous or uncomfortable; I was a shy and watchful child given to daydreaming.

In my teens, I would often take long walks around the cliffs of the Gower Peninsula alone and, looking out to sea, waves crashing against the rocks below, wonder what lay far off in the distance. Those raised by the sea are blessed with the gift of an infinite horizon that nourishes thoughts of what lies beyond. Was it this, or the constant coming and going of the water, I wondered, that nurtured an early sense of restlessness and encouraged it to grow? For, despite the beauty of my birthplace, I couldn't wait to escape. I wanted to see the world, to understand how it worked. I did not yearn for fame or fortune; what I wanted more than anything was what I thought of as wisdom, with little awareness of what it really meant. I left home at seventeen and rarely looked back. While my early years were defined by repeated upheaval, those that followed came close to nomadic.

As the silver-haired doctor continued to speak I found myself mentally totting up the number of places where I'd lived before making a home in the Sibillini mountains. Closing my eyes for a moment, a kaleidoscope of sights and sounds and smells came drifting back. The chatter of students and clinking bicycle bells in the City of Dreaming Spires. The whiff of fresh waffles in Brussels where I worked as a *stagiaire*, or intern, with the European Commission's environmental division. The crowing of roosters in the old Alsatian farmhouse where I lived in Strasbourg while on another internship with the European Court of Human Rights. And after this the succession of places where I worked as a journalist: from Paris to Berlin, to Miami and then Mexico, that vibrant, chaotic, exuberant country where I lived with my daughter and her father in the shadow of the simmering, smoking Popocatépetl volcano before my daughter and I returned to London. At this point the kaleidoscope in my head jammed, the memory of that break-up too painful to recall. But by then, I had counted more than twenty-five changes of address and I was not yet out of my thirties.

The sun was just creeping over the crest of Mount Sibilla as I looked up at its peak and reflected on what it was that had drawn me to this place. For in the early years after making a home in Amandola, I had often still felt a strong pull to the sea. I found a cove surrounded by woods and cliffs a little like the one where I swam with my sister as a child, on the Conero peninsula, an hour and a half's drive away on the Adriatic coast, and in summer preferred leisurely days there rather than sweating up a mountainside. But in the wake of the earthquakes, unlike my friend and neighbour Luisa who couldn't bear to look at the Sibillini, I found myself identifying much more strongly with the mountains that enveloped my adopted home.

Perhaps, because of the ferocious energy they had unleashed, I began to comprehend a little more clearly why mountains have been revered by spiritual traditions through the ages and sometimes viewed as an axis linking three levels of the cosmos: Heaven, Earth and Hell. For just as the Vatican once decreed climbing Mount Sibilla to be a mortal sin, the ascent of sacred mountains, like Mount Kailas in Tibet, is still deemed heresy due to the supernatural powers they are thought to possess.

There had been times when I experienced a strange sense of this otherworldliness when walking in mountains elsewhere in the world: once when standing amid the ruins of the former Incan citadel of Machu Pichu, high in the Peruvian Andes, looking out across the Sacred Valley. But it was only later, when walking above the cloud line in the Sibillini, that I really came to appreciate this sensibility of mountains occupying a mysterious liminal space. I saw then how their very size and ancient origins invited a different perspective. For where the wide-open horizon and constant movement of the sea engender thoughts of exploration, the sheer magnitude and age of mountains stir a tendency to reflection and introspection – an appreciation of the deep time in which they exist, far beyond our own brief lives.

Many speak of each place on earth being imbued with its own unique intangible quality. Some call it spirit. Others a life force embodied by the ancient Greek goddess Gaia or Andean Pachamama, the ancestral mother pregnant with possibility. In Amandola I felt it in the cool morning air as I leant out of my bedroom window and watched dawn wash the highest peaks of the Sibillini salmon pink.

As if reading my thoughts, next up to the microphone that day was a local landscape photographer who spoke with intensity of the influence of the landscape surrounding us. He talked at some length about the origin of the Italian word for landscape, *paesaggio*. How its root *paese* is frequently used to denote the place a person is from. For unlike its English equivalent, often taken to simply mean a particular kind of topography, the Italian concept of *paesaggio* is heavily weighted with a sense of belonging.

Yet as a word *paesaggio* only came into use at the time of the Renaissance when painters needed an expression to describe the way they were portraying nature in their work. For such artists *paesaggio* was a matter of personal interpretation. It implied imagination. It was a creative act. 'So we too must remember that our *paesaggio*, the soul of this place we are from, our sense of belonging, calls us to engage our imagination. We need to become creative to revive what we have lost in the earthquakes,' the photographer Giorgio implored his audience.

As the morning wore on there were lively discussions led by experts in art, architecture, history and literature about the strong traditions and culture of the region dating back to antiquity. Including that of the age-old practice of transhumance whereby livestock was herded up to high pastures in the summer and in winter guided further down the mountain slopes to graze. This custom, which lasted to the middle of the last century, once saw the great mountain looming directly in front of us, Mount Priora, support thirty-six full-time shepherds.

There were further musical interludes too. Recordings were played of *musica popolare*, the traditional folk songs once integral to the rhythm of life in these parts, with different songs for different tasks throughout the agricultural year. There was, of course, a lengthy pause in the middle of the day for lunch during which a small truck loaded up the plastic chairs from that morning and drove them higher into the mountains. By the time we'd clambered up to the place where they had been arranged, on the terrace of an old, abandoned house in the small hamlet of Balleria di Rubiano, the last feeble rays of the autumn sun were fast disappearing. It grew colder. But the view was spectacular. The old house was within sight of Mount Sibilla's voluptuous peak. From here, beyond the crumpled quilt of fading green in the valleys below, tinted reddish-gold here and there with early leaf-fall, you could just make out the distant stain of the Adriatic.

It was to this windswept place that the Apennine Sibyl's hand-maidens were said to have descended on moonlit nights. Here that they entranced shepherds and travellers with their dancing, hence its name Balleria, before cajoling them deep underground.

But that night the Moon was on the wane. There would be no seductions, said Adolfo, our guide for the afternoon, to laughter and shouts of *che vergogna!* – shame! – as he took his place at an improvised podium at the edge of the terrace.

Adolfo was a columnist for one of the oldest newspapers in Italy *Il Resto del Carlino*, founded after unification, which took its curious name, roughly meaning 'the change you get from a carlino', from the ten-cent coin, or *carlino*, that once circulated in central Italy and was often given in lieu of small change. Adolfo, a slim, erudite man, had grown up walking ancient trails in the Sibillini and spoke at length of his sorrow at seeing the mountain communities he knew from childhood become *fantasmi muti*, silent ghosts, in the aftermath of the earthquakes.

'It is as if our history has been cancelled and we are entering a period of post-history,' he said, as the final sliver of the sun slid behind Mount Sibilla's crest. 'The scream that shook these mountains and tore them apart left us questioning ourselves, asking how we can find balance and steadiness on this shifting land,' he said, as if addressing the peaks now shrouded with scudding clouds. 'It is in times like these that we turn for answers to our native son Giacomo Leopardi, that seeker of truth and meaning and to the wisdom found in his poetry.' He returned his gaze to the seated gathering, before starting to read aloud stanzas from Leopardi's *Canti*.

Time seemed to stand still as we sat listening in hushed silence. The wind picked up and leaves on the skeletal trees close to the terrace fluttered in agitation. The temperature dropped uncomfortably low. But no one made a move to leave. How many evacuees from disaster areas would sit rapt by poetry in the wake of tragedy, other than in Italy, I wondered. Surely it did happen elsewhere. But I had never before witnessed such a scene.

The words of Leopardi floated around us. First, verses from '*Il tramonto della luna*', The Setting of the Moon, in which Leopardi writes of darkness falling:

> Behind the Apennines
> . . . the moon descends, the world loses its colour
> . . . and darkness falls on hill and valley;
> the night is desolate
> singing a mournful melody . . .

Then words from Leopardi's '*Canto notturno di un pastore errante dell'Asia*', Night Song of a Wandering Shepherd in Asia, in which he first laments the disappearance of the *silenziosa luna* and the indifference of the silent Moon to the suffering of those over whom she casts her light, before speaking of the regeneration she can engender.

We should take heart in Leopardi's words and the possibility of renewal, said Adolfo, and in the writings of a young contemporary Italian author, the Sicilian-born secondary school teacher Alessandro D'Avenia who was inspired to bring the poet's words to a new generation. D'Avenia's book *L'Arte di essere fragile: come Leopardi può salvarti la vita*, The Art of Being Fragile: How Leopardi Can Save Your Life, was, by chance, published the day after the October 2016 earthquake. It went on to become a number-one bestseller in Italy and was subsequently published as far afield as China and Taiwan – feelings of fragility clearly weighing heavy on us all.

As Adolfo spoke of D'Avenia, I thought once again of the photograph of me and my sister with our parents on the cusp of their fourteenth move. A year or so before this photograph was taken, I remembered, my mother had contracted severe meningitis and barely survived. My sister and I were forbidden from going near her for fear of infection. But I clearly recalled standing alone outside her closed bedroom door in the middle of the night and being aware she might die. In the way that most children take their childhood experiences to be normal, I was not conscious of the effect this had on me at the time. But the more Adolfo spoke of fragility the more I wondered if it was this early lesson in the precariousness of life that gave me a sense from a young age of how close we all walk to the edge. How all our lives can be torn apart at any moment by random events.

I began to question too if it was really by chance that I had sought refuge and consolation in a landscape liable to sudden rupture, or if there was something else at play. Something about this landscape that felt familiar. For as Adolfo continued to read out D'Avenia's words they relayed to us how life is not defined by equilibrium, but tension. How the art of living is to consider ourselves constantly reborn. And while poetry may make us look what he called 'our mutilated world' in the face, it is capable of unleashing energy too, of restoring meaning and a sense of place.

'We are fragile. This leaping earth of ours is fragile. Our relationships, our loves are fragile,' Adolfo said in conclusion, gathering his notes together with a tap like a teacher bringing class to a close. 'It is love that allows us to accept our fragility, and, despite it, learn the art of repairing life, rebuilding communities, flourishing.'

As we picked our way back along a narrow path to our cars in the dusk, I prayed that he was right.

In the aftermath of the earthquakes, I sometimes felt overwhelmed by this sense of fragility, both my own and that of the world around me. I found my dreams, and even my waking thoughts, filled with images of fractured landscapes, yawning chasms, me falling.

Writers such as Jules Verne, Lewis Carroll, J.R.R. Tolkien and, seven centuries earlier in Italy, Dante Alighieri, conjured up hidden worlds deep underground to challenge convention or logic or stir up existential terror. But they were writing at a time when little was known about what lay beneath the earth's surface. Today we know more about the forces that shape our planet. Central to our understanding is the widely accepted theory of plate tectonics which explains how colossal sections of the earth's crust are constantly on the move, albeit at the speed, on average, that our fingernails grow, above a volatile mantle of semi-liquid rocks that convect away the heat of our planet's molten core.

So, when a few weeks after returning from Amandola that autumn, I learnt that one of the pioneers of this theory would be visiting London, I asked if we could meet. But it was not Xavier Le Pichon's professional achievements as one of the world's leading geophysicists that drew me to him. It was his radical shift in perspective on life that intrigued me. After years spent studying the fragility of the physical world, the French professor, a devout Catholic, became so concerned that the rigour of science was making him lose touch with humanity that he turned his back on his career at its height and went to work for a time with Mother Teresa, caring for the destitute of Calcutta.

The professor was in his early eighties when we met one afternoon in a wood-panelled room of Burlington House, Piccadilly, headquarters of the illustrious Geological Society of London. He was there to address a conference to mark the fiftieth anniversary of the theory of plate tectonics. He looked tired, so we did not speak for long; he had travelled that morning from the retreat centre he founded in southern France for those with learning difficulties. But I wanted to ask him about the analogy I read he liked to draw between the pressures that lead to the sudden rupture of the earth's surface and the way communities fracture unless flexible. In keeping with the theme of the day, he talked science first. Reminding me of my university studies and of how, in the lower layers of the earth where temperatures are high, rocks are able to deform without fracture. They become ductile. They flow. And how, in the upper few miles of the earth's surface where temperatures are low, rocks become rigid so their weaknesses cannot be expressed. They react by reaching the limit of their resistance and then suddenly – at this the professor clapped his hands together – 'There comes the roar, a bang, a major commotion, an earthquake,' he said, tipping alarmingly backwards in his chair.

'Human society is similar,' he then said, his demeanour softening. 'Communities which are very rigid and do not take into account people who are in difficulty tend not to evolve. Or only evolve by very strong commotion, what in French we call *révolution*. Fragility is the essence of men and women,' he said finally. 'It is at the heart of all humanity.'

When I left the bespectacled professor that day and stepped out into the bustle of a busy London street, I felt sure he was right: that all of nature's systems, from the earth's crust to each of us as human beings, only evolve when pliable and accommodating of frailty.

But how far, I wondered, do I, or any one of us, apply this principle to ourselves when navigating precarious terrain? Especially when most societies today place so much emphasis on strength, while denigrating vulnerability.

Chapter 7

As strong aftershocks continued to pound the nerves of those at the heart of Italy during the winter months that followed, I had little choice but to remain in London. One evening, feeling homesick for Amandola and despondent at my inability to help my friends and neighbours there, I finally took down the box I had kept for so long on my study shelf. The box of secrets abandoned a century ago in my attic.

If I couldn't be physically present in my mountain home, then at least I could touch traces of its past and of those who once lived there, I thought, as I spread the contents of the box across the carpet in front of a fire in my living room and tried to find some order in the dates of the miscellaneous material. The easiest to place in time was a small booklet, little bigger than the palm of my hand. It was a gift distributed by the Italian postal service to mark the start of a new century. A calendar that was nothing short of a miniature work of art.

On the front, beneath the greeting '*Buon Anno Nuovo 1901*' and a gilded crown of the former Kingdom of Italy, was a carefully drawn picture of two young postmen with handlebar moustaches in tightly buttoned jackets and red peaked caps, one astride a bicycle, with satchels brimming with letters slung across their chests. On the back was a delicate pastel watercolour of the Rome skyline bathed in the pink of dawn; in its foreground two small figures looking out across the river Tiber, as if contemplating what lay ahead.

Flicking through the booklet's sixty-eight densely printed pages, the concerns of man and the motion of our planet at this juncture in history emerged. On the very first page the rotation of the Earth and arc of the Moon across the night sky was recorded in minute detail, noting the exact time, to the hour and minute, that the Moon would be full, waning, new and waxing in each month of the coming year.

Beneath certain dates in each lunar cycle was a note of the timing of the *tramonto*, the hour of sunset at which the devout would be called to fall to their knees to recite the Ave Maria prayer.

Following this was a moving testimony to the crucial role that postmen played in people's lives long before the advent of instant communication. It was a touching reminder to all who received the gift of the calendar that:

'It is the postman who delivers news to those who love, those who aspire to a more beautiful moment in life, those who expect reproach or are called to duty. These poor agents, who work in all seasons, bringing joy, pleasure and sometimes pain and who feel great compassion for those who cry out, or mourn or are saddened by the news they bring.'

It was also a polite request: 'that the brave individuals who render this service, and who are poorly paid for their trouble, be treated with courtesy and kindness.'

I felt a sudden pang as I thought of what Italy's *portalettere* would be called on to do in the years that followed. How, besides bringing joyful announcements of a birth, or marriage, or the imminent arrival of a loved one home, 'these poor agents' would be delivering news of so much sorrow. News of a loved one killed in the catastrophic earthquake that would engulf Sicily and Calabria seven years later. Or of one of the hundreds of thousands of Italians who would die a few years after that in the First World War. News of those struck down by *l'influenza Spagnola*, the Spanish flu that would claim even more lives than the war itself had done. Then of those who would fall victim to the horrors of Fascism and perish in yet more years of war.

Putting the booklet aside, I picked up a thinner pink and white catalogue bearing the sticker of the Alati Angelo music shop at via Tre Cannelle in Rome. On its cover was a photograph of the Italian tenor Enrico Caruso staring dreamily into the distance. Had those in my house been opera lovers, I wondered. Had its rooms once echoed with the world-famous tenor's rich tones? Then opening the catalogue out fully, I was surprised to find its centre pages written in English, under the heading 'His Master's Voice Records for British and American Troops in Italy'. Flipping to the front cover again, I saw, half hidden under the music shop sticker, the date June 1918, five months before the end of the First World War. This centrefold was illustrated with a drawing in pink ink of the Statue of Liberty towering above a New York skyline and an American doughboy soldier wearing puttees and a lemon-squeezer-style soft cap. The soldier was seated at a table, pen in hand, writing a letter. Taking out my laptop, I couldn't resist searching online for some of the songs the catalogue listed and sat listening to crackling 78rpm recordings of Caruso singing Verdi's 'La Forza del Destino', Australian baritone Peter Dawson singing 'The Green Hills o' Somerset' and the Metropolitan Dance Band playing 'The Bugle Call Rag'.

How war weary British and American soldiers must have longed to return home; Italian soldiers too, trudging back to small communities like Amandola from the treacherous terrain of the Dolomites where so many lost their lives. Amandola, I was once told, had sent more than a thousand men marching north, woefully unprepared and underequipped, to defend their still fragile young country against the expansionist forces of the Austro-Hungarian empire after Italy entered the First World War in May 1915. A thousand men was more than a fifth of its population at the time and in the main square there was a touching plaque, often hung with garlands of flowers, that listed the names of the eighty-eight husbands and sons who did not return. Beside it was the inscription:

'Remembered with the pride and affection of a mother.'

As I continued to sift through the material, I grouped together a curious assortment of papers, including an obscure legal document; an exercise book full of handwritten notes in Latin; the book of stipends; a missionary almanac; and the illustrated local journal from 1910. The corners of this journal, the Rivista Marchigiana Illustrata, had been partially nibbled away by mice. But leafing through it, I came across an article berating Italian politicians of the day as spineless creatures or 'molluscs' for ignoring the problem of so many of their countrymen sailing away from Italy's shores.

I knew the turn of the last century was a time when Italy was in the throes of mass emigration to the United States and South America, especially Argentina and Brazil. I remembered once glancing through a phone book in Buenos Aires during the years I reported from there and noting that at least a third of the city's residents had Italian surnames. But I had no idea how many might have left Amandola in search of better fortune in the New World.

I thought of the more recent reverse flow of humanity struggling to reach Italy's shores in flimsy craft, more than half a million in five years before the country's populist government clamped down, and how perilous their homes must have felt to impel them to leave. How precarious home felt now to those living in the heart of Italy as the ground beneath them continued to shake.

Then I remembered the envelope that first caught my eye when builders handed the box down to me from the attic – the one sent from America in 1906. There were more than fifty letters and postcards in the thick bundle of correspondence. But, fanning the sheaf across the carpet, one envelope with a blue and white 5c stamp bearing the stern features of Abraham Lincoln stood out. The postmark certified it as having been dispatched from Essex Street Station, Boston, at 5.30 p.m. on 1 January. But a second Italian stamp showed it did not arrive in a local Le Marche sorting office until two weeks later before finally being delivered to the seminary in Fermo where the former occupant of my house must have been studying to become a priest.

Some of the many century-old letters hidden away in the attic, including that sent from Boston on 1 January 1906

Several of the envelopes gave the name of my predecessor as Don Federico, though I had no idea what age he would have been when he received them or what family he had, either in Amandola or elsewhere. But when I slipped the Boston letter from the envelope, I saw it was addressed to *carissimo fratello*, dearest brother, and was signed Donato Bellesi, which seemed strange as I imagined a brother would have simply signed his Christian name. The letter was eight pages long and written in neat script that flowed smoothly along faint lines making it easier to read than I could see some of the other letters would be.

I felt a momentary qualm about sifting through another's personal correspondence, long abandoned though it was. It had taken me years to be able to bring myself to look through my own mother's most intimate papers, and not just because her loss was too raw. I had grown up listening to my mother typing in the room next to mine as I lay in bed and had longed as child to know what she was writing. But as I grew older, I sensed the night hours she spent alone with her typewriter were a form of private communion.

As in many families, there was much that was never spoken of in ours. But children understand much more than they are conscious of. At a visceral level I sensed an underlying sadness in my mother. I grew accustomed to what was left unspoken. To concealed truths. A sensibility that perhaps informed my later working life. When I finally came to read through the folder of my mother's writings, I questioned whether she would have wanted this. Besides her poems and the partial manuscript of an unfinished novel, I found several typescripts. Some were little more than streams of consciousness, but as I read them, I found my childhood fears confirmed. Despite my mother's great warmth and gregarious nature, they offered a glimpse into her inner life: unspoken words of sorrow at lost love and unfulfilled dreams. My heart broke. Although we had always been close, I finally understood much more clearly how constricted she felt her life had been. I realised more clearly too the influence, whether conscious or unconscious, this had on my own fierce struggle to lead a life free of constraint.

While my mother's death was sudden, the result of an undiagnosed tumour, I believe she must have known I might one day come across her night-time musings. She had always been scrupulous about de-cluttering and had, I knew, burnt most of her writing. As painful as it was to read what she had left, I was glad to finally hear her authentic voice, speaking to me as a woman, rather than as the daughter she sought to protect from her own anguish.

It cemented a conviction that our voices carry an importance we cannot imagine far beyond our death.

So, presented now with the century-old collection of letters and journals spread before me, I saw them as more than a collection of mere memorabilia. Perhaps this was a legacy Don Federico too might have intended would one day be found, albeit one hundred years later. With such thoughts I set aside my misgivings, sat back on my heels and held the pages of the letter before me up towards the light.

After a brief preamble, complaining about the incompetence of the Boston postal service in delivering letters to the wrong address, Donato wrote of the difficulty he and his wife Rosa were having finding work to support themselves and repay a 600-lire loan taken out for their passage to the United States:

'*Certo che America non è più America*,' – America is not America any more, he lamented. 'It's not as people in Amandola say: that women here earn more than men. In six months we have only paid off 200 lire. If we had come ten years ago, we would surely have accumulated a fair amount of money by now. Still, I assure you, things here are much better than in Italy,' he continued. 'Just one day of work is enough to live for one week.'

The letter went on to speak of the number of Italians – thirty to forty thousand, Donato estimated – who lived in the same area of Boston as he and Rosa, and how the couple still struggled because they did not speak English. The culture shock those from remote rural communities must have felt when arriving in such a burgeoning city is clear from Donato's awe-struck description of 'the electric railway that moves in the air here supported by iron poles.'

But it was a sense of the life the couple left behind that touched me most. Their heartache at having left their children, their *angiolette* or little angels, with relatives in Amandola. 'Today I received a letter with photographs of my little ones and was very comforted to see this portrait of them both together,' Donato wrote.

There were echoes of longing too for the beauty of his mountain home where he spoke of yearning to be able to walk again in the Sibillini, together with Don Federico, to hunt and trap wild birds and enjoy the 'very pure air up there which I can't wait to breathe again.'

When he goes on to describe what he calls the 'shocking' practice he observed on the streets of Boston I could only smile. This practice was that of allowing sparrows and pigeons 'to walk around freely, encouraged by rich people who give them food, so they fly into their very hands'. Indeed, there were so many of these birds strutting freely around, Donato wrote, presumably aghast they were not destined for a cooking pot, that 'near the town hall there are trees which, in the evening as the sun sets, are so filled with sparrows their branches appear covered in snow'.

While the letter hinted at the hardship faced by those who left their homes to seek a new life abroad, it also offered me the first glimmer of insight into the character of the priest whose home had become my own. That he loved walking in the mountains and hunting as a young man.

I was certain there was much more to be gleaned from the letters spread out before me. But it was getting late, and I was tired. I set about tidying away the material, including the sheaf of impressive lithographs: portraits of prominent figures from Italy's tangled past, including ones of General Giuseppe Garibaldi and Giuseppe Mazzini, champion of the Risorgimento that saw Italy's long-warring states finally, in 1861, become a unified kingdom and Camillo Benso, Count of Cavour, the new kingdom's first prime minister.

It was only then that I noticed a neatly folded sheet of yellowing paper tucked between the lithographs. The paper was brittle and rustled like a dry leaf as I carefully prised it apart. When I did, any trace of weariness vanished, and I felt my skin prickle at the realisation of what I had found.

Chapter 8

The frail, tissue-thin paper I held was a finely drawn map. Almost translucent in places, it bore the watermark of a royal crest. Curled beneath the watermark were the words '*Leggi e Decreti del Regno d'Italia*', Laws and Decrees of the Kingdom of Italy, and the date 1914.

Maps, especially old maps, have always felt to me like a doorway into another world. One full of adventure and secrets of the past. A key to seeing life as others saw it long ago. This map I had inadvertently inherited was no different. Roughly the size of an old broadsheet newspaper, it was covered with both narrow and wide contour lines to denote a sharply undulating landscape. Across its centre were a series of straight lines in black and red ink, and to one side two small uniform circles surrounded by dense downward pen strokes to signify two steep hollow peaks. It was not obvious at first where any of these topographical features were located. But peering more closely were two place names I recognised.

The first of them Acireale, a city on the east coast of Sicily. The second Zafferana Etnea, a small town close to Mount Etna, Europe's most active volcano, that made the headlines in recent years when explosives experts had to blast a diversion channel in one side of the volcano to stem a flow of molten lava threatening to engulf it. To one side of the old map, that predated such events by a century, was a handwritten *legenda*, in such small looping script it was hard to make out at first. But as I strained my eyes one word leapt out at me: *terremoto* – earthquake.

The earthquake the map recorded was one that struck an area east of Mount Etna on 8 May 1914, one innocent red line marking the place the earth tore apart on that spring day. Besides this marker there were other black lines crawling across the map tracking the direction in which other faults had yielded over the previous fifteen years, years in which the great cities of Messina and Reggio Calabria succumbed to seismic disaster, burying tens of thousands of innocents alive.

But how and why would such a map have come into Don Federico's possession, I wondered, a priest who lived in the Sibillini mountains more than three hundred miles away. The number of elaborate stamps and signatures belonging to various government ministers and military officers at the bottom of the map suggested it was intended for official use. Regardless of how he came by it, why would a man of the cloth have considered the map of such significance that he had chosen to preserve it together with his most intimate possessions?

From the small number of personal effects I found in my mother's bottom drawer after she died – a childhood book of autographs and drawings by soldiers heading off to Germany during the Second World War, a train ticket from her honeymoon, congratulatory telegrams on the birth of her daughters, a few cards, letters and photographs – I was certain of one thing. That those things we hold on to as years pass possess a very special meaning, despite how incidental they may seem to others.

I felt sure this map of Sicily he'd kept held the key to a hidden past, if only I could unlock its secrets. Perhaps one connected in some way to the more recent trauma suffered by those in the Sibillini mountains.

The Japanese have a word for objects, especially old objects, that have, through their handling, absorbed some essence of the person to whom they once belonged: *tsukumogami*. As I held the map in my hands I began to think more deeply about the life and times of the priest who had left it concealed in my attic. Perhaps he too was someone who shared a deep concern for the fragility of our natural world and a hundred years earlier felt the need to understand more about the vulnerability of his native land as I did now. Had we both in different ways become earthquake detectives? Had he, as a priest, perhaps travelled to Sicily to provide solace to survivors of these earlier earthquakes? If he had, what scenes of despair he must have witnessed. At the time of the Messina quake the Catholic Church held far greater sway than it does today. In the wake of that disaster the Catholic hierarchy was quick to attribute the catastrophe to a lack of devotion among the faithful and encouraged survivors to turn to the church for salvation.

Who do we look to and who do we blame today when our world collapses, I asked myself: science, the media, crooked politicians and criminal networks seizing construction contracts and overloading cement with sand? In the case of the tragedy that befell the city of L'Aquila just forty miles to the south of Amandola only seven years earlier in 2009, it was all of these.

With hindsight I realised how naïve I had been in not taking the L'Aquila quake as a warning. Especially in light of everything that subsequently emerged.

Like all those asleep within a wide radius of that medieval city, perched like The Eagle of its name high in the Abruzzo mountains, I was shaken awake by a violent rattling of windows and doors when the Apennines gave a great heave at 3.32 a.m. that 6 April. When I threw open the shutters that night to make sure the bell tower of the church of Saint Augustine was intact, except for the faint sound of a pendulum brushing the lip of its great bell as it settled in its yoke and the distant barking of dogs, all was quiet.

At the time I had just returned from an assignment in Iran and was on deadline to deliver a long dispatch. So I did not immediately drive south to L'Aquila to report on the disaster as I might otherwise have done. Only later did I learn that, in the weeks leading up to the earthquake, a series of tremors had prompted scientists and civil protection officials, whose job it is to predict, prevent and manage national disasters, to convene a special meeting to assess whether the so-called seismic swarm could be a precursor to a major quake.

The mood in the city that spring had been tense. For weeks an amateur geologist had been issuing dire warnings of impending disaster on the basis that he was observing rising levels of the odourless radioactive gas radon in the air. His claims that this signalled much greater earth movement was imminent were dismissed by officials who denounced him for inciting panic. But the atmosphere was tense when they crowded into a room at the end of March to discuss the matter and scientists warned that, though unlikely, a major quake could not be ruled out.

Despite their urging caution, one civil protection official, Bernardo de Bernardinis, emerged from the stuffy meeting room and not only declared the situation posed no danger, but in a now infamous and widely reported aside, went further and told worried Aquilani they should simply sit back and enjoy a nice glass of wine: 'preferably Montepulciano d'Abruzzo DOC'.

When the city began to shake more intensely a week later, on Palm Sunday evening, many elderly Aquilani ignored his advice. They held to the wisdom of previous generations by huddling in open spaces or bedding down for the night in their cars. But those used to relying on the internet and television news heeded de Bernardinis's words and stayed indoors. By dawn three hundred and nine men, women and children lay entombed beneath the rubble. Sixty-five thousand lost their homes.

Even as survivors were crawling from the wreckage, two businessmen, whose phones were being tapped as part of an investigation into corruption, were recorded bragging about the construction contracts the disaster would bring their way. 'I was laughing in my bed at three thirty this morning. It's not every day we get an earthquake like this,' one crowed. When the recording was made public, protestors took to the streets wearing T-shirts with the slogan 'We weren't laughing'.

The infiltration of organised criminals into the Italian construction industry was and is, sadly, nothing new. Days after the quake, the bestselling author of *Gomorrah*, Roberto Saviano, wrote a searing indictment in *La Repubblica* of the way the Mafia routinely gorged itself on Italy's natural disasters, regarding them as 'a paradise of profit'. '*Quando la terra trema, il cemeto uccide*' – when the earth shudders, cement kills – he said, reminding his countrymen of what happened when the mountains of Irpinia to the west and south of Naples convulsed thirty years earlier in the winter of 1980, killing three thousand people and rendering a quarter of a million homeless.

The Irpinia disaster remains burned into the national psyche as an act of God made worse by human greed; tens of billions of pounds of government funds and international relief were siphoned off by one of Italy's oldest Mafia networks, the Camorra, in league with corrupt politicians. The disaster was seen as a watershed in the history of southern Italy. A time when a way of life in ancient settlements dating back to the Normans, Lombards and, in some cases Romans, was lost. A time when compact societies of what were described as 'meek and tenacious people, proud of their sobriety and silence' were transformed and communities disintegrated.

The infiltration of the Mafia into the construction trade became only too clear to me when I applied for permission from the regional authorities to start work on repairing my house and found nine mentions in the paperwork of anti-Mafia measures designed to prevent the systematic penetration of criminal networks into reconstruction projects by means of dubious subcontractors.

Ironically, one of the few buildings in L'Aquila that withstood the 2009 quake was its prison, where eighty men facing more than four hundred counts of Mafia-type associations were being held.

In the aftermath of the L'Aquila quake, de Bernardinis and six of Italy's leading natural disaster experts were convicted of manslaughter for failing to provide citizens with clear information about the dangers they faced. After years of legal action, the six scientists were eventually acquitted by Italy's supreme court, while the conviction of de Bernardinis was upheld. But the trials outraged the international scientific community and led to furious debate about how scientists should communicate levels of risk and respond to public demands for forecasting in the face of unpredictable forces of nature – a debate few could have imagined then would become a matter of pressing concern to us all when we found ourselves in the grip of a global pandemic.

In the immediate aftermath of the quake, Italy's then prime minister, Silvio Berlusconi, breezily instructed the many thousands of Aquilani reduced to living in tents after their homes collapsed that they should treat the experience as a 'camping weekend'. But once the former premier had wrung whatever political capital he could from the disaster, the city was left in the hands of construction tycoons, crooks and speculators.

It wasn't until some years after the disaster that I made the long and winding ascent into Abruzzo's Gran Sasso mountains where the eagle's nest is perched and witnessed the aftermath for myself.

The Gran Sasso are where the Apennines reach their zenith: the 9,500–foot Corno Grande, or Great Horn marking their highest point is, more often than not, wrapped in cloud. And the Calderone, or cauldron glacier cradled close to its summit, which once lay claim to being Europe's southernmost such ice mass, has now succumbed to global warming, causing it to split in two and recede at such a pace that it will surely one day soon disappear altogether.

The densely wooded slopes of the mountains here are one of the few places in the world where critically endangered Marsican brown bears still find a home, though they too are now threatened by the encroachment of human activity. But it was the fall-out of human folly in the wake of natural disaster that I was preparing myself for up ahead. For those who live in the shadow of seismic disaster speak less of the physical damage such disaster causes than the emotional scars they are left with when what follows is so callously mishandled. For this I had come prepared.

In the aftermath of the L'Aquila earthquake, I had followed the publication of a series of deeply personal letters written by one bereaved father who lost his two children and his father when the roof of their family home collapsed on that terrible night. Every year, on the anniversary of the earthquake Giustino Parisse, a former newspaper editor, sat up late into the night and poured out his feelings in a letter he addressed to his fifteen-year-old daughter Maria Paola and her seventeen-year-old brother Domenico. Some of these were later made public. Each letter was gut-wrenching. Each full of the father's pain. Some brimmed with anger and disgust at the corruption and self-interest the disaster exposed. The fact that rampant political cronyism and administrative chaos had magnified the destruction caused by nature a hundred-fold. The way many who lost their homes were haphazardly relocated to what were supposed to be temporary satellite settlements with little regard for existing social networks, destroying the fabric of communities with roots dating back to the Middle Ages.

But the most heartbreaking were the letters in which Giustino begged his children for forgiveness for not having been able to save them as every member of the family lay trapped beneath fallen masonry in their beds. The way his son's last words as he cried out '*Papà! Papà!*' haunted him every hour of every day and, he wrote, 'broke the soul of those condemned to stay.'

Giustino and his family were born in the village of Onna, a few miles from L'Aquila, a place I imagined much closer in character to Amandola than Abruzzo's once bustling regional capital. Before the 2009 earthquake Onna had been home to around three hundred people, forty of whom were killed when the village was reduced to rubble. It was to Onna I went first, to meet Giustino.

It was early afternoon by the time I pulled my car to the side of the road by a huddle of wooden huts erected as temporary accommodation for those who lost their homes. While waiting for Giustino I walked slowly along a nearby brick wall covered with black and white photographs of how Onna had once looked. One a sunlit lane flanked by whitewashed houses, their balconies overflowing with trailing plants. Another an improvised altar covered with a lace cloth and bowls of flowers on the corner of a cobbled street during a festival. There were snapshots too of family gatherings, religious processions, groups of smiling young men in their Sunday best, arms draped across each other's shoulders.

Beside the photos Giustino had written a few words that spoke of the *silenzio dei giorni sereni e assolati*, the silence of clear and sunny days that Onna once enjoyed. A silence broken that day, as I waited for him to arrive, by the clanking of machinery clearing away rubble.

I heard Giustino approach before I saw him, his hacking cough echoing through that ghostly place. As we walked together through the ruins he pointed out what each place had been before it was reduced to dust: a shop here, a friend's house there, a corner where children used to play. He then led me to a handful of the few new houses rebuilt since the quake. All were clustered around a small courtyard and had arched doorways, iron balconies and concrete balustrades so fresh you could almost smell the wet paste.

'As you can see it's all *finta*' – a pretence – he said with a sweep of his arm and a drawn-out coughing fit. It was true. Each house was a pastiche of those pictured in the old photos of Onna. A perfect example of the contested Italian custom of rebuilding dwellings *dov'era – com'era*, 'where they were, as they were', in the wake of disaster, in an attempt to replicate local style regardless of whether the character and social cohesion of a community had been retained.

The place was deserted. All the houses stood empty, their windows dark and doorsteps thick with dust. Many had been put up for sale by owners who accepted government compensation for the loss of their homes and watched them being rebuilt only to decide they could no longer live somewhere so lacking in soul, Giustino explained.

When we finally made our way to the place where Giustino's own house once stood, his cough worsened and seemed to echo from somewhere deep underground. 'I look at the world now as if I am still peering out through a hole in this rubble,' he said, turning away so I could not see his eyes. The site before us was nothing but a crumpled mass of concrete and stone, overgrown with weeds.

In the years following the earthquake, Giustino left his newspaper job and dedicated himself to writing books about Onna, about how it had once been, both his own personal recollections and from the time of its origins dating back nearly a thousand years.

'I don't give a damn about my house being rebuilt,' he said in a voice that was both angry and sad as he walked me back to my car through a damp veil of mist. 'What I care about is the history of this community! If we lose that we have lost everything,' he said, bringing his hands together with clap and raising his eyes skywards, as if in prayer.

After I left Giustino I drove on to L'Aquila and, in the fading light, saw its skyline criss-crossed with so many cranes it looked like it was in the grip of an alien invasion. As I walked along thoroughfares radiating out from the main market square, the Piazza Duomo, the next day it was clear much of the city centre still lay in ruins. But there was one street almost entirely lined with the neon-lit estate agents' offices. In their windows were photographs of grand old houses that, as in Onna, had been rebuilt with government money dov'era – com'era, and were now being sold by owners wanting to capitalise and move elsewhere.

On the evening before I left L'Aquila its streets glistened with a steady rainfall. In some places, where cobbles had collapsed, rainwater collected in dark pools. The Piazza Duomo was almost entirely deserted that evening as I stood looking up at the partially repaired facade of the church of Santa Maria del Suffragio, beloved by Aquilani as the Chiesa delle Anime Sante, the Church of Blessed Souls. When the great neoclassical dome of the church, designed by one of the Vatican's chief architects of his day, Giuseppe Valadier, collapsed in 2009 the wounded building became a sacred symbol of the destructive power of the earthquake.

But as I stood before that place of blessed souls, I became aware of a presence behind me. I turned to see a figure wearing a top hat, patchwork trousers and a brown velvet jacket with a giant bow at the neck. The person's face was covered with a silver mask, so that, at first, I could not make out if it was a man or woman. But by the way the figure moved, with a slight sway, I realised it was that of a woman – short, slightly stooped, and I judged not young. With one hand she held aloft an outsize black and white umbrella. With the other she clutched the handle of a small cart onto which she'd strapped an old-fashioned radio that seemed to be playing a talk show at low volume. When I asked her name and what she was doing she just smiled and let go of the cart. Reaching into her pocket she brought out two blue and red balls and started juggling them with one hand. She was a clown, a pagliacco, though there was nothing cheerful about her demeanour.

'È *troppo triste*, it's too sad, walking these empty streets alone,' she said finally, slipping the balls back into her pocket. 'I come here at night and try to remember how these streets were when I was a child.' And this? I asked, glancing down at her trolley. 'It's so I can at least hear other voices,' she said, the mask hiding the expression on her face.

With that she moved off, dragging her radio for company, her melancholy summing up the spirit of the broken city.

It has sometimes felt as if that strange encounter with the clown in L'Aquila was something I imagined. But her mournful words and those of Giustino, as he spoke with passion of the importance of the history of his devastated community, echoed those I heard the day of the concert in the forecourt of the old yeast factory on the outskirts of Amandola. The longing of the former newspaper man and strange clown in L'Aquila for everything that had been lost was as palpable as that of those gathered for that concert in Cremore who yearned to connect with the ancient culture of the Sibillini as a way of retaining their sense of identity and communal belonging.

It took me time to understand how the local landscape, the *paesaggio*, the photographer Giorgio spoke of that day, was so much more than its strikingly beautiful physical scenery that had drawn me to settle there. That it was the layer upon layer of history and tradition laid down by families rooted in that landscape for generations which made Amandola and other mountain communities like it what they were. I came to see much more clearly how, given time, buildings could be repaired. But what could not, if people left and never returned, was the continuity of individual family stories of which the heart and soul of each unique community was made. How, once this was broken, something utterly precious was lost.

Chapter 9

On moonless nights the Sibillini can feel like a foreboding presence: an immense, impenetrable dark wall stretching south to the heights of the Gran Sasso where the eagle of L'Aquila lies wounded. Beyond the murky summit of Monte Vettore, the Sibillini's southernmost cloud-making peak now permanently scarred by seismic shifts, there lies a high plateau called the *Pian Perduto*, the Lost Plain.

The Lost Plain was once a glacial lake. But long before this, before the peaks of the Sibillini were sculpted by ice, the plain lay beneath the tropical waters of a prehistoric sea. Throughout the aeons it lay submerged; calcite shells of countless deceased organisms settled on the seabed and built up deposits of limestone which today form the well-drained karst landscape for which the high plateau is known. This landscape provides perfect growing conditions for a tender-skinned type of lentil, *lenticchie di Castelluccio*, so highly prized it is served in fine restaurants from the Champs-Élysées to Fifth Avenue. The place after which these lentils are named is the small village of Castelluccio.

Perched almost a mile above sea-level, on a rocky outcrop over-looking the Lost Plain, Castelluccio is one of the highest settlements in the Apennines, leading some to refer to it as 'Little Tibet'. When the earthquake of 30 October 2016 razed much of it to the ground, its hundred or so permanent inhabitants, all of whom miraculously survived, were helicoptered to the coast. But before this, the tiny village used to attract tens of thousands of visitors each year from all over Italy, and far beyond, drawn there by a true wonder of nature. For beside the much sought-after tender-skinned *lenticchie*, at a certain time of year this landscape is covered with a profusion of poppies, narcissi, violets, clover, oxalis, gentians, cornflowers, buttercups and many other species of wildflower. When these bloom in sequence in late spring and early summer the explosion of colour weaves such a rich tapestry of red, yellow and blue, and other shades in between, that it carpets the entire vast plain.

I had witnessed the spectacle of *la Fioritura*, the Flowering, many times with friends and it never failed to enchant. But following the earthquakes, the three roads leading to Castelluccio from the north, west and east – the road from the east coming from Amandola – were so damaged they were closed. The Lost Plain's carpet of flowers was left to bloom and wither, witnessed only by the birds.

By the time I was next able to return to Amandola the army jeeps and fire trucks manned by anxious crews stationed for months in the main square after the earthquakes had moved out. Some had been dispatched to prevent looters from entering areas utterly wrecked by the quakes. Others to stand sentry at barricades on roads leading deeper into the Sibillini, to places such as Castelluccio, which buckled, cracked and slumped when the mountains danced.

But one squad of emergency workers remained and took up residence in a disused warehouse on the outskirts of Amandola. From there they fanned out each morning to inspect buildings at risk of collapse. At lunchtime I would see them hunched over plastic trays in a makeshift canteen attached to a local supermarket, bantering and swapping tales. With this continuing presence of so many men in uniform Amandola still felt under siege and a heaviness hung over the town like a fog.

With little prospect of being able to return to my home any time soon, I took to renting an attic room in a house on the outskirts of town with equally panoramic views of the Sibillini. Sometimes, when I could not sleep, as I had in my own home, I opened the window and sat, wrapped in a blanket, waiting for the sky to lighten and the sound of birdsong.

The chorus of birds competing to be heard often began in what felt like the dead of night, when the Moon still hovered above the mountain peaks and the full beauty of the surrounding landscape had yet to be revealed. Within an hour or so sunlight would creep over the furthest summits, glancing off the highest crags before slowly seeping downwards across the forested slopes and meadows to reach the terracotta rooftops of small villages in the distance and eventually those nearby. Almost as if some ghostly stagehand were waiting in the wings for the right moment to flick the switches and illuminate a lavish set.

In that strange liminal space between slumber and becoming fully awake I sometimes had a fleeting sensation that the unfolding scene was the backdrop to a performance in which most of the cast had fallen sick, leaving those that remained struggling to keep the production afloat. Except this was not fiction but cold, hard fact. My thoughts turned quickly then to places like Castelluccio and other virtually deserted communities lying phantom-like, in dark folds of the mountains.

Even though I was prohibited from returning to live in my home, as winter turned to spring, I sought solace when I could in its increasingly neglected garden, noting with sadness the absence of some of my most beloved trees that had long since reached the end of their natural life. Treading through the tall damp grass, I sat beneath an old cherry tree that survived at the far end and tried to summon up the sense of calm I had experienced a few years earlier during the time I spent in a Zen training temple in Japan while in the depths of grief at the sudden loss of my parents. There, in the temple of Nisodo, each day had begun long before dawn with hours of sitting *zazen* meditation in the company of the women whose lives I was chronicling. Cocooned by their kindness, I began to glimpse something of the wisdom of their practice: that of observing the ever-changing weather patterns of the mind without being constantly carried away by them.

As I watched the petals of my cherry tree float in the breeze, I remembered the gnarled cherry tree that stood in the temple's courtyard and how the paths beyond the translucent rice-paper doors of the meditation hall were carpeted with its fallen pink petals. I thought of how their transient beauty is seen by the Japanese as a symbol of both the fleeting nature of life and its ability for renewal.

But in those early years after the earthquakes, it was hard to imagine how the battered communities of central Italy could be revived. The task of reconstruction was enormous. In Amandola and its outlying villages and hamlets alone, more than nine hundred public buildings, commercial premises and private homes were rendered temporarily or permanently uninhabitable. One map of the *centro storico* showing its stricken buildings shaded orange or red according to the level of damage sustained, looked like a flaming dragon, with my own house, shaded orange, a few hundred metres from the beast's head.

My days then were consumed by endless queueing in the town council's technical office and meetings with my friend Francesca to try to understand the deluge of decrees being issued by the Italian government to regulate the reconstruction process. Though Francesca always greeted me warmly, a broad smile lighting up her striking dark features, her slender frame seemed to sag and grow ever more slight each time we met. And the studio she shared with her brother Raul, a towering structural engineer, was thick with tension as their team of assistants, heads bent low over technical drawings, grappled with interminable government forms.

As months slipped by my notebook filled with calculations. What I thought initially was a matter of simple repairs to a damaged vaulted ceiling and its supporting wall quickly escalated into a more complicated project. When Raul clambered under the eaves he discovered a central beam holding up a portion of the roof had shifted and there was nothing to stop it moving further in the event of another major quake.

I was fortunate in that I had an insurance policy with a British company that covered earthquake damage as standard. But in order for Italian authorities to grant permission for work to begin on any buildings for which eviction orders had been issued they demanded assurances that each structure not only be repaired, but also strengthened to minimise the likelihood of future damage. This made sense to improve the country's housing stock as far as possible for future generations. But since my insurance policy did not cover any work considered an improvement to the property I was caught in a bind.

Few in Italy had any kind of insurance against earthquake damage, I soon discovered. Little wonder since the Italian government had in the past largely covered the cost of reconstruction and repairs and was promising to do so again. It was hard to imagine how a country so prone to repeated seismic disaster, and with an increasingly struggling economy, could afford such largesse. One estimate placed the cost of repairing damage due to the 2016–17 earthquakes at more than twenty billion pounds, some of which would be met by the EU Solidarity Fund. But all such funding came with strict conditions and technical criteria, and it was these that were constantly changing.

Francesca was confident most of the work not covered by my insurance policy could be supplemented by this state funding and I was grateful for such generosity. But this signalled the beginning of a complicated process of negotiation between Francesca, regional government officials answerable to the *Commissario Straordinario Ricostruzione Sisma 2016* – the extraordinary commissioner for earthquake reconstruction – and loss adjusters dispatched from England. I could see that I would be left to pick up any financial slack.

Although my Italian was fluent enough to hold my own in most conversations, I struggled, even in English, to understand the technical terms for much of what was being discussed. The multiple *catene*, or chains that were not chains but rather steel rods, that needed to be inserted from outer to inner walls and secured at either end by *chiavi*, keys or large steel plates with a screw mechanism that would hold them steady should the ground shake. The *cordolo*, or ring-beam, a band of steel that would encircle the eaves and be attached to a metal harness, like an equine bridle, beneath the apex of the roof to keep it from ever collapsing like a deflated soufflé.

To help me understand, Francesca directed me to a website that would give me a clearer picture of what each process would involve. One short film that showed craftsmen repairing a *camorcanna* vaulted ceiling of the kind on my top floor – a wood and reed structure rather like an inverted coracle boat from my native Wales – revealed a skill and tradition handed down through generations.

But who knew when any of this work would begin?

'It will be ten years, maybe twenty, before many places are rebuilt. Look at L'Aquila. Its centre is still more or less in ruins,' Oreste said to me one morning when I met him in the market, his fears echoed by all throughout The Crater. With his livelihood destroyed and his young daughter and wife Manuela no longer able to live in their family home, Oreste's salt and pepper hair had turned almost entirely grey within just a few months. In the past we would always joke a little together. But that day there seemed little that could raise his spirits.

In the haste of the evacuation, it was hard to know where many Amandolesi whose homes were damaged, some beyond repair, had gone. The small encampment of caravans and trailers parked on flat land close to the sports stadium gradually dwindled. All that was left there was a row of a dozen or so Portakabin homes, transported in as a last resort for those with nowhere else to go. But most were left to make their own arrangements; either receiving a small government subsidy to rent whatever alternative accommodation they could find or going to live with friends or relatives.

Among them were Antonio's daughter Barbara and her family, who Antonio and his grandson Alessandro had watched in horror as they fled their swaying home. While Antonio and his wife Giuseppina's newer home on the farmstead had withstood the quakes, the older adjacent building where Barbara, her husband, Alessandro and his brother lived suffered substantial damage. Like so many forced to evacuate their stricken homes, the extended family moved in together, and now lived with Antonio and Giuseppina.

Wounded as Amandola was, it was fortunate it had suffered no fatalities as a direct result of the earthquakes and I knew other places had fared so much worse. Some had already been consigned to obliteration from the map, their underlying geology considered too unsafe to contemplate any kind of reconstruction on the same site. One community condemned to oblivion was Pescara del Tronto, the small village sixteen miles to the south of Amandola where the two little sisters remained buried in each other's arms under the rubble for sixteen hours.

After months of negotiation with the authorities, my journalist friend Francesco and I were granted permission to enter Pescara del Tronto's *Zona Rossa* and that of its devastated neighbour Arquata del Tronto, but only if accompanied by emergency workers, three firemen on duty in the area that day. It was a warm spring day and the heat was building. The climb to Arquata from the via Salaria, the old salt road that cuts through the Apennines, was steep. We moved in single file, wearing hard hats and heavy boots. The sky was a brilliant cobalt blue and there was not a cloud in sight. It was the sort of day when, in another time and place, a small Italian community would be purring with activity. Children playing in the street. Mothers standing in the shade, swapping recipes or local gossip. Old men sitting on benches in the piazza clutching walking sticks or playing cards. Old ladies in housecoats tending potted plants. But all was silent that day except for the plaintive *peeee-uu* of buzzards circling high above.

Perched on a rocky outcrop in the lee of Monte Vettore, Arquata is the only municipality in Europe to straddle two national parks – that of both the Monti Sibillini and the Gran Sasso. Its most distinctive feature from afar is the crenellated tower of a medieval fortress around which the settlement had grown over centuries, surrounded by forests of fir and beech. But as we drew near it was clear little of

Arquata remained but debris and dust. In what was once the main square all that was left of its church was a tall iron crucifix propped defiantly upright amid the rubble.

Following the line of an old Roman road we skirted further around the base of Vettore to the nearby village of Pescara del Tronto. I dreaded what we would find, and my fears were confirmed. The eerie desolation of the place had the air of a war zone. It reminded me of a place where I once stood, close to the Israel's southernmost border with Egypt, inside the Gaza Strip, in the aftermath of heavy shelling. There were car chassis crushed beneath collapsed houses, once gently bustling streets lined with small houses flattened. Peering into the darkness of one home with only part of a wall standing I saw a bookcase still full of books; pots and pans in what must once have been a kitchen; a pizza oven that looked as if it was suspended precariously in thin air; a marble mantlepiece with a portrait of the Madonna tacked above, and shower fittings exposed to the elements.

But it was the profusion of improvised crosses made of red tape and pinned in the dust to mark the site where people perished that chilled my blood. Nearby lay the intimacy of their shattered lives: bedding, family photographs, clothes spilling out of suitcases packed for a summer holiday. For the number who lived all year round in Pescara before it was destroyed was less than one hundred and fifty, many of them elderly. But this number would swell during summer months, as it had in the summer of 2016, with children and grandchildren returning to spend time with their parents and grandparents. In the early hours of that 24 August, fifty-two of those who were either visiting or permanent residents lost their lives under the rubble.

The silence of that desolate place was broken now and then by the soft flapping of the pages of a book caught by the wind as it lay in the dust beside a pair of wire cutters. Gently lifting the spine of the book, I read its title, *Paesi e Uomini*, Countries and Men, and on its cover saw a photograph of a woman with long plaits and a trilby-style hat I recognised as typical of the Quechua people of South America. I thought of the person in whose lap the book had last rested, a mother or father perhaps, keen to fill their child's imagination with dreams of a world yet to be discovered. I uttered a silent prayer that they had survived.

Book and wire cutters lying in the dust of the destroyed village of
Pescara del Tronto

In the months that followed I drove back and forth along the coast
in search of those who did survive and were now housed in hotels
requisitioned by the government. Those who were now known by the
doleful name *i terremotati*, the earthquaked people, as if they themselves had ruptured. Certainly, their psyche had. They were traumatised. Security was tight in such places to protect the *terremotati* from
unwelcome intrusions, not least by the media. This made me wary
about taking notes and those I did take were fragmented, perhaps a
reflection too of my own unsettled state. Besides, people were weary
of talking about all they had gone through. What good did it do them?
   But of those I did manage to speak to, the generosity of one family
reminded me of one fundamental truth: that it is very often those
who can least afford to share what they have, or who find themselves
in the most difficult circumstances, who are the most generous and
thoughtful in the way they treated others. For this family I met at
the end of a long day on the coast were one of several living in a
small concrete box of a hotel, in two adjoining rooms that housed
four generations: a great-grandmother, her son and his wife, their
recently married daughter and her husband and their newborn baby.
The newly-weds had taken the baby out for the day. But even without
them there it was hard to see how the family were managing in
such cramped surroundings. There were bags piled up against every
wall containing the few belongings they had managed to salvage

from their home in Pieve Torino, close to Visso, the epicentre of the October quake.

Despite this, seeing my tired face, the elderly couple ushered me in and offered me coffee from a small stove in a kitchenette in the corner of one of the rooms. As I sat perched on the edge of a bed, they spoke with pride of their medieval home in Visso which had been in the family for generations and of their hope it would one day be repaired.

'You must come and spend Christmas with us there when our house is rebuilt,' said Domenico, the seventy-five-year-old head of the family. But, from his hollow look, it was clear he feared he might not live to see that day. When I got up to leave, his elderly mother, confused and distraught, clung on to the strap of my shoulder bag, convinced it was hers and I was trying to take all the worldly goods left to her.

During the long nights that followed, as I looked out at the Sibillini mountains from my rented attic room, I thought often of what Giustino Parisse had said as he stood peering down at the tangled ruins of his home in the small village of Onna, near L'Aquila: '*I don't give a damn about my house being rebuilt . . . What I care about is the history of this community. If we lose that we have lost everything.*'

It was then that I was reminded of the unique and intimate insight into the history of Amandola contained in the letters and other material hidden away in the attic of my stricken house.

I knew something of Amandola's rich and often troubled past from the stories Antonio told as we worked together in my garden and from speaking now and then with one or other of the town's local historians. I knew that the start of the last century when the letters from my attic were written were years of extreme turmoil for Italy. Years in which more than a million Italians lost their lives in two world wars and twenty million more sailed away from home shores, many of them never to return.

But how, I wondered, had the priest Don Federico and his family fared through all this? What if I could recover their story? Dig down through the fractured layers of Amandola's past. Piece it together in the hope it might throw some light on how Amandola and other places like it in the Sibillini had recovered from hard times in the past and might, perhaps, flourish once again in the future.

I remembered, too, a scene I had come across once by chance in Japan while strolling down a quiet backstreet in the coastal city of Kamakura, one-time seat of the ruling shoguns. Glancing through a window there I saw an old man bent low over a bench, deep in concentration, working at something that glistened in the light. When I stopped to talk to his apprentice, who was sitting on the doorstep leisurely smoking a cigarette, he told me in broken English that the old man was a master of the art of *kintsugi*. Seeing my puzzled look, he stubbed out his cigarette and beckoned me inside with a finger to his lips, motioning to a corner where I could stand. From there I quietly observed the old man applying a layer of glistening golden lacquer to the crack in an azure porcelain bowl, his brush gently stroking the place where it had broken.

I knew nothing of the art of *kintsugi* at the time, though in recent years it has become well known in the West. But at its core the purpose of the ancient Japanese practice is to mend a damaged pot in such a way that the places where it broke remain visible and tell its story, thereby rendering it more precious.

It seemed to me then that telling the story of one small community in the earthquake-stricken heart of Italy I had come to love might be a way of performing a kind of narrative *kintsugi*. Not hiding Amandola's past or present scars. But in bringing them to light, allowing the place and its people to shine. And in this Don Federico would become my silent accomplice.

In Search of Don Federico

'*Ma la città non dice il suo passato, lo contiene come le linee d'un mano.*'
'But the city does not recount its past, it contains it like the lines on the palm of a hand.'

Italo Calvino, Le città invisibili (1972)

Chapter 10

Near the end of his life, the emperor Hadrian retreated to the seclusion of his small island villa within the estate he built on the slopes of the Tiburine Hills east of Rome. There, surrounded by the tranquil waters of a wide moat, he is said to have written a memoir of his rise to power and love of poetry, music and philosophy. This autobiography was lost. But two millennia later, the Belgian-born French writer Marguerite Yourcenar imagined his final thoughts on life in her novel *Mémoires d'Hadrien*, written as if the ailing Roman emperor were addressing a letter to his adoptive grandson and eventual successor, Marcus Aurelius.

Reflecting back on his mostly peaceful rule and passion for building, Yourcenar has Hadrian muse that while building means collaborating with the structure of the earth 'to put a human mark upon the landscape', reconstruction requires a different skill. It calls for an understanding of 'time gone by': a recognition that only by understanding the spirit of a place can its future be ensured. Since it is only 'beneath the stones, we find the secret of the springs,' Hadrian reflects.

These musings of the ailing emperor were invoked one afternoon in a darkened upper room of Amandola's town hall when the town was chosen by academics at Cambridge University as the focus of a case study into post-earthquake reconstruction a year after the disaster. This had come about through a family connection of an energetic professor of architectural history from Rome then working in Cambridge, Antonello Alici, whose uncle lived in Amandola and who had become increasingly concerned about the uncertain prospects of small communities in the Sibillini mountains in the aftermath of the earthquakes.

Over time, I followed the comings and goings of Antonello's visits to Amandola in the company of a growing number of academics and students and attended a conference he helped organise in the hushed cloisters of Jesus College, Cambridge. As image after image of Amandola's wounded buildings flickered up on a screen in a darkened lecture theatre over a thousand miles from the Italian mountains I had a vague sense of what it must be like for victims of crime or other misfortune to see their lives suddenly exposed and projected into the public sphere.

Over the course of two days, I watched engineers, architects and professors pore over charts and diagrams and talk numbers. I listened as one likened those working in seismic disaster zones to CSI detectives hunting for clues to weak spots in buildings and winced as another referred to reconstruction as a 'sexy topic' since it was now tied up with identity politics in academic circles. So, as hands were shaken and group photographs taken, I began to wonder in what way Amandola would really benefit from such an academic initiative.

Yet Hadrian's imagined words gave me pause for thought. For if the stones in Amandola's cobbled streets and beyond could speak, the stories they could tell would stretch back into antiquity. Before the earthquakes I had only ever heard a few of their tales. But with so much around me now in ruins and in need of rebuilding the ghosts of the past were felt more keenly. As I walked through Amandola's narrow streets and the countryside beyond, the town as it once was began to come alive in my imagination. I thought of how ancient voices speaking in long-forgotten tongues had echoed through this mountainous terrain even before the first stone of what would become Amandola was laid. Indeed, proof that the town and its territory was occupied long before the birth of Christ sits suspended in time behind glass in an archaeological museum on the coast.

The early inhabitants of this region of Italy, the Piceni, were thought to have been a warlike people with little artistic ability of their own. But an elaborate banqueting cup with lions' claw feet used for mixing wine and honey during festivities found years ago in the high valley of the river Tenna tells a different story. The bronze chalice, now known as the *Dinos di Amandola* and thought to be of ancient Greek origin, is believed to have been brought here in the fifth century BC by an aristocratic class of Piceni who settled in the area and were eager to display their wealth after establishing trade routes across the Adriatic.

There beside the chalice lies another marker of ancient enterprise along this river valley: a large, rounded boundary stone etched with cryptic markings by those who eventually eclipsed the Piceni. Its arrows and letters part of a code denoting the limits of parcels of land given to Roman centurions as a reward for their army service during the reign of the first Roman emperor, Caesar Augustus. These were the times when the myths of the ancient sibyls were born. When those craving some kind of certainty in their lives looked to oracles, priests and shamans as intermediaries between the world of humans and that of the gods and spirits in whom they believed. When even the simplest scratches on a piece of bone or shell were seized as auguries about future events.

It was not until after the fall of the Roman Empire, when the papacy took control of these lands, that Amandola as a more clearly defined settlement began to take shape. But even then, the whispered prayers and hushed voices of monks and nuns in remote monasteries and convents here were overshadowed by those of growing conflict. When the Church tried to sequester land for the common people, the militias of the papal Guelphs clashed repeatedly with the Ghibelline supporters of the increasingly powerful local noble families. In an effort to put a stop to the battles, the beleaguered population on the three neighbouring Sibillini foothills of Castel Leone, Colle Marrubbione and Agello was brought under the protection of the Church of Rome and a mile and a half of high walls with five gates were built around them to keep out the opposing forces. It was then that Amandola was first declared a free and independent *comune*. The year was 1248 – a century before Dante Alighieri wrote his *Divina Commedia* and more than two centuries before Christopher Columbus set sail for the 'New World'.

There are few physical traces left that hint at the hardships these early Amandolesi must have suffered throughout the tumultuous early centuries of the town's existence. But a walk to the far end of the *centro storico* offers one tantalising clue. Concealed behind a rusty protective grille lies the mossy entrance to what remains of a network of secret underground tunnels. These tunnels were hewn out of the bedrock of Castel Leone where much of the old town, including my house, was built. In times of trouble, they were the only means by which embattled Amandolesi could steal beyond the town's protective walls and, under cover of darkness, fetch food and supplies from the surrounding countryside.

With the power of the feudal lords curbed, however, Amandola flourished. The population grew and the weaving and wool-dyeing industry thrived. As Amandola's renown increased, wool merchants started exporting their high-quality yarn and woven fabric to clothe the papal court in Rome and to Florence, Venice and beyond this to northern and central Europe. Certain families within the town prospered. Guilds and a new aristocracy were born. Grand palazzos and country houses were built with each powerful family insisting on constructing its own churches – one in town and one on their country estate. Little wonder, then, that Amandola had so many churches: at one time there were six surrounding its square alone, though only that of Saint Augustine now remains.

To flaunt their new wealth, the Amandolesi also built a small theatre on the high ground of Castel Leone where the families of rich merchants and the nobility could don their finery to attend plays and balls. Over the years the theatre was enlarged and became ever more elaborate, being both a place of entertainment and a status symbol intended to outshine that of other communities in the area. At one time there were well over a hundred such jewel-box theatres throughout Le Marche, of which Amandola's La Fenice, with its multiple gilded balconies, was considered one of the finest.

But Amandola's success aroused jealousy and its people came under frequent attack. Neighbouring hill towns launched running battles in an attempt to breach its defences. Papal taxes increased. Brigands abounded. And, as in all of Europe, by the middle of the fourteenth century Amandola was beset with recurring outbreaks of *la Pestilenza*, the Black Death. In one of the first waves of disease in 1349, according to some estimates, nearly half of its population – as many as seven thousand souls – perished.

Long before the advent of modern geophysics some thought the plague the result of an ancient virulent infection escaping from the bowels of the earth during an earthquake. But most believed it to be divine retribution for those who sinned and, as a consequence, many priests refused to bless those who became infected. There must have been those in Amandola, however, who took a more benevolent view for in the fifteenth century, on the town's outskirts, the small church of Santa Maria a Piè d'Agello was built as a place of protection for those suffering from disease. Even today it is still known as the plague church. Painted on its walls is a beautiful fresco of the Madonna with her mantle spread wide.

Just a short walk from my house one can find evidence of the fear and superstition surrounding death at a time when few defences against such insidious threats existed. I must have passed it many times, but it was only after the earthquakes that I took note of the date carved into the ornamental keystone above a tall thin window of one of the smaller palazzos in the *centro storico*. The date was 1509 and beside it a lopsided double crucifix looked as if it had been chiselled by an unsteady hand.

It was, I discovered, a *finestra del morto*, a dead man's window, such as was common in houses in central Italy in the Middle Ages. Some trace the origin of these windows back to the time of Italy's ancient Etruscan civilisation; to the belief that the souls of the dead return to inhabit the places where they perish. To prevent it these strange windows were created and bricked up without mortar. This allowed bricks to be easily removed when someone died so that their corpse could be handed out, feet first, into the street. After the body was taken away, the window would be bricked up quickly again to confuse the soul of the departed and bar it from re-entering the house.

How many times must bricks have been removed from such windows as plague swept repeatedly across the globe throughout the centuries? And again when earthquakes struck. Few records of early quakes in the Sibillini exist except one which struck with such great force on a January day in 1703 that an estimated ten thousand people were buried alive at its epicentre in Norcia – the same Umbrian settlement at the heart of the October 2016 quake.

I could find no record of how many perished in Amandola in that first recorded quake. But so calamitous was it that, as a mark of respect for the dead, an order was issued in Amandola for all plays, balls and carnival festivities in the town to be suspended for ten years, while wealthy citizens were forbidden from wearing garments decorated with threads of silver and gold. Many of those who survived undertook a walking pilgrimage to the shrine of the Virgin of Loreto, fifty miles away on the coast, to pray for divine help.

Periods of severe famine and disease followed. The woollen industry went into slow decline. And, at the end of the eighteenth century, invading Napoleonic forces reached Le Marche. Attempts at resistance were met with severe repression. In the hamlet of Rustici, on the outskirts of Amandola, where farmers revolted, entire families were massacred in retribution. To the disgust and outrage of the

Amandolesi, French soldiers also entered the church of Saint Augustine in the main square and dragged the mummified body of Amandola's patron saint Beato Antonio into the pulpit and paraded it before the congregation with mocking sneers.

It was only after Napoleon's troops were routed by those of Austria early in the nineteenth century and papal authority was restored that the town's fortunes once again improved. Though the woollen industry was slowly petering out, the number of artisans making shoes and furniture flourished. By the mid 1850s the town's population had swelled once again to nearly twelve thousand. And, despite this still relatively modest size, Amandola was elevated by Pope Gregory XVI to the status of *città*, a city.

The reason for this was explained to me one afternoon by Amandola's mayor, Adolfo Marinangeli, as an attempt to mollify jealousies between Amandola and the regional capital of Fermo, which was then, and still is, the seat of the archbishop. As a *città*, the mayor reasoned, Amandola would have been deemed a suitable place for the archbishop to stay overnight, though where he would have slept was unclear. Mayor Marinangeli, a bustling engineer, was quick to add that it was he who lobbied the president of the republic to have Amandola's city status enshrined in law two centuries later. A curiosity of sorts for a place with such a small post-earthquake population, but one celebrated with its elaborate coat of arms.

It was Adolfo Marinangeli too, in his capacity as an engineer before he became mayor, who oversaw the refurbishment of Amandola's main square, Piazza Risorgimento, levelling and resurfacing it with new cobblestones, in the years before the earthquakes. Throughout many centuries the elongated triangle of the piazza had been a congested crossroads through which mail wagons en route from Ascoli Piceno to Macerata would pass. One surrounded by hostelries and grand palazzos. But over time the square was made more spacious, and after Marinangeli saw it was repaved with gleaming new cobbles, and its colonnade and lamp posts were strung with hanging baskets, it featured on television as one of Italy's *borghi più belli*, one of the prettiest places in the country.

A hundred years earlier, when Don Federico would have swept across the square in his clerical robes, an English visitor arriving in Amandola had a very different first impression. His name was Edward Hutton and he was both a well-known writer and renowned

Italophile whose books about Italy were widely read. His travels in this mountainous area are detailed in his book *The Cities of Romagna and the Marches*, published in 1913, and begin optimistically enough. After setting out from Ascoli in a horse-drawn *diligenza*, 'little more than a broken-down wagonette', he writes enthusiastically of being overawed by the 'amazing splendour and beauty of that wonderful road' through the Apennines that brought him to Amandola and describes looking at the town from a distance and seeing a 'little place of rosy brick piled up on a precipitous hillside'. But as his *diligenza* pulls into the Piazza Risorgimento at nightfall he describes it as 'bleak' and the town itself as 'threaded by rude and stony streets between gaunt houses.' It is only after he is led by hand over the cobbles in the dark to an inn in a far corner of the piazza that he says he found the place 'full of light and warmth' and 'the best company in the world.'

Seated there that night in the inn, he describes being surrounded by 'priests from the mountains' and children who sang and danced for him and shepherds who 'blew me mountain airs on their pipes and told me tales of the snow, of witches and the evil eye.' So enchanted was he that he finally concludes: 'When I think of Le Marche, Amandola appears in my mind as the heart and rose of a country which for friendliness and charm is second to none to Italy.'

Could Don Federico have been one of the mountain priests Hutton encountered in the inn that dark night? Had he too been serenaded by shepherds who spoke of witches and the evil eye? In truth I knew very little about this mysterious priest or any others who once lived in my house. But like all intimate histories, the bare bones of their lives lay in the depository of family records: Amandola's *anagrafe* – its register office.

Armed with the few details gleaned from the material from my attic, I began to follow the trail that the records held there pointed towards. The more I did so the more intrigued I became when a grand sweep of Amandola's, and Italy's, more recent turbulent history started to unfold.

Chapter 11

Amandola's *anagrafe* sits on an upper floor of the town hall above the colonnade in the piazza. Its imperial-style facade bears the date '*Anno 1939*', a reminder of the mark left on the town by Mussolini's Fascist regime. Lining the walls of the wide stone staircase leading up from the ground floor is a series of photographs, most of them from an earlier time. Faded black and white images of Amandolesi promenading in the piazza. Wives in floor-length gowns and wide-brimmed straw hats. Husbands in waistcoats carrying canes. A town band holding trombones and trumpets, serious expressions on their faces. A troop of soldiers in heavy coats in the snow beside horses covered with blankets and sacks bulging with supplies.

But there is another image too that draws the eye. It shows the town square packed with people, all eyes turned towards a speaker on a wooden podium. Behind him, on every column of the colonnade, the word '*Duce*' is stamped. Some in the crowd are holding up bundles of rods, the infamous *fasces* adopted by Mussolini to signify strength through unity. Who were those people holding *fasces* aloft, I wondered, fervently hoping none belonged to the family who once lived in my house.

When I had first mentioned my search for the story behind the letters in my attic to the friendly local optician Alfredo, a keen collector of old photographs of Amandola, he had slipped the sign on the door of his shop in the piazza to *chiuso*, closed, and beckoned me into his back office. There he flipped open his laptop and together we scanned through hundreds of digitised photos of town celebrations and gatherings in the early decades of the last century in the hope we might find one or two of Don Federico and his family. But few were annotated.

However there too, in among the many images, were others of mass attendance at Fascist rallies in the town. Some showed *camicie nere*, blackshirts, grandstanding in front of what used to be the *casa del fascio*, their local offices, now a deserted building behind the town hall. Such scenes were, of course, typical of rallies held across Italy in the mid 1930s. Some were expressly organised to fund Mussolini's colonialist ambitions in Africa at which women were encouraged to drop jewellery into military helmets and priests their pectoral crosses – a propaganda drive dubbed *Oro alla Patria*, Gold for the Fatherland, which according to some estimates hauled in more than thirty tons of gold and ninety of silver, worth in excess of one billion pounds sterling in today's money. For this was a time when support, in public at least, for *Il Duce* was mandatory. When many citizens with prominent roles, such as doctors, pharmacists and teachers were forced to become members of the Fascist party if they were to continue working. It is a time, as one Italian friend put it, about which '*c'è una damnatio memoriae*', a taboo, a period most prefer to forget, afraid of what they might find if they dig too deeply.

Unlike in Germany where de-Nazification, or *Vergangenheitsaufarbeitung*, working through the past, was actively and officially pursued for years after the end of the Second World War, Fascism was never rooted out with the same zeal in Italy and, in some areas of public life, not least politics, the ghost of *Il Duce* has continued to stalk the country ever since. So, seeing such images at the very start of my search for the truth about the more recent past was unnerving.

But I knew that I was getting ahead of myself. That I needed to go back to the beginning. To the time when Don Federico and Donato were born in order to understand more about their family, and Amandola itself, during these tumultuous years.

There was a queue of people waiting to see the town registrar when I first entered his office, so I feared a polite but perfunctory dismissal of my request to dig back through a hundred years of the town's records. But Moreno, a smartly dressed man I judged to be in his early forties, with thick-rimmed reading glasses and a shock of dark hair, was a model of efficiency. The queue dwindled quickly. And when I explained why I had come, about the cache of hidden letters, I could see a flicker of interest stir behind his stern gaze.

He took my enquiry as a challenge. And, like Alfredo, slipped a wooden block against his office door to indicate it was temporarily closed. Then he beckoned me to follow him up a further flight of stairs to a cramped garret room it was not obvious from the main square existed. The room was full of metal filing cabinets and shelves of marbled ledgers where Amandola's oldest birth, marriage and death records were kept – local annals of the most important events in the lives of those who once lived in the town: newlyweds exchanging nervous glances; young couples rocking a newborn in their arms; mothers, wives, daughters, heads covered in black lace, whispering the moment loved ones took their last breath.

I would return to that dimly lit garret more than once with Moreno and, with the tantalising smell of fresh coffee wafting up from the offices below, hover as he patiently walked his fingers through drawers full of dog-eared pink index cards, Bellesi being a common name in Le Marche. '*Eccoci qua!*' Here we are! Moreno said finally, a note of triumph in his voice, when he unearthed the first trace of those whose lives would come to absorb me. As I bent closer, I saw the name Bellesi Federico followed by those of his parents. His father, Cesare. Mother, Anna Maria Teodori. And the full name they gave their son, Federico Francesco Nunzio, when he was born on 9 October 1882. Alongside this was the exact time, a quarter past nine in the morning, at which baby Federico's first cry was heard echoing through Amandola's narrow cobbled lanes.

Further searches revealed both Cesare and Anna Maria were born before Italy itself was born as a nation – before Italy's national hero Giuseppe Garibaldi and his thousand redshirts, his *Mille*, landed in Sicily at the start of a campaign that would see their country freed from foreign domination. Both were in their twenties when their son was born a citizen of a unified country which they must have prayed had finally found some measure of peace.

Two years after Federico was born, Anna Maria gave birth on 9 April 1884 to a daughter, Rosa Palma Carolina. For a long time we could find no trace of a third child, another son, the *fratello* who wrote to Federico from Boston of his longing to breathe the pure mountain air of home. But as I gradually pieced together what I could of the Bellesi family tree, its branches increasingly distorted by loops, arrows and crossings-out, I eventually found a connection. Donato, it transpired, was not Federico's brother at all. He was a cousin. Born seven years earlier than Federico, in 1875, he was the son of Cesare's brother Luigi, though at that time, and sometimes still today, Moreno explained, cousins were referred to as *fratelli*. But there was more to it than that.

A few stark words on both Cesare's pink index card and that of his brother Luigi provided the first clues to what must have been a childhood marked by hardship and sorrow for young Federico, his little sister Rosa and their cousin Donato. These records showed that Cesare became a widower less than two weeks after Rosa's fifth birthday, when Federico would have been just seven years old. Their mother Ana Maria died of tuberculosis at the age of thirty-six in the spring of 1890, a time when Amandola must have been in the grip of a severe outbreak of the disease. For within a few weeks of her death Donato's mother Filomena also succumbed, leaving the three children, Federico, Rosa and Donato, partially orphaned and united in grief.

When I discovered the death of Federico's mother, I berated myself for not noticing before that there were no letters from her among his treasured collection. Why, I asked myself with a sudden pang, had it not struck me before as odd that his father seemed to concern himself so much with matters of laundry. One I opened had simply read: 'Send me the dirty items and I will send back the clean ones. We are all well and I hope you are too. Greetings from me and Rosina. Your affectionate father, Cesare.'

Now I understood they must have been written in haste, and the reason could be found in the two words written on the back of his tattered index card. These listed his employment as *inserviente comunale*, town servant, 'a menial position, perhaps a porter or some kind of cleaner' Moreno mused as he handed me the card. I realised Cesare must have been writing to his son, by then in a seminary, at the end of a hard day's labour: hauling packages up the stairs of the town hall, or sweeping Amandola's streets, or swabbing its hospital wards.

There was no mention of Cesare ever having remarried, even though he too was only in his thirties when widowed. He must have been left to raise his young children alone. So, had Federico been sent to a seminary as a way of easing his father's burden of care, I wondered. With such thoughts, the thread of Don Federico's fractured life slowly began to unravel.

I felt a surge of tenderness towards this person I would never know. Perhaps it had something to do with the realisation that he had been the same age when his mother died as I was when mine narrowly survived a severe bout of meningitis. Sometimes it's hard to distinguish between what we ourselves remember about our childhood and what others tell us about it afterwards. But the feeling of dread that I might lose my mother when I was so young was buried deep. So how, I wondered, had this young boy found his feet after his childhood world was thrown into turmoil? While I had gone out into the world in search of answers, had he sought and found steadiness through faith? And what of the rest of his family: his sister Rosa and cousin Donato? Had Donato and his wife found stability, work, the new life they sought in America, I wondered. And where were their *angiolette*, their little angels they so pined for after crossing the Atlantic? Had their children joined them in Boston and were their descendants still there?

I was left with many questions. And yet it was as if a door had opened and, invited or not, I had stepped unobserved into a room full of strangers who might, with time, turn and talk to me.

One faint echo of Don Federico's early voice lay buried in the pages of a notebook I had paid little attention to at first. The notebook was missing its cover and binding and was full of Don Federico's trademark small, tight script, heavily slanting to the right. When I first found it, I thought it little more than student scribblings. Routine ecclesial tasks he had been set as a young seminarian. But when I returned to look at it and saw the word '*Impressioni*' on the first page it was clear some of what it contained was of a more personal nature.

There I found pages filled with handwritten poems. Verses by some well-known and lesser-known Italian poets. Literary figures he perhaps admired, whose work he must have copied out as a boy during the long days he spent far from home in the seminary in Fermo. Most were poems about nature. Poems about mountains and autumn, the stars, a bay tree, a farewell to a lake. When I read them, it was as if I were hearing Don Federico speak for the first time. They were expressions of loneliness and yearning for the natural world.

In one poem '*Cavalcando*', Riding, by Augusto Ferrero, a son speaks to his mother of a recurring dream he has of riding on horseback through the mountains by her side: 'I would like to be next to you like this always in my life,' it read. 'When you are by my side my bewildered soul finds peace.' In another poem '*Perché?*', Why?, a small girl stands by the side of a bed on which the body of her brother lies and asks her mother why he is cold to the touch.

While most of the poems were intimate and lyrical, there was one, '*Rondinelle di Dogali*', Swallows of Dogali, by Augusto Mazzucchetti, that hinted at an early understanding of the follies of war. It related to an infamous episode not long after the unification of Italy when a battalion of Italian soldiers were slaughtered in what is present-day Eritrea as their young country attempted to assert itself by establishing an empire. It was written as if addressing swallows migrating north from Africa to Italy and was a lament for the mothers of soldiers who died so far from home: 'Do not build your nests under the eaves of those who died. Do not disturb their mothers with your cries,' it read, carrying echoes of the constant shrill chatter of swifts that circle the sky above Amandola.

The only trace of Don Federico's own words, among everything he left behind, was contained in a letter he wrote just a few weeks before the dawn of the twentieth century, on 11 November 1899, when he would have been seventeen. It was the earliest letter in the collection of correspondence and was but a brief, plaintive note addressed to his *zia*, his aunt, in which he apologises profusely for not having written sooner. The reason, he explains, is that he has been cloistered in '*raccoglimento*', meditation or prayer. The main thrust of the letter, however, was to first ask his aunt what he should do with his laundry and then, after saying he has been unwell, ask her to appeal to his *nonna*, his granny, to knit him some socks. 'Those I have are not warm enough,' he pleaded, before scribbling one final line sideways along the page to tell his aunt the food she sent did not arrive. It could be a note written by a young student trying to manage on his own today – cold, hungry, unsure how to deal with dirty washing.

Six weeks later, at the end of December 1899, his aunt replied to say she is sending him another food parcel – *una bella ciambella*, a rich cake made with eggs – with the request he say an Ave Maria on her behalf because she has a cold. From these letters, it is clear her nephew did not return to Amandola to spend Christmas with his family. Nor did he the following year, as another short note from his father written four days before Christmas 1900 talks of Cesare enclosing a long vest and ten lire for his son's *piccole spese*, small expenses, with the caution he should not spend it all at once. This note ended with his father saying he is *contentissimo* that his son is feeling better, and his feet are warmer. So, presumably, *Nonna* had knitted her grandson more socks.

But any difficulties Don Federico faced keeping warm and fed paled in light of the struggles of the soul that he, and the young men studying to become priests alongside him in the seminary in Fermo, must have felt at the start of the last century. For the story that unfolded within its walls of espionage – dead-letter drops, threats of excommunication and burning the building to the ground – seemed beyond belief until I went to see the place for myself.

Chapter 12

The facade of Fermo's old seminary is bleak: a towering brick wall in a narrow lane in the medieval centre of the city. The building is now home to a prestigious conservatoire, and as I stood looking up at it on a chilly spring day, the strains of an accomplished pianist echoed down from one of its small high windows. Basking in the music for a moment, I imagined Don Federico as a teenager in one of those upper rooms, with cold feet, copying out verses of his favourite poems and yearning to be back in the Sibillini mountains. But even from Fermo's vantage point on a high escarpment, the poet Giacomo Leopardi's Monti Azzuri are mostly lost in the clouds.

Close to the former seminary there is a touching statue of Leopardi dressed in a tailcoat, feet crossed at the ankles, head bent low over a book. Leopardi was of a noble family from Recanati, thirty miles to the north of Fermo, who felt suffocated by the rigours of his religious upbringing and parental restrictions. He had a delicate constitution, suffered ill health throughout his life and died of cholera at the age of thirty-eight. But the statue portrays him as a young man, perhaps in his early twenties, the age at which Federico too, I knew from his hidden letters, was bent over books in this very place.

Venturing inside, I expected to be challenged. But no one questioned why I was there, at first. Down a wide flight of stone steps, I found the former cloisters that now house the conservatoire's administrative offices where serious young men and boys in cassocks and Roman collars would have carried prayer books before hurrying to class. The door to the chapel was barred shut so I continued up an internal staircase to the top floor where I imagined the dormitories once would have been. At the end of a long corridor there I saw a custodian bent over a squat desk lit by a hooded glass lamp and felt a shiver of unease. His presence reminded me of the plump babushkas who sat, arms folded, on each floor of the National Hotel where I stayed in Moscow during the Soviet era in my twenties before setting off alone on the Trans-Siberian express. Their task had been to keep tabs on guests and report suspicious activity to the KGB. But as the conservatoire's custodian got up from his desk and beckoned me over, I was relieved to find he was nothing like the brusque Soviet babushkas and was instead there to help. He listened patiently as I explained why I had come and apologised that he couldn't allow me into any of the upper rooms as classes were in session. Besides, he said, the building had been entirely transformed. But he was able to take me up to the flat roof to see the view, and the panorama that opened up was of the sea not the mountains: a vast expanse of the Adriatic shimmering in the distance.

As I took a deep salty breath, I felt a familiar sense of freedom looking towards the horizon and wondered if Don Federico had felt it too. If his perspective changed when he moved closer to the coast. Perhaps he too had felt the stirrings of restlessness the sea instilled in me. I knew from a pamphlet buried among his papers that he sat a series of exams in the seminary in 1903, when he would have been twenty-one. But other dates suggested it took him longer than the customary twelve years to complete his religious instruction.

It was possible that, like Leopardi, he had suffered from ill health and missed several years of study due to illness. But there was another explanation that also played on my mind. That Don Federico might have experienced doubts about his future path, possibly even leaving the seminary for a period before eventually returning, either voluntarily or at the urging of his family. For beyond the walls of the seminary Italy was in turmoil at that time. After Papal States like Le Marche were incorporated into the new Kingdom of Italy in 1870, with Rome as its capital, Pope Pius IX declared the church 'despoiled'. The quick-tempered, epileptic Pio Nono of the statue from my attic excommunicated the king and all his successors and shut himself away in the Vatican Palace. He then forbade the faithful from playing any part in the democratic politics of what he saw as a godless new country: one in which outdoor religious processions and services were banned, schools were secularised, Church property was confiscated, and priests were conscripted into the army.

By the turn of the century, as Don Federico walked in clerical robes through Fermo's steep and winding streets, he must have felt harried by the tension in the air. Anti-clericalism had been festering for decades. Much of the population was going to bed hungry. Social unrest, worker strikes, increasingly violent clashes with socialists, communists and anarchists were met with harsh repression. In 1900, amid protests at rising food prices, King Umberto I was shot through the heart by an Italian-American anarchist as he stepped from his open carriage in Milan.

Within the walls of the building where I now stood there was growing conflict too. And that day in Fermo I felt myself pulled back in time, imagining the atmosphere of fear and suspicion that pervaded the seminary during the years Don Federico was there. There was no way of knowing what his hopes and fears, his dreams and thoughts, would have been at this time. But he and others must surely have battled with feelings of paranoia. For these were the years when a fierce crusade, begun by Pio Nono and enforced even more stringently after Pius X ascended the papal throne in 1903, was being waged to stamp out any attempt at modernising the Catholic Church. A time when even the slightest suggestion that the Church come to terms with developments in modern society and contemporary thinking in areas such as the natural sciences was deemed utmost heresy.

To ensure those on the path to holy orders were not tainted by such modernist ideas, or poison as they were called, seminaries were virtually shut off from the outside world. Visits home were severely restricted, women forbidden from entering and an undercover network of thought police began to operate more akin to the McCarthyite witch hunts pursued against communists during the cold war.

At the heart of this insidious web was a secret service Pius X set up within the Vatican, in which the Pope himself was given the codename *Mama*, which oversaw the work of spies and double agents in parishes and seminaries throughout Italy and beyond to root out anyone suspected of modernist sympathies. Anyone overheard expressing a liberal view or suspected of harbouring doubts about matters of doctrine, often on the basis of little more than rumour, faced expulsion from the Church, demotion or exile to a remote country parish.

True to the fiercely independent spirit of Le Marche, one of the principal challengers within the church to such blinkered thinking was a former student of Fermo's seminary called Romolo Murri who was born in the small nearby village of Monte San Pietrangeli. Increasingly frustrated with the Church's unwillingness to modernise,

Murri stood as a candidate in parliamentary elections in March 1909 and was immediately excommunicated.

All of this has been widely chronicled by eminent historians of the Catholic Church. What has not is what happened afterwards in this one small corner of Italy. The place where Murri was born, where his links were strong, and his progressive ideas found fertile ground in the minds of the young. The fact that, following Murri's election to parliament, a group of seminarians from Fermo wrote to congratulate him on his success and began asking questions of him, and of themselves. Questions like: *Facciamo bene a farci preti?* Are we right to become priests? 'Some of us have begun to have doubts,' they wrote in one of a series of letters. 'Amid all this turmoil how can we keep our faith? How, in all conscience, can we promise to carry out rituals in which we see no virtue? Should we disrobe and embrace the secular life? Would we do more good as laymen than if we continue on the path we are on?' When several of their tormented private letters were mysteriously intercepted and made public, what followed was the stuff of fiction.

After thanking the conservatoire custodian and taking my leave, I retraced my steps down to the ground floor, stepped back into the narrow lane and followed it along to where it joined a wider thoroughfare in search of the scene where some of this played out. I was looking for the original entrance to the seminary and found it tucked around the corner with the words '*Clericorum Seminarium*' still engraved in the stone above a tall black door, now firmly locked. Just a few yards from the door, embedded in the brick wall and sunk in shadows, was a box-like recess. Above it a stone plaque bore another inscription which, from memories of schoolgirl Latin, I translated roughly to mean '*Here lies succour for those abandoned by their parents*'. Beneath this was the date *MDLXX*, 1570.

This dark recess, roughly the height, width and depth of a woman's arm, was now covered with a rusty iron grille. But during Don Federico's day it would have yawned open, ready to receive bundles of pitiful humanity laid there when no one was looking. The stony hollow still bore the grooves where what used to be known as a *ruota dei trovatelli*, or foundling wheel, slowly turned. A place where women could leave babies they lacked either the means or will to nurture.

A little further along, higher up in the wall, was an elaborate stone lintel carved with the image of a woman wearing a crown and a capacious long cloak. Her arms spread wide so the cloak billowed to shelter a huddle of kneeling mothers, each one offering up her child. The carving reminded me of Piero della Francesca's gloriously serene *Madonna of Mercy*, the gilded centrepiece of his tempera and oil polyptych which now hangs in the museum of Sansepolcro in Tuscany. But while the carving before me might have drawn inspiration from the great Renaissance masterpiece, the scenes it witnessed during Don Federico's day were more like something that might have taken place in the depths of the Dark Ages.

Beside the locked door above which the carving loomed was a sign identifying the building as the Ospedale di Santa Maria della Carita, otherwise known simply as an *orfanotrofio*, or orphanage. Unknown perhaps to most of the nuns who dedicated their lives to looking after the children abandoned here, this orphanage also provided succour, and a secret lifeline, to struggling souls in the seminary next door. There must surely have been some nuns who wondered why letters to and from seminarians were being sent via the *ospedale* instead of directly to their place of learning. But there must have been others who understood perfectly well that this place of sanctuary was also being used as a dead-letter drop for illicit correspondence. Those who knew this must have been aware that their complicity in sanctioning such activity put them in grave danger, exposing them to the risk of severe sanctions by the church.

It is not clear how some of the seminarians' letters passed via the nuns were eventually exposed. Perhaps one of the sisters had become suspicious and sought to curry favour with those in authority. In my mind's eye, I saw a veiled figure stealing out of the orphanage at night, hugging the wall close to the foundling wheel before knocking on the seminary's black door on the pretext of delivering some culinary delight to the office of the rector or principal. Or perhaps one of the nuns had simply made a mistake and passed the letters to those in charge of the seminary without realising the maelstrom of misery this would unleash.

What followed, however, soon passed into the public domain. Once the content of the students' letters became known, a campaign of intimidation was launched to identify those responsible. One local liberal newspaper stirred the pot by saying the majority of seminarians in Fermo agreed with the letters, even though they had been too afraid to identify themselves by name. In a state of panic at the consequences, the students who penned the letters wrote to Murri again and begged him to return the originals since this was the only solid evidence by which their identity, through handwriting, might one day be known. They were surrounded by spies, they said, and felt like lambs about to be sent to the slaughter.

After this the situation escalated further. The Catholic press became involved and published threats that the seminary would be burnt to the ground if those who wrote the letters and signed themselves simply *gli amici del Seminario*, friends from the seminary, did not come forward. Students then began to be interrogated, one by one, in confession. And the ordination of those due to become priests that summer was put on hold. When eleven seminarians, fearing the consequences for their brethren, eventually acknowledged penning the letters, most were instantly expelled or banished to serve in remote parishes where little was heard of them again.

An account of these dark days written by a Catholic priest and academic decades later carried the names of some of those directly and indirectly implicated. There was no mention of Federico Bellesi. Whether he secretly harboured similar sympathies or yearned for the freedom to explore modern ideas I would likely never know. But, surrounded by such ferment, it seems almost inconceivable that he would not have had some doubts about the path that lay ahead.

Clues to the closed mindset of those in whose care he found himself could be found not far away from the orphanage, however: back along the narrow lane that opened out into Fermo's expansive main square, the Piazza del Popolo, in the musty newspaper archives of the Biblioteca Civica, the municipal library. Under the strictures of Pius X's papacy, seminarians were only permitted to read approved newspapers such as the archdiocese of Fermo's weekly *La Voce delle Marche*. Glancing at *La Voce*'s front page on 15 February 1906, Don Federico would have seen a headline announcing '*La bancarotta del darwinismo*', The Bankruptcy of Darwinism, above an article that stated: 'God is in no hurry; sooner or later, by logical necessity, science must bow to revelation.'

So, these were the confines of Don Federico's world as a young man. A man with a clear passion for nature. Someone with a love of walking in the Sibillini mountains and the sense of freedom that comes with it. How he must have longed to return there.

Chapter 13

Today some say that in Italy hope is a national virtue. 'A feeling with an almost mythological quality,' the Italian writer Mario Di Vito observed in his book *Dopo: Viaggio al termine del cratere,* Aftermath: Journey to the End of the Crater, published in the aftermath of the 2016 earthquakes. One that is 'waved about on every minimally national-popular occasion' offering false promise of an Italy that will always make it, despite everything, he lamented. An Italy that scores in the last minute. 'Italy with flags.' Italy that is not afraid. 'Poor Italy that rises from the ashes like a Phoenix,' Di Vito wrote.

But hope deferred makes the heart sick, as the proverb goes. Hope requires some effort be put into realising whatever it is you wish to happen and believe possible. Otherwise, it is simply vague optimism, worse still denial and deception. And there was little evidence on the part of those at the heart of government that the problems of the *terremotati* were any longer a priority. As time passed and so many political promises offering help to the earthquake-stricken region and its people were broken, hope was in short supply.

Much of central Italy remained at a standstill. So many businesses were ruined, with livelihoods lost; so many remained far from their homes, housed in temporary shelters or packed into hotels commandeered far away on the coast – it felt as if a vast swathe of the country's interior had fallen into a coma. Some began to talk of a deliberate strategy of abandonment. A gradual forced depopulation of the heart of Italy: the thousand-square kilometres of The Crater. A rewriting of the region's history in favour of more densely populated, hence politically attractive, places on the coast.

Some who had clung on in the area in the belief that permission to begin work on rebuilding would be granted relatively swiftly, gave up and decided to abandon their damaged homes for good. The hardship of those reduced to living in wooden shelters or Portakabin containers parked on the outskirts of stricken communities ground on. In Amandola, the number living in such containers gradually dwindled. But a dozen or so with nowhere else to go remained cooped up, the few with jobs relieved to leave each morning, the elderly whiling away the hours as best they could.

One day I stopped to talk to an elderly lady I regularly saw trudging up the hill from the containers with a crumpled bag of dried cat food tucked under her arm. Her name was Vincenza. She was seventy-five years old and had lived her entire life in a house with medieval origins beside the church of Saint Francis at the far end of the old town. When the church spire was toppled by the earthquakes it had narrowly missed the roof of her home. I recognised which house she meant immediately when she told me this; it was one of those that always had a spectacular display of flowers spilling from pots on every windowsill and, even after the earthquakes, still did.

Vincenza went every day to tend the pots outside her childhood home, its front door now sealed shut, and then went to feed her beloved twenty-four-year-old cat Pippo. The night of the August earthquake it was Pippo who sensed impending danger first. 'I didn't hear the roar that other people heard. But Pippo jumped onto my bed meowing, which he never did. Then everything started shaking, the walls and roof crumbled, and plaster fell onto the bed. I grabbed Pippo, pulled pillows over us both and told him, "We'll die together." I thought it was the end. It was *un buio pesto*, beastly dark. I knew we'd never make it down the stairs. One more shudder, I thought, *e siamo fritti*, we're fried. When it stopped my house was ruined.'

Ever since the earthquakes Vincenza had kept Pippo safe and warm in a room above a shop in town, offered by a friend, since she could no longer keep him with her. Would I like to see why, she asked, and then led me back down the hill to the roadside layby where the containers were parked. There she lived in a monk-like cell, perhaps six feet by twenty, with a camp bed, a bedside table and a cupboard for her few salvaged belongings. To the side of the container there was a makeshift kitchen and shower block shared with others made similarly homeless.

Vincenza had no children, was widowed, and held out little hope of her home being repaired for many years. The *comune* had promised to build a block of flats near the disused railway station to house the displaced. But work had yet to begin. 'I feel like I'm suffocating here,' she said, but still managed a smile and uttered the phrase heard so often in Italy: *tiriamo avanti*, we carry on.

Vincenza then introduced me to her temporary, or not so temporary, ninety-year-old neighbour Primetta, who shared two adjacent rooms in the prefab with her sixty-year-old son Adriano. Primetta sat perched on the edge of her neatly made bed, hands clasped and dressed in a snowflake-patterned fleece jacket and skirt, feet thrust into slippers with thick socks up to her knees. She hardly registered us as we entered and greeted her but continued staring at the door with rheumy eyes, as if waiting for someone, or something. When I asked when she hoped to be able to return home, her wizened features wrinkled into a smile at a question she could not answer.

Amandola felt in a state of stasis. With the rules and building regulations constantly changing, little progress was being made on any reconstruction or repair projects. The authorities had announced they were giving priority to approving work on houses that could be repaired more quickly in advance of those most severely damaged or totally destroyed. Their logic for this was that it would restore as much housing stock as possible in the shortest amount of time.

In theory, it meant approval would be given for work to start on my own home. But there was little sign of this happening any time soon. Even though the damage was relatively light compared to that of so many, the list of 'works to measure' in Francesca's reconstruction and strengthening plan ran to ten pages and totalled more than £50,000. Like every architect and engineer throughout The Crater she was having to navigate her way through the labyrinth of bureaucracy and constant updates to regulations before government officials would issue a *permesso* to allow builders to start work.

There were occasional glimmers of light, however. Although a thick chain remained looped around the iron gates of the Hotel Paradiso, over the previous twelve months engineers had managed to shore up the damaged walls of an old red-brick palazzo in the hotel grounds so that Oreste, his mother, wife and child could finally be reunited. And when I called in on Oreste and Manuela one afternoon they finally had some happy news. Their young daughter was to be joined by a baby brother; '*un figlio del terremoto*,' a son of the earthquake, Oreste called him with a smile I had not seen on his gentle features in a long time.

*

Meanwhile, some of those whose houses had not been damaged but who had left Amandola unnerved by the continuing aftershocks, did slowly return. Among them were my neighbour Luisa and her husband Dom. After passing the first winter following the October quake in an apartment near the coast, they came back to live in their house down the lane from mine. On the many days when the frustrations of dealing with the welter of paperwork and regulations surrounding attempts to repair my home became too much, their friendship and patient explanation of the country's arcane bureaucracy were a great comfort and help. Since Dom worked such long hours, Luisa and I would sometimes go for a walk in the mountains. Or we would sit talking in the couple's airy sitting room overlooking Amandola's baroque Porta San Giacomo archway with its four pinnacles, two bells, elaborate ironwork and giant clock that once stood on the face of Saint Augustine's church.

As the hands on the clock clicked inexorably forward, and the reality of the present felt overwhelming, our conversation would often turn to the past. Luisa, I learnt, was born in Rome. But her grandmother's family had a farm in the small village of Garulla, some way up in the mountains from Amandola. Dom's family also farmed land there for generations and the couple met when Luisa was visiting her grandmother one summer. After they married and she moved to Amandola she taught English in the town's technical institute for more than twenty years. As someone committed to the importance of education, she was aghast when I told her of the lengths those in charge of Fermo seminary had gone to in order to stamp out the merest hint of progressive thinking by young seminarians in Don Federico's day. But did I know, she said, that Dom too had spent some time in the seminary in Fermo as a boy, albeit half a century later, long after Pius X's spy network was disbanded?

'Dom started training as a priest?' I asked, startled at the thought that her husband, whose passion in life was restoring classic cars, might instead have spent his days wearing a cassock.

'Not exactly. He was the only boy in a family of five sisters and his mother believed he would have a better education in the junior seminary than the local school. But he was so homesick he pleaded to come home, otherwise I might not be here,' she laughed.

Like Dom's mother, Don Federico's father Cesare must have believed
he was doing what was best for his son. But perhaps he also comforted
himself with the thought that the boy could provide him with both
spiritual succour and some measure of material comfort in his old age.

'It's true that not only was there a certain status to having a priest
in the family but becoming a parish priest in those days was also
a way of making money,' said Luisa. And not only because of the
steady income they were assured. There were priests both in Italy and
elsewhere in times past who were notorious for purloining bequests
intended for the Church. Some even acted as intermediaries for
collectors in other countries when it came to choice items of furniture,
silverware and paintings. Knowing this made me feel a little uneasy
about the provenance of the paintings hidden away in my attic.

Over the years, after I bought my house, I had occasionally asked
around to see if anyone knew anything of the priest from my house.
No one I asked had and I thought little of it at the time; we were
talking about someone who lived there over a century ago, after all.
But back then my questions had been nothing but idle curiosity. It
was only now they assumed more of a sense of urgency.

Now that I understood how young Don Federico had been when he
lost his mother, I would have liked to know how old he was when
he was first sent to Fermo. Most boys entered a junior seminary at the
age of eleven or twelve, as Dom had, said Luisa, though there were
many who were sent as boarders to start their religious education
as young as six or seven. How, I wondered, would his father have
felt had he known of the intrigue and venom, the threats of excommunication and of burning the seminary to the ground, directed at
students while his son was there. With no mother to confide in, would
his son have told his father or sister or anyone else in the family? Or
did he keep quiet, knowing they had struggles of their own?

When I returned to look at his collection of letters in search of
answers it was clear he was under pressure to succeed on the clerical
path, regardless of whether it was one he himself had chosen or one
that was chosen for him. In one letter sent from Rome in February
1900 his Uncle Antonio reminds his nephew of the *sacrifici* everyone,
above all his father Cesare, is making to ensure Federico can continue
with his studies.

Many of the letters were hard to decipher, however, and when I
mentioned this to Luisa, with her customary kindness and generosity

she offered to help. As spring turned to summer two years after the earthquakes, we spent many hours seated side by side at her round mahogany dining table and, with the letters spread before us, began our detective work.

When together we read, in another letter from the same Uncle Antonio, of a severe outbreak of flu which had hit Rome that same year 1900, Luisa fell silent and seemed lost in thought. Her maternal grandfather had died in the Spanish flu pandemic that swept the globe twenty years later, claiming more than fifty million lives, she explained. This had left her grandmother struggling to raise five daughters alone in Rome where the family lived. Her grandmother had been forced to take whatever humble work she could to support her children and had little choice but to send two of her daughters to a convent. One of them, Luisa's mother, was just six years old. Once a week, on a Sunday, their mother would visit the two girls and, sometimes, bring them one boiled sweet each. 'My mother used to tell me how she would unwrap her sweet and take just a few licks before wrapping it up again to make it last,' said Luisa. 'She missed her family so much.'

It was a stark reminder of how harsh life was, not only for Luisa's grandmother but for most throughout these years, like Don Federico and his family. And as we continued reading the letters there were further reminders of this. And of the pressure Don Federico was under from his family, not least as a brother to his younger, also motherless, sibling, his sister Rosa, or Rosina as she signed herself.

None of Rosina's eight letters in the collection are dated but some have the tone of a demanding teenager. One is devoted almost exclusively to an urgent appeal that her brother buy her a black chiffon scarf '*di ultima moda*', of the latest fashion, to cover her head when attending mass. Her instructions for exactly what she wants and where she wants her brother to buy it – a famously expensive shop in Fermo at the time – fill two pages. 'If they try to sell you something different, I don't want it . . . *Ai capito*' (*sic*), you understand, she warns, before signing off: 'I kiss you and send you dearest wishes. Your affectionate sister Rosina.'

Even when Federico satisfies his sister's whim, he receives scant praise for having done so. 'I liked the material,' is all Rosina says of the scarf he must have sent her, before continuing, 'Now I want to take care of myself.' What she means by this, she explains, is that she wants to have her photograph taken, even though she knows this is expensive. Again, it seems her wish was granted. 'I look beautiful,' she tells her brother in a later letter. I dared not think how many hours Cesare would have spent sweeping Amandola's streets or carrying heavy packages to pay for such luxuries. Did the photographs still exist, I wondered. How I would have loved to see what Rosina looked like at that young age.

One small insight into a cottage industry prevalent in Amandola at the time comes in another of her letters where she talks of *i bachi*, the silkworms she and her father are cultivating to help make ends meet. This was the first time I heard mention of there having been a tradition of sericulture as well as wool production in the area. There was no sign of mulberry bushes in my garden when I bought the house, but perhaps the Bellesi family once cultivated a small plot of land somewhere else in the countryside.

Despite the demanding tone in some of Rosina's letters, they also convey her sisterly concern for her brother's welfare. 'Are your feet still hurting?' she asks in one. 'Do you still have toothache?' she asks in another. There was talk too of food parcels she was planning to send to him containing salami, bread, pizza, *ciambella*, walnuts and, in one, a large quantity of *castagne*, sweet chestnuts. In this letter she says she is preparing to send fifty kilos of chestnuts by horse and cart, perhaps, Luisa suggested, as part payment for his tuition.

Chestnuts are certainly abundant in the Sibillini mountains, and the annual *castagnata*, or chestnut festival, is one of Amandola's autumn highlights. But in hard times past, sweet chestnuts, rich in protein, were a dietary staple, either roasted or ground to flour as a substitute for wheat, Luisa explained. An abundance of chestnuts would have been cause for celebration and, in another letter, Rosina boasts that the markets of Amandola were overflowing with them that year. 'Imagine the envy of the *Sarnanesi* at that!' she gloats.

Luisa and I both laughed at this blatant display of triumphant *campanilismo*, which roughly translates as loyalty to the bell tower, the still prevalent rivalry that exists between Italian towns, villages and even neighbourhoods within earshot of different church bells. 'Even today there is great rivalry between Amandola and Sarnano, as well as Comunanza and Montefortino,' Luisa said of the three neighbouring towns. 'Each one wants to be thought of as the best. Especially Amandola!'

The first time I encountered such *campanilismo* was thousands of miles away in Mexico where I sometimes heard my daughter's father Enrico spar good-naturedly with his close friend Gerlando, who hailed from a neighbouring small Umbrian hill town, even though both had lived in Mexico for many years. But there seemed to be a sharper edge to Amandola's sense of superiority. I once heard Amandolesi spoken of, not altogether good-humouredly, as 'those people with their nose in the air'.

It was true that Amandola had once been very prosperous; the place where noble families in the area chose to live. Some spoke of a time when *contadini*, peasant farmers and farm labourers, were forbidden from entering the piazza in rough wooden clogs to prevent its cobbles from being soiled. And if they did enter, they were not permitted to wear shirts with collars as this was regarded as the attire of *signori*, gentlemen.

But the more layers of Amandola's history I began to peel away the more of its troubles I came to understand. For I also heard stories of darker episodes. One, particularly troubling, involving a local nobleman, was told to me by someone who, as a child, had lived in the little lane where my house stood. At the time, she said, the lane used to reek of salted hides hung out to dry by the butcher who ran a shop in the basement of the house facing mine. She did not know exactly where or when the crime had taken place but did not speak of it as if it was in some distant medieval age. She gave only scant details, saying it involved an unwilling young woman, perhaps still a girl, and the birth of a baby whose body was later found abandoned in a garden. The story was vague and, out of respect for those in the town whose lives it might touch, I did not press for details, knowing that the trauma of such things can seep down through generations.

As Luisa and I continued to read the letters we found no mention of Don Federico going to Sicily in the aftermath of the earthquakes that first levelled the city of Messina and after this the small communities in the shadow of Mount Etna. Nothing that might explain the presence of the map in my attic recording such disasters. The last dated letter in the collection was written on 30 December 1909, almost exactly a year to the day after Messina was destroyed, but makes no mention of it. Instead, it is another in which Don Federico's Uncle Antonio complains of ill health, saying he has lost his appetite from living so far away from the Sibillini.

There was no envelope for this last letter, however, so it was not clear where Don Federico, by then twenty-seven years old, was living. The only clues to where he went after leaving the seminary lay in a handful of postcards, all but one of which had the advantage of both a postmark and an address. The most beautiful of all was a hand-painted card simply signed *Federico* in which he sends affectionate greetings to his sister and father to wish them *Buona Pasqua*, Happy Easter. On the front he had painted a delicate vase of violet and ochre pansies surrounded by ferns against a glinting background of mottled gold. To my untrained eye the small picture showed some skill and made me wonder if Don Federico might once have cherished hopes of a more artistic life than one as a man wedded to the church. I had no idea how old he would have been when he made it because this was the one card that was undated. But it both enchanted and intrigued me and I kept it propped in front of my keyboard for months as I wrote.

It was in three of the remaining postcards that I saw Don Federico finally addressed as *Egregio Sacerdote*, esteemed priest. All three were brief Christmas and New Year greetings postmarked December 1910 or January 1911 when he would have been thirty years old. Each was signed with names I did not recognise and addressed care of the provost of Monte San Pietrangeli, the small village where the rebel priest turned politician Romolo Murri was born. Was it mere coincidence that this is where Don Federico went first after leaving the seminary, I wondered. Even though the village was less than thirty miles from Amandola, further along the river Tenna valley towards the Adriatic, I had never been there and felt drawn to go. I wanted to understand how Don Federico's life had unfolded after the troubles of his youth.

Chapter 14

The one place where I believed I might be able to put more flesh on the bones of what I already knew about Don Federico was near to his old seminary, down a steep cobbled lane from Fermo's Piazza del Popolo. But when I arrived I found it guarded by a fierce custodian, a sturdy woman with a steely gaze.

When I began by asking if she could confirm at what age Don Federico first entered the junior seminary, which seemed a simple enough question to me, she bridled. 'No,' the keeper replied, crossing her arms. This was, she said, 'sensitive information'. My heart sank. But just then the phone rang, and she retreated behind her corner desk. While I waited, I surveyed the tightly packed shelves of ecclesial volumes dating back centuries in the only room in the archbishop's historical archives open to the public. When she put down the phone, her mood was more relaxed.

There were certain records she could check, she said, disappearing into a back room and emerging with two hefty bound tomes dating from 1909 to the 1920s. The first of these confirmed the date on which Don Federico was fully ordained: 24 October 1909, just months after threats were issued to burn his seminary to the ground. From this it was clear he had been among those whose ordination was put on hold while a witch hunt was conducted to root out so-called heretics. Though there was no mention of any of this in the volumes the keeper held close to her chest, or at least none she was prepared to share with me.

There was, strangely, no mention either of his ever having been in Monte San Pietrangeli, birthplace of the rebel Romolo Murri, despite the postcard in my attic confirming this. The first entry was from 1913 when Don Federico was appointed *parroco*, priest, of the parish of SS Vincenzo ed Anastasio, a former sixth-century Benedictine monastery tucked away on the forested slopes of *Monte Amandola*. I had trudged past this monastery many times on my mountain hikes and, after the earthquakes, seen the entrance to its solitary chapel boarded up because of damage and overgrown with giant daisies. But it was there, surrounded by the mountains, that Don Federico had spent the next eight years serving a quiet rural parish while the world beyond was convulsed by revolution and war. For despite so many Amandolesi having marched north to fight in the First World War, there was no mention of him ever having served as an army chaplain, even though clergy were not exempt from military service until 1922 unless on medical grounds.

With so many men away fighting, Don Federico must have been left with only women, children and the elderly in his care. Those unable to read or write would have made their way through the mountains to his door to plead for help. Bent low over his desk, beside the chapel where Benedictine monks once sung the Liturgy of the Hours, he would have spent many hours penning letters in his immaculate hand in search of news of loved ones on their behalf. When the news they most feared came, it was he who would have delivered it and provided them with comfort.

His life must have been one of relative ease compared to theirs. For the records showed that, while there in the mountains, Don Federico was in receipt of both parish benefits and tithes from the one hundred and seventy acres of woodland, stands of sweet chestnut and pastures that belonged to the Church. Under the prevailing system of *mezzadria* the local families who worked the land and the shepherds who kept their flocks there would have been obliged to give him half their yield. As they toiled, Don Federico would have been free to roam the mountains and, when he could, travel the eight miles back and forth, by horse or on foot, from his parish to visit his father and sister Rosina in Amandola. Shaking off his shoes at the front door, the same threshold I was to cross all those years later, he would have climbed the stone stairs into our shared house and told them of the troubles of his flock.

It was in those early years of the twentieth century that the elegant Gran Caffè Belli in Amandola's piazza first opened its doors. And I imagined copies of newspapers would have lain on tables there then, as they do today, not censored as they had been while he was studying in the seminary. It was most probably there that Don Federico first read reports of the earthquakes that struck Sicily in 1914, the ones recorded on the map left hidden under my eaves. When disaster befell the island six years earlier, he would still have been a student and unable to help. But by 1914, Don Federico had agency. Like parish priests throughout Italy, he would have begun a collection for those whose lives were wrecked, just as every church and community had done in the wake of the Messina earthquake. But in the long nights he sat alone in his mountain cloisters, surrounded by frescoes of angels and saints, had he dreamt of doing more than this?

When I told the keeper about the earthquake map of Sicily in my attic and asked if she thought it possible Don Federico had travelled to Sicily to help, she could find no mention of it in the records. 'Ma si, è probabile,' she replied, thinking it not just possible, but quite likely.

How and when he might have had the opportunity to go was unclear, however, as the records were sketchy. From Don Federico's time in a quiet mountain parish close to home they jumped forward to 1922 when it seems he became more ambitious. In February of that year, at the age of forty, he entered a *concorso*, a competition, to move up the ecclesial ladder, which saw him move from the Sibillini to take up the position of *parroco* of a prominent church in the expanding seaport of Civitanova, fifty miles to the north-east of Amandola, on the Adriatic coast.

Throughout the years he spent in the mountains, the persecution of those in the priesthood who had more open ideas eased. Benedict XV had ascended to the papal throne and disbanded his predecessor's network of spies. Perhaps it was this atmosphere of greater openness that encouraged Don Federico to apply for a more challenging position. If it was, then he could not have been more wrong. For not only was 1922 the year Benito Mussolini's Fascist blackshirts marched on Rome and Italy's two-decade-long totalitarian regime was born, but it was also a year of change in the Vatican too. Just a few days after Don Federico arrived in Civitanova, the papacy once again changed hands. This time it passed from the more moderate Benedict XV to autocratic Pius XI. Whatever personal views Don Federico might have held he would have now found himself severely fettered.

The struggle between the dictator, a visceral anti-cleric known in his youth as *mangiaprete*, priest-eater, and the stubborn, dogmatic, authoritarian Pius XI would determine every aspect of his and his countrymen and women's lives in the years that followed. In the early years, in an effort to consolidate his power, Mussolini established a truce of sorts between Church and state. A series of pacts was agreed that recognised Roman Catholicism as the country's sole religion, accepted the validity of church marriages and reinstated religious education in schools. They also paid compensation for Church property and lands seized when the Kingdom of Italy was created and bestowed on all future popes the title of head of state of the newly created sovereign territory, the tiny Vatican City, with its own police force, railway station, radio and newspaper. Soon after these pacts were finalised at the end of the 1920s, however, relations quickly deteriorated as Mussolini showed his true colours and the autonomy of the Church was steadily eroded.

What happened, I wondered, during all this to the young man I imagined chafing at the straitjacket imposed by his superiors on all those in the seminary where he studied? I wanted to believe my silent companion through the trials of Amandola's past had a tender heart. That he had been adventurous and brave. That he knew how to stand tall in the face of adversity. But was this true? Perhaps he had simply bent to prevailing winds. Perhaps his move from the mountains to the coast marked a fundamental shift to more traditionalist views.

Until then I had been unable to do little more than intuit Don Federico's innermost thoughts and feelings about the tumultuous times in which he lived from the fragments of his life concealed in my attic. Closer inspection, for instance, of the book I first assumed was a guide to conservative sexual morals had revealed a more progressive text. One chapter entitled 'Signs of the Inferiority of Women in Marriage' was in fact a criticism of the subjugation of women and the way many were treated as material possessions, not only in Italy but in other European countries. At the time of writing the book in 1912, its author Roberto Michels was a militant socialist, though he later went on to support Mussolini. I had no way of knowing when or why Don Federico acquired the book. Perhaps he had been encouraged to read it by his cousin Donato or sister Rosina. But it seemed to suggest a broad mind.

The records offered only the briefest glimpses into the evolution of Don Federico's character as some of these turbulent events unfolded. But they make it clear that, once he arrived in Civitanova, Don Federico was very careful about sticking to the rules and enforcing the expected strict moral code. In his first four years they note he reduced the number of co-habiting couples in the parish, opposed the opening of any so-called 'locked houses', *case chiuse*, state-sanctioned brothels, saw the number of those taking Holy Communion swell and greatly increased the number of confessions heard to around thirty thousand every year, a measure of the guilt that must have weighed on his flock in the rampantly repressive climate. He also refused to carry out baptisms late in the evening in people's homes, as might, I imagine, have been requested by parents fearing their infants would not survive to see the dawn, insisting that all baptisms must be carried out during regular hours and in church. But the records also hint at Don Federico having suffered from a rather delicate constitution, as his lack of military service also suggests, in the several mentions made of him suffering from a sore throat if he talked too much.

In a more positive vein, he also founded a mobile library, a church choir and parish newspaper and started contributing occasional articles to both the local archdiocesan newspaper and the national Catholic newspaper *Corriere d'Italia*. As was customary, few articles then carried bylines. But scouring yellowing back copies on a return visit to Fermo's beautiful old library, I found one, almost certainly written by Don Federico, with a rather preening tone. It was a glowing account of a visit by the archbishop to Civitanova in July 1926 which, besides a lengthy description of how cheering crowds thronged the streets and tossed flowers from windows as he passed, referred more than once to the conscientious attention paid to the archbishop by the *giovane parroco*, young (*sic*) priest, of San Pietro, the very church of which Don Federico himself was priest.

Such telling insights aside, what really interested me was what happened to Don Federico as Mussolini's dictatorship tightened its grip and descended into the depths. When it banned Catholic youth organisations and started challenging religious instruction in schools. How, I wanted to know, had he behaved in the face of the expulsion of Jewish children from state and private schools in 1938 when the country's heinous race laws barred Jews from teaching, serving in the military, working in the civil service and much else? There were certainly many pro-Fascist priests, though there were some too who risked their lives by providing safe haven for those in danger of imprisonment and transportation to Nazi concentration camps.

When I asked the keeper about such things her mood changed once again. All Church records in the archive during and after the

1930s were closed, she said, turning on her heel and making it clear it was time for me to leave.

As I made my way back to my car, I had to question whether the benevolent portrait of Don Federico I had constructed in my mind was valid and to wonder who he became in the face of his country's brutal regime. The only personal note in the records was a brief mention of the fact that Don Federico's father Cesare had moved to the coast to live with him in Civitanova after his son took up his new post. I knew that after Rosina married she too had moved away from Amandola, to the small *comune* of Serravalle di Chienti, thirty miles to the west, where her husband found work. Cesare would have been in his sixties by then and must have struggled to maintain the rambling family home alone until, exhausted by a lifetime of labour, his son took him into his care.

At least this might explain why all the letters and other written material recovered from my attic were dated from the 1890s and the first two decades of the twentieth century, but petered out after that. With no one to care for it, I imagined the doors to my house had been locked, its shutters barred, and precious items hidden away in darkness.

Instead of taking the most direct route back to Amandola from Fermo by following the banks of the river Tenna, I chose the road that runs above the valley floor, hugging the crest of a high spur of land where Monte San Pietrangeli sits. I wanted to know what had happened to Don Federico during the years that were missing from the records. A possible answer to those immediately following his troubled ordination lay close by. For earlier in the week, I had called a priest in Monte San Pietrangeli to ask for his help and after a few days he called back to say he had found something interesting which he would explain when I got there.

The sun was sinking behind the Sibillini as I drove on, windows down, the scent of wet grass and pine needles drifting on the breeze. I imagined Don Federico riding on horseback in his clerical robes down the same winding country lanes. Then I wondered how long it would have taken a horse and cart to travel this old road between Fermo and Amandola, especially one laden with the fifty kilos of sweet chestnuts Rosina once dispatched to her brother.

The tall wooden doors to the large church of Santi Lorenzo e Biagio were barred shut when I arrived and there was a familiar

notice pinned to the door *'chiuso a causa di danni da terremoto'* –
closed due to earthquake damage. The far end of the small village
was otherwise deserted. So I supposed the figure heading towards me
at some speed must be the parish priest Don Lorenzo, even though,
rather than clerical garb, he was dressed in a dark-blue football strip
that clung to the contours of his ample girth. He had unruly dark
hair, a moustache and long sideburns tapering through a fashionable
shadow of stubble.

From his appearance, I judged Don Lorenzo to be a little older
than Don Federico would have been when he served the same parish,
but close enough in age to sympathise with the difficulties one of
his predecessors might have struggled with, albeit a century earlier. I
also guessed Don Lorenzo was not a man to miss a meal, so when
I offered to take him to supper he nodded with enthusiasm and led
the way up the narrow main street towards a square where knots
of old men stood around chatting. Don Lorenzo greeted each with
a wave and a few words. 'Eh, Luigi. Are you sleeping with men or
women now?' he called out to one wizened figure on the other side
of the road. 'Women,' the man said, hitching up his belt and letting
out a deep laugh. 'Ah yes, but how many?' Don Lorenzo shouted
back, his face crumpling into a broad grin as he dodged a car and
crossed the road to slap the old man on the back.

I trailed behind as Don Lorenzo dipped into the doorway of an
old hotel, past a tall, copper-fronted bar, into a back dining-room
where the *padrona* emerged from the kitchen wiping her hands on her
apron and, arms spread wide, ushered us towards his *tavolo abituale*.
With a napkin folded into the neck of his football shirt, he ordered
the special of the day for us both and tucked with enthusiasm into
his plate of *penne all'arrabbiata*. There was a delicious smell of fresh
basil and *parmigiano* wafting in the air and a faint hum of football
commentary coming from a TV fixed high on a far wall, to which
Don Lorenzo, fortunately, had his back turned. As I told him more
about what I had found in my attic he listened, eyes fixed on his
plate, now and then raising his head to return the greeting of other
diners as they entered the room. For Don Lorenzo was a warm and
open character, made more voluble with wine. And after finishing
his pasta and wiping a piece of bread, a *scarpetta*, across his dish to
soak up the last traces of spicy tomato sauce, he told me what he
had discovered looking back through old parochial diaries.

Federico Bellesi had come to Santi Lorenzo e Biagio as a *cappellano*, chaplain, in February 1910, he said, but just thirteen months later had left and been replaced by another chaplain. After this he had been sent to serve another parish in Montefortino, a small *comune* neighbouring Amandola, where again he stayed for only a short time before being dispatched to the remote rural parish of a former monastery higher up in the Sibillini mountains.

Don Lorenzo thought it unusual in those days for a young priest to serve for such a short time before repeatedly moving or being moved on. But Santi Lorenzo e Biagio was once a *collegiata*, a collegiate church home to several priests living in community, he explained, and he believed the provost there during the first years of the twentieth century was very conservative, strict, old school. 'Perhaps they clashed, and the provost asked for Bellesi to be sent elsewhere,' he speculated. I thought back to the day I stood looking out to sea from the roof of the old seminary in Fermo and of the persecution of those suspected of progressive sympathies at a time when a careless word in a refectory was enough for a clergyman to be exiled to a distant village curacy.

But there was something else, said Don Lorenzo. He had found mention of a book written about the former monastery of SS Vincenzo e Anastasio on the slopes of Monte Amandola that was published in 1934; its author was a certain F. Bellesi. It was too much of a coincidence. It had to be Don Federico.

When I told Don Lorenzo about the earthquake map of Sicily buried among Don Federico's papers, he made a connection that had not crossed my mind. 'Perhaps he intended writing a book about earthquakes too one day,' Don Lorenzo mused. 'Priests often took to writing books as they grew older.' The thought that Don Federico might have planned to write a book about the fragility of his native land, as I was now, was tantalising, though there was no record of him having done so.

In Don Federico's day much less was known about the forces of nature that forged the mountain ranges which run the length of Italy, let alone the cause of the sudden convulsions to which they are prone. But just seven years after Messina was laid to waste, on the morning of 13 January 1915, another severe earthquake struck much closer to Amandola in the central Apennine town of Avezzano, killing nearly the entirety of its population of 30,000. Both the quake itself and its aftershocks would certainly have been felt by Don Federico in his Sibillini mountain parish sixty miles or so to the north as the crow flies.

'Those of us born on this land know the earthquakes will return,' Don Lorenzo continued. 'Some can live with the knowledge of this fragility. Others do not have the inner resources. To live with earthquakes means to invest yourself in a place, not just physically, but in your inner life too.'

As he spoke, I recognised how invested I had become in this land of trembling mountains. How it had worked its way into my psyche, and it was this that was driving me to explore its past and fret about its future. But more than this, I realised once again how, deep down, I had long been aware that in one way or another we all live on *terra ballerina*, on dancing earth. From all I had seen through my work and through my own experiences I was sure of one thing: that life itself is full of uncertainty and that, however much our minds try to convince us otherwise, life-changing thunderbolts can come at all of us, at any time, from any quarter.

Monte San Pietrangeli was far enough away from the epicentre of the August 2016 quake for Don Lorenzo's church to have survived this first major shock with little damage. But the earthquake of 30 October was a different matter. As I slowly finished my meal, Don Lorenzo told me what had happened that day. How he had risen shortly after sunrise and opened the doors of the church early, at 7 a.m., because he suspected some of his elderly parishioners might have forgotten to turn their clocks back and he wanted them to be able to sit and wait quietly for the first mass of the day.

Since his arrival in Monte San Pietrangeli four years earlier, Don Lorenzo had thrown himself into the life of the community. A keen footballer, he had been coaching a youth team the night before. He needed a shower and a shave, so retreated to his bathroom behind the apse of his church and changed into a bathrobe and slippers. A small bell would ring in these private quarters if anyone crossed the threshold. Since it was silent, he prepared his usual milky coffee and went to get ready. Through the buzz of his electric razor, he did not pick up the first deep rumble, the *boato*, so many heard on that October morning. But as the walls and floor of the bathroom began to judder, then violently shake, his feet, still wet from the shower, slipped sideways on the tiles. He dropped his razor and grabbed at the sink to try and stop himself from falling. As he did so he caught sight of his reflection in the mirror, his deep blue eyes widening in terror as he sank towards the floor.

Sprawled out on the tiles, he heard the sound of crashing masonry beyond the bathroom walls. 'I have been in six strong earthquakes in my life. But I knew immediately this one was different,' he said. 'It was stronger than anything I ever experienced before. Even in those very first moments I knew some people would leave and never return. Earthquakes always transform. They change things. They select,' he said, as if seismic events followed some sort of cosmic psychic plan. 'Would you like to see the church?' he asked finally, as the *padrona* brushed away my attempt to pay for our meal.

It was dark as we walked back down the hill and Don Lorenzo led me through a side entrance into a cavernous, dank, underground space in the bowels of Santi Lorenzo e Biagio lit by a single bare light bulb. I followed him up a winding staircase, through a sacristy hung with white surplices and crimson cassocks where he flicked a row of switches to illuminate the main body of the church. The grandeur of the space that then lit up was breathtaking. A series of spotlights trained upwards revealed a panoply of elaborate frescoes: tempera and oil paintings that adorned every wall and the cupola and alcove surrounding a golden altar. The grand domed ceiling fifty feet or so above our heads came alive with colour and the sweeping motion of angels and saints. Towering marbled columns ran the length of the aisles and a grand organ with silver pipes occupied a balcony in a lateral recess.

'*Molto bella, no?*' Don Lorenzo said, seeing the smile on my face.

'*Bellissima.* Truly,' I replied, wondering how it was possible that such grandeur was created for such a small community.

The population of Monte San Pietrangeli is little over two thousand these days. But it was once a place of refuge for noble families fleeing persecution during the French Revolution, Don Lorenzo explained. As a way of thanking the community, they commissioned Giuseppe Valadier, who designed L'Aquila's Church of Blessed Souls, to build Santi Lorenzo e Biagio in grand neoclassical style.

At first glance, the church appeared intact. But as Don Lorenzo walked me down the nave, I saw deep cracks running across the ceiling and walls. The most serious damage could only be seen from above the dome, he said, and was likely to cost nearly a million euros to repair. Despite the church being closed to worshippers on the grounds of public safety, Don Lorenzo was still living in his private quarters behind the apse.

It was late evening by then. I was tired and not looking forward to negotiating the winding road back to Amandola in the dark. 'I have to leave early tomorrow for Rome,' said Don Lorenzo. 'But you are welcome to stay in one of our spare rooms if you don't mind seeing yourself out in the morning.'

The bedroom was austere, and the bed sagged and creaked. Struggling to sleep, I wondered what had happened within these walls to cause Don Federico to leave with such apparent haste. I began to wonder too what had happened to his cousin Donato, whether he and his wife Rosa ever returned to breathe the pure Sibillini air they so longed for.

After a fitful night, I had an uneasy feeling that was beyond any rational explanation. I was not expecting the building to be utterly deserted when I woke and called out 'Buongiorno' several times, thinking a housekeeper would be there. But when I walked through the sacristy, I found myself in the body of the boarded-up church, alone. There was no lighting to illuminate the frescoes. The painted figures on the great domed ceiling were sunk in shadows. I let myself out.

Chapter 15

At times Amandola has an ethereal air. In the summer months the Sibillini can disappear behind a shimmering heat haze, as if they had been nothing but a dream. Then, as night falls, and the heat subsides, a strange hush descends with even the chorus of swifts falling silent. It was on a night such as this I imagined the broken figure of a man stepping out into the dark and trudging through the streets of the *centro storico*, half sleepwalking, half dazed with shock. He does not notice the boy dressed in pyjamas trailing in his wake. Even when the man strays beyond the town's cobbled streets and into the countryside, the boy still follows, afraid for his father.

In the year this happened, every household in Amandola was dealing with the fallout of *La grande guerra*, the 1914–1918 war to end all wars. Many were caring for loved ones returned from the northern front: some with physical injuries, some, left trembling and shaking, labelled *scemi di guerra*, or fools of war. Our man was neither injured nor *scemo*. But he was frantic. He felt he had lost everything and feared for the welfare of his seven children. A decade earlier, he and his wife had endured years of painful separation from their first-born two young daughters and gone in search of a better future for their family. In the summer of 1905, the couple had sailed four thousand miles to the New World to take whatever work they could find. The journey was torturous, conditions on board abominable and the living hard on their arrival. They worked long hours and saved what they could. But they gradually became disillusioned with *l'America*. The man's wife was so homesick for her children and their life in the Sibillini she could bear it no longer. Or at least that is what she told him when she insisted one day that she must return as soon as possible, and he should follow as soon as he could.

What she did not tell him was that the owner of the factory in Boston where they both worked was constantly pursuing her. She was a renowned beauty, strong and determined. But she was struggling to fight off his advances. She knew her husband was a proud and jealous man and feared what he would do to the factory owner, and perhaps her, if she told him the truth. Besides, she was pregnant with their third child and implored him to allow the baby to be born in Italy, cradled in the beauty of their mountain home.

And so she made the arduous journey back across the Atlantic alone. After she left, the factory owner fired her husband and in the autumn of 1909 he returned too. Back in Amandola, the man worked first as a cobbler, then as a butcher, and, in the hours of light that remained at the end of the day, he tended a small plot of land. Through long hours of labour, he added to the savings they brought back from America and deposited most of it in a local bank. The rest he invested in barrels of wine which he sold by the jug in a makeshift bar in the basement of his butcher's shop. After a few years he was able to begin building a house for his growing family. But one day he discovered all his wine was spoilt. He opened the taps on his barrels and watched their contents flood, like a torrent of blood, into the river Tenna. Years later, at the start of the Great Depression in 1929, the bank that held his savings went bust.

This story was told to me by the son of the boy who followed his father through the streets at night, dressed only in his pyjamas. The father of the boy, the man who felt he had lost everything, was Don Federico's cousin, Donato Bellesi. The boy was Donato's eldest son, Leido. It was only after the earthquakes, as my fascination with the Bellesi family grew, that I discovered five of Donato's grandchildren, now advanced in years, still lived in Amandola. That so many stayed so close to their roots was testimony to how deeply attached the Amandolesi are to their mountain home; a visceral connection that made it all the more distressing when so many were forced to abandon it, either permanently or temporarily, after the earth shook.

Two of the five grandchildren even lived in the same lane as my house. One was very elderly and too frail to receive visitors. The other, a gentle stooped man who also suffered from ill health, I had often stopped to talk to in the piazza over the years without realising the connection. A third, a retired headmaster and former mayor of Amandola, I also knew well by sight. But of all Donato's grandchildren, it was Attilio, the son of Leido, who was most forthcoming and one afternoon he came to meet me in my house.

When I led Attilio into the garden that day he stood, feet planted in the long grass, eyes searching the wall of the house that forms its far boundary. Over the years, the Virginia creeper and climbing roses I had trained up the wall had grown tall, so it was hard for him to make out what he was looking for. But as I held the foliage back with a stick to reveal a small low window with a crossbar grill, Attilio gave a little laugh of delight.

'That was my bedroom window when I was a boy. I grew up in that house and used to look out into this garden and sometimes come here to play. But I haven't been here for over seventy years,' he said, turning slowly to look around.

Attilio remembered the garden as one large vegetable patch with a shaded arbour close to the house where his mother would sit as a young woman, knitting and gossiping with Don Federico's sister Rosina. Rosina sometimes returned to Amandola from Serravalle during the hot summer month, he explained, so that her deaf and mute son Licio and daughter Ana would know something of the place that had been her childhood home.

'I don't think I ever went upstairs,' Attilio told me when I led him inside. 'But as a small boy I always thought of this house as *signorile ma un po'scura* – elegant, but a little dark. You have done well to open it up to so much light,' he said, as we climbed to the top floor and stood looking out at the mountains. For a few minutes Attilio seemed once again lost in thought and as I stood quietly by his side, I was conscious that my own imprint on the house was less than traditional. While many houses in the *centro storico* had heavy wooden shutters and dark furniture, my own shutters were white and most of the furniture light and modern.

Many houses declared *inagibili*, however, were being surreptitiously reoccupied all or part of the time by their increasingly desperate owners. So I had begun to feel more comfortable about opening the shutters again when I was in the house, and sun streamed in as we sat downstairs in the living room, talking over cups of tea.

After Donato and Rosa returned to Amandola the growing family lived in the house directly opposite mine, in the quiet pedestrian lane leading down to the main square, Attilio explained. But unlike the front door of my house, which opens onto the lane, that of the house opposite opens onto the square. It sits under a shaded portico next to what was once the butcher's shop where Donato worked. The family lived on the floors above. Saddled with debt and nearly ruined after his dream of building his own home collapsed, Donato found solace in music, said Attilio. With the windows overlooking the piazza open, his grandfather would play the clarinet or saxophone late into the night. The sound of it was so beautiful, people stood in the square beneath the open windows, listening and gently swaying as the notes of the vibrating reed drifted on the night air.

This was a time when many were struggling. When Italy was grappling with spiralling inflation and there was growing anger that territorial gains promised in return for her men fighting with those of the Allied powers in the First World War had been largely ignored.

Donato was not one of the thousand men who marched north from Amandola, pitifully equipped, in the struggle to hold back Austrian forces in the Alps. He did not witness the appalling loss of life in the Battles of Isonzo, nor the shelling of the mountains there in winter to trigger avalanches that buried his compatriots alive. By the time Italy entered the war in 1915, he and Rosa had six children and he could have claimed an exemption on the grounds of having a large family and land to work. Though he had, in fact, been declared unfit for active duty when he first became eligible for conscription in his early twenties due to *deficienza toracica*, problems with his lungs.

But soldiers returning to small communities like Amandola at the end of the war brought with them new political ideas. Contact with a wider, rapidly changing world sowed discontent with social inequalities that had existed for centuries. In areas like Le Marche, heavily dependent on agriculture, there was growing opposition to the injustices of the system of *mezzadria*, a system which gave a landlord the right to the labour of an entire peasant family living on his land, including the right to evict at will. In 1920, at the height of Italy's *biennio rosso*, its so-called Two Red Years of intense social unrest, a time when I imagined Don Federico still living in relative isolation in his small rural parish in the mountains, many Amandolesi took part in national strikes.

While his cousin lived far removed from such ferment, Donato's political awareness, awakened no doubt by the conditions of factory workers in the United States, intensified. First, he became a confirmed socialist. Then, following a split in the Italian Socialist Party, he veered further to the left and became a communist. So much so that when his youngest child, a daughter, was born at the height of the Russian Revolution in 1920, he named her Lenina. But after Mussolini came to power this had to be changed and she was renamed Rina.

I was so intrigued when Attilio told me this, I checked it later in the register office records and found two entries. The first, a pink index card in which Lenina's name had clearly been scratched out and her new name written over it. The second, an entry in the register of births, marriages and deaths dated 1933, which noted that the name Lenina had been suppressed as 'an offense to national sentiment'. Rina would have been thirteen years old at the time. And by then, Amandola was firmly under Fascist control, as was the rest of Italy. When I saw this, I thought of the images Alfredo, the optician, had shown me of Fascist blackshirts grandstanding in front of what used to be the *casa del fascio*, behind Amandola's town hall. And of the photograph that still hung in its stairwell of a speaker addressing a packed crowd with the word '*Duce*' stamped on columns behind.

It struck me then how both the Catholic cleric and his communist cousin would have very likely had more in common than their brotherly bond and shared passion for their beloved Sibillini mountains. That both had almost certainly had to wrap a shield of silence around what they felt and what they feared. Don Federico under the suffocating strictures of the anti-modernists, Donato in the face of the brutal Fascist regime.

Once again, I saw in the physical landscape in which both men were born, and to which I was strangely drawn, a mirror. How the structure of the Sibillini created a place of hidden depths where much was concealed or at least not obvious to the casual eye. Not only treasures such as truffles and great art, and, in my case, a cache of letters and abandoned paintings. But also potential threats: underground fault lines and caves and, if you believed it, the secret lair of an ancient temptress with the power to lure in strangers.

Given all this, I could only imagine Donato's horror when his eldest daughter Filomena was briefly co-opted to work as a secretary in the *casa del fascio*. Much of the time Attilio spoke with great theatricality, waving his arms and exaggerating pronunciation for emphasis, a manner that must have made him an engaging teacher of Italian history and philosophy. But when he told me what happened to his Aunt Filomena – Mimena, as he called her – he leant in close and spoke in a quieter tone, and with obvious affection.

'Poor Mimena. She was a teacher, an educated woman. It was she who taught me to read and write,' he said. But when Filomena, unmarried, became pregnant, her father Donato threw her out of the house, and she was forced to go and live in one of Amandola's most wretched quarters on the outskirts of town. When Attilio's father Leido learnt of it, he stormed back to his father's house with his sister in tow and insisted she be allowed to return home.

'Only my father could talk to *Nonno* like that,' Attilio said, with a note of pride.

As he said this, I remembered the delicate statue recovered from my attic of a young girl reclining against a red cushion with a faded red silk rose in her hand. The relief lettering on the base of the statue identified it as a portrayal of Santa Filomena, the patron saint of infants. One of the postcards that had lain alongside it – a black and white image of snow-capped mountains sent to Don Federico in Amandola in 1918 – was signed *saluti affettuosi tua nipote*, affectionate greetings from your niece Filomena. Thinking of both, I then wondered if her uncle had also intervened on Filomena's behalf.

Attilio did not know, he said. He was just two years old when Don Federico died so he had no recollection of him. But he did know that his mother and Don Federico's sister Rosina became close in the time they sat knitting in the garden. And his mother, he remembered, always encouraged him to refer to Don Federico as *zio prete*, uncle priest, and spoke of him as *un uomo galante*, a gallant man. This seemed to me to be a curious way to describe a priest, and when I asked Attilio what it meant, he smiled.

'Well, I remember my mother saying there was something *particolare* about his character,' he said, and I could have sworn he winked.

'*Particolare?*'

'Well, yes. He was something of a, shall we say, *Don Giovà*.'

I had no idea what he meant at first. When it dawned on me *Don Giovà* might be short for Don Giovanni, I nearly spat out my tea.

'Of course, he was *un uomo bravo*, a good man. A very educated man,' Attilio added quickly, perhaps sensing he had said too much.

But in that moment, I came to see Don Federico in a new light. Until then, the thought of his difficult childhood, growing up without a mother, the bitter acrimony and repression in the seminary where he trained, had saddened me. But this hint, if I understood it correctly, that he might not have totally denied himself the pleasures of female company I found rather heart-warming.

I was not raised a Catholic. The dogma of a Church that dissuaded my grandmother, a staunch Catholic, from attending her own daughter, my mother's, wedding because she was marrying a Protestant, left my parents with no desire to induct my sister and me into the faith; we were christened into the Church in Wales. So, I was unhindered by the idea that a priestly wandering eye might constitute a cardinal sin. Apart from attending midnight mass on Christmas Eve, religion played very little part in our upbringing. And yet there had always been something in me that yearned to understand what the writer Lawrence Durrell once called 'the meaning of the pattern'. A yearning that had drawn me to write about the lives of women choosing to follow the Buddhist path.

But as I caught my thoughts straying I realised I needed to pay attention. Attilio had eased himself back in my leather sofa and moved the conversation on to a subject he felt more comfortable talking about. This was his father Leido's escape from near death at the hands of German soldiers during the Second World War. The story he began to tell me opened my eyes to one of the darkest periods in the last one hundred years of Amandola's history.

What happened to Leido took place in the aftermath of Italy switching alliance and signing an armistice with the Allies in September 1943, after Mussolini had fled north to run his puppet Republic of Salò on the shores of Lake Garda. When, as Allied forces advanced from the south following their successful invasion of Sicily and German troops flooded into north and central Italy to try to halt their progress, Amandola found itself a hundred miles behind Germany's front line. The lives of those caught behind this bitterly defended Gustav Line were plunged into turmoil and Amandola became a microcosm of the confusion of war. Resistance in the Sibillini was fierce. While Fascists continued to grandstand in the piazza, higher up in the mountains, in small communities like Montemonaco and Montefortino, bands of partisans found sanctuary. From there they plotted acts of sabotage and launched lightning attacks on German forces billeted below, all of which resulted in violent retaliation.

Amandola's strategic position between the mountains and the coast turned it into a hub for German intelligence. The building in the piazza which now houses the bank whose staff have been so kind to me over the years, became the nerve centre where orders for brutal reprisals were meted out. Before the war the building had been a hotel called L'Albergo Italia. The same hotel, or perhaps its successor, where the English writer Edward Hutton once sat surrounded by priests and shepherds who blew mountain airs on their pipes and told tales of the snow and of the evil eye. But during these latter years of the war L'Albergo Italia was said to have housed between twenty and thirty *Wehrmacht* officers along with a certain number of collaborators and *Gebirgsjäger* mountain troops from the Austrian Alps whose ability to speak Italian allowed them to infiltrate partisan ranks.

In the chaos surrounding Italy's surrender to the Allies, three thousand mostly British and American soldiers held in a prisoner-of-war camp thirteen miles away in Servigliano broke through a wall and escaped into the countryside. Anyone caught harbouring them, including my gardener Antonio's family, was liable to be shot. Bodies of men, women and sometimes children were discovered in remote locations at dawn. Some were without shoes, after being marched barefoot over rough ground or through snow, to the place where they were killed. Those left in a ditch by a road were quickly found. Others made to march further into the mountains, to places like *Gole dell'Infernaccio*, Hell's Gorge, had to wait much longer for a Christian burial.

Italian soldiers throwing off their uniforms were treated as deserters and executed. Testimony to one such summary execution, that of a young conscript from Puglia named Angelo Biondi on 2 October 1943, is engraved on a stone plaque in Amandola's main square. The story behind it unfurled as Attilio sat sipping tea in my house that day with the sunlight thinning and shadows growing longer in the room.

When word reached German intelligence that two deserters had been spotted in the surrounding countryside, the men were hunted down by the Waffen SS and marched into town. One was saved when his wife, an Amandolese, fell to her knees at the feet of the SS commandant about to shoot him. Biondi, however, was paraded in the piazza and made to kneel in front of an assembled crowd. Before he was killed, the twenty-three-year-old infantryman handed his wristwatch to a young boy who was then forced to witness him being shot.

It was just before dawn the following day that Attilio's father Leido was stopped by German soldiers who were scouring the town for more deserters, escaped prisoners and hidden weapons. He was thirty-three and recently returned from serving as a grenadier in Sardinia.

'Word had gone out that they were rounding up young men,' said Attilio. So Leido, afraid he would be forced back into uniform, waited until it was dark and then stole out of the family home at the end of my garden. Hugging the walls of houses in lanes leading to the top of Castel Leone, his plan was to descend its steep leeward slope and from there escape into the countryside. But he was stopped by a German patrol.

'Anyone out at this hour must be attempting to flee. Anyone attempting to flee must be frightened of something. And anyone who is afraid is an enemy,' one of the soldiers barked in Italian.

Leido, who had become a butcher like his father Donato, pleaded that he was on his way to check on goods in a storeroom in the Piazza Alta. As he fumbled in a pocket to retrieve keys to the store, the soldiers pushed him against a wall and demanded to see his documents then marched him home at gunpoint. As Attilio spoke, I imagined the sound of German jackboots marching his frightened father past my front door.

A few days earlier, Leido had buried three hunting rifles and a demijohn full of ammunition under a pile of earth and stones in his back yard. As the soldiers searched his house, his wife and children stood trembling in their nightclothes. When the soldiers found nothing, and were satisfied Leido's papers were in order, the Italian-speaking soldier turned to Attilio's younger brother and grabbed his cheek, pinching it hard. Was his father telling the truth, the soldier demanded? As the terrified boy nodded, afraid to speak, the soldiers turned on their heels and left.

Within hours of his father's near arrest, the ground began to shake, violently. At 9.28 a.m. on 3 October 1943, a strong earthquake struck twenty miles south of Amandola. The quake caused widespread damage close to its epicentre in the ancient hill town of Offida, destruction made worse by the fragility of buildings already weakened by wartime bombings. Yet there are few official accounts of this quake. Field surveys were hampered by the lack of cars and petrol for engineers to assess the damage. Most local newspapers had suspended publication due to a shortage of paper. Amandola was spared the worst of it. But Attilio, just a young boy at the time, remembers fearing the world was coming to an end.

'Time is a *traditore*,' a traitor, Attilio sighed. 'I remember all this as if it were yesterday.'

When, after months of assault on German defences at Monte Cassino, the Allies finally broke through the Gustav Line in the spring of 1944 and marched into Rome early that June, German troops were rapidly withdrawn to defensive positions further north. There they dug in at the Gothic Line that snaked across the Apennines from Pesaro on the Adriatic coast to the marble crags and gorges of the Apuan Alps and Massa-Carrara on the fringes of the Mediterranean. As the German forces retreated, they blew up bridges, roads and power stations to hamper the advancing Allies, causing havoc for villages and towns left in their wake. To disrupt their retreat, Allied warplanes targeted key lines of communication. It was this that caused the most lasting damage to Amandola's connection with the outside world, rendering it yet more remote in the years that followed. For the Allies set their sights on the mountain-to-coast railway line that had only been completed amid great celebration thirty years earlier. One bombing raid succeeded in blowing up the tracks and they would never be repaired.

But these days in which Amandola stood on the firing line also brought an unexpected bonus. As one of the last German convoys to pass through the town pulled out, taking with it animals rustled from local farms to boost the German soldiers' food supplies, a great roar from the skies was heard. The Amandolesi, huddled in their homes to avoid confrontation with the departing troops, recognised it as the sound of an approaching warplane. Those who dared approach a window witnessed a scene of unfolding carnage. A plane with the red and blue roundel of the RAF swooped low and strafed the convoy. While the German soldiers were able to scramble for cover, the tethered animals stood no chance. Most were killed instantly. As the last of the convoy sped off, a few men emerged from their homes and any animal left writhing was put out of its misery. All were swiftly butchered and the Amandolesi, who had not eaten meat for months, carried off legs of mutton and cuts of beef.

When, on 21 June, a convoy of Allied armoured vehicles carrying a corps of Polish soldiers descended a mountain road from Montefortino, Attilio remembered the cheers that went up: '*Siamo salvi, siamo salvi!*' We're saved!

In their haste to leave, German troops left an assortment of munitions abandoned in fields and buildings they occupied. 'Children who found them and played with them were sometimes killed,' said Attilio. 'But the metal they contained was valuable. Some collected it to melt down and make tools and farm implements.'

When Attilio said this, I realised it was the most likely explanation for the odd collection of metal scraps I found in my house when I bought it. And almost certainly explained the live ordnance precariously perched on a shelf that nearly destroyed the place before I began its transformation. But who, I wondered, would have placed it there? As far as I knew the house had been closed and more or less abandoned, except for Rosina's occasional summer visits, long before this, when Cesare moved to live with Don Federico in Civitanova sometime after 1922. It was then that I made an interesting discovery.

For some time, I had been looking for traces of the uncle who had written to Don Federico from Rome, first complaining of the flu and then of losing his appetite because he missed the Sibillini mountains so much. Once someone left Amandola, their paper trail generally petered out. But trawling through the records again one day with the registrar Moreno, we found mention of an Antonio Bellesi who, after cross-checking, we realised shared the same parents as Don Federico's father Cesare; Antonio was his younger brother.

Written in very small, almost indecipherable lettering on the reverse of Antonio Bellesi's pink index card was a brief note of where he had lived in Amandola on two separate occasions. It was the address of my house.

Moreno's eyes widened and he let out a soft whistle before he handed me the card: 'This man is a *leone!*' a lion! he muttered as he read out the details. The record showed that Antonio had married three times. His first wife Eugenia died in 1910 in Rome, but before her death they were registered as living in my house. Perhaps this presence of Cesare's brother and his wife having moved in with him and Rosina at that time explained why I found the rooms in the house split into such a maze when I bought it.

Then, sixteen years after the death of his first wife, Antonio married again. But his second wife also died, three years later, in 1929. Ten years after he was widowed for the second time, Antonio married for the third time, at which point he was once again registered as living, albeit briefly, in my house. According to the records, two months before this third marriage, when Antonio was eighty-three years old, his wife to be gave birth to a son. Shortly after this final marriage Antonio and his wife and child moved to Fermo where Antonio died in 1945.

'A lion – a lion, I tell you,' Moreno repeated, shaking his head with a smile as he read out these details.

I was curious to know if Attilio remembered anything about his great-great-uncle from the time he lived in my house, but he remembered very little. He did recall once peering into the cot of the newly married couple's young baby when Antonio's bride brought the infant to show him off with pride to Attilio's mother. 'But I was very young then,' he said with a wistful air. 'And I don't believe they were in your house very long.'

Chapter 16

Ever since I began following the fortunes of the family whose lives were once so entwined with my house, I had never been able to put a face to those whose stories I was unravelling. But Attilio's cousin Luigi had an old sepia photograph he wanted to show me and so we arranged to meet one morning, on the shaded terrace of the Gran Caffè Belli. As espresso machines hissed and sputtered in the background and a steady trickle of customers sauntered past, Luigi slid the photograph between our cups and saucers and declared, with a note of pride: '*La Banda musicale Città di Amandola!*'

Leaning forward to take a closer look, I saw it was a formal portrait of a musical troupe of around three dozen men and boys clustered on the steps of a colonnaded building. The boys in the front row were seated cross-legged on the ground, wearing oversized caps with shiny peaks perched at odd angles and small trumpets resting on their knees. Behind them the older members of the band wore the same peaked caps with buttoned-up jackets and held a variety of wind instruments, from trombones to trumpets, clarinets and saxophones, and one a giant curved brass horn almost as tall as the man himself.

Nearly all the men sported *baffi*, moustaches of varying degrees of extravagance: some modest chevrons, others waxed handlebars or wispy spaghetti whiskers. All had serious expressions on their faces and looked directly at the camera. All, that is, but one man. The one on whom Luigi placed his finger with the words '*Ecco Nonno!*' – This is Grandpa!

Even if I had not come to feel a curious sense of kinship with the Bellesi family, I would have picked Donato out as the most striking figure in the crowd. His *baffi* was an elaborate handlebar with the ends teased up into a half-Moon curl and he had a firm jaw, aquiline nose, intense dark eyes and a bearing that verged on the military:

shoulders back, chest expanded. And while some men stood with arms casually crossed, musical instruments cradled in their arms, Donato held his clarinet to his left shoulder as if it were a rifle and he a soldier on parade. Instead of wearing his cap he held it by the brim in one hand to reveal a full head of short-cropped dark hair peaked above a broad, unlined forehead. But it was his seeming determination not to look at the camera that marked him out; his head was half-turned and he was staring into the distance.

It was hard to tell how old he was when the photograph was taken, perhaps in his early to mid-forties. Luigi did not know. Luigi was the son of Donato's youngest son, Ledo. Born two years after Allied warplanes strafed German troops on the outskirts of Amandola and slaughtered the terrified beasts tethered to their trucks, he was nearly ten years younger than Attilio. As such, his recollections of his grandfather were more vague. He was also harder to read than his cousin. Where Attilio was exuberant and increasingly expansive each time we met, Luigi was more reserved, more formal, with short-cropped grey hair, pensive eyes and a firm jaw but little else of his grandfather's more severe look. As Amandola's one-time *primo cittadino*, or mayor, and former head of the town's primary and middle schools, as well as schools elsewhere in Italy, he was, he told me, a stickler, for *buon comportamento*, good behaviour.

If the photograph was taken when Donato was in his mid-forties then Italy would just have seen the end of the First World War. Since he was exempt from military service on the grounds of ill health, he had not borne witness to the carnage in the mountains of the north. But perhaps the photograph was taken after his savings were lost and dreams of building his own home were ruined, and this accounted for his stern look and the searching eyes his grandson shared.

Again, Luigi did not know. His own father rarely talked about his upbringing, he said. All he knew was that Donato became an invalid in later life and died of heart failure at the age of eighty-five in 1960 on the exact same day of the year he was born, 14 September. The little that Luigi did remember, however, further opened the door at which I felt I stood looking in on his family's past.

One thing he was sure of, he said, was that his grandfather was '*molto stimato*', very well regarded in the community and that, like others who travelled across the seas, he too would most likely have sent back what little money he could spare as a donation to the church in his *paese* of origin in the hope that it would bring good fortune. Proof of this flow of money sent by those who sought their fortune overseas could be found close by, said Luigi, who offered to show me.

Stepping out into the warm sunshine, I followed him down the flight of wide, shallow steps that led from the piazza to the grand stone portal of Saint Augustine's church where the mortal remains of Amandola's patron lie encased in a glass coffin. For centuries, Amandola's faithful have turned to Beato Antonio to intercede on their behalf in troubled times. This humble priest, so vilified by French soldiers during the Napoleonic Wars, was the son of a poor farmer who, in the fourteenth century, worked land close to the monastery in the mountains where Don Federico later went.

Legend had it that, following his death, Beato Antonio miraculously saved Amandola from enemy onslaught and from the worst of one wave of the plague in 1523. Thereafter, he was often called upon by farmers to intercede on their behalf when the land was parched and rain late in coming. Hence the beautiful mural above the church altar of a dark-robed figure surrounded by clouds, hands raised in supplication.

But it was a marble plaque to the rear of the church that Luigi wanted to show me. One bearing the date *MCMVI*, 1906, the year after Donato and Rosa arrived in Boston. The plaque was erected in recognition of money donated to the church by emigrants who it described as '*Amandolesi apud Indias Occidentales commorantium*' – literally, the Amandolesi in the West Indies, a term sometimes mistakenly used at the time to refer to those living anywhere in the Americas.

'Many who left faced great hardship and prayed to Beato Antonio to protect them,' said Luigi, explaining that it was these remittances that helped pay for the church's murals to be painted on what were, until then, largely white walls.

And what of his great-uncle, Don Federico, I asked, as we retraced our steps down the nave. 'I never knew him. He died before I was born,' Luigi replied. 'And the house where I came to live? Did you ever go there?' No, said Luigi. It had stood empty, abandoned, for as long as he could remember, certainly long before I bought it.

But then, as we emerged blinking into the sunlight, Luigi stopped on the threshold, momentarily lost in thought. There was something

I might be interested in, he said. Now he remembered, there was a glass cabinet that stood for many years in the corner of one of the classrooms in Amandola's primary school when he was headmaster. 'It had an inscription carved into its wooden frame that read '*Dono del sacerdote Federico Bellesi*' – gift of the priest Federico Bellesi, said Luigi, running his thumb and forefinger through the air as if tracing the lettering from memory. The cabinet was tall and narrow and about as high as his waist, he said, 'and I remember it was full of fossils and rock samples.'

'What sort of rocks?' I asked, aware I was switching from relaxed conversation into a more interrogatory mode that sometimes embarrassed my daughter. Luigi shook his head. He did not know. Simply a collection that his great-uncle believed would interest the children. 'Very probably he was passionate about the natural sciences,' he said.

As he said this, I imagined the shelves of the cabinet full of fragments Don Federico plucked from the ground as he roamed the mountains, finally free to indulge his intellectual curiosity. Relics of creatures that thrived when the Sibillini lay beneath a primordial sea and were later turned to stone. But the thought that really intrigued me was that the cabinet might also have housed lumps of lava hurled into the Sicilian sky long ago, setting it ablaze, before crashing to earth and solidifying. If so, it might be further evidence that Don Federico did indeed once travel to the island in the wake of the Messina earthquake and returned with mementos of his unforgettable journey south?

If he had gone to Sicily, his primary duty would surely have been to provide succour to those in need. But if Luigi was right, that his great-uncle nurtured a deep love of the natural world, as the poetry he collected also suggested, perhaps he might also have used that voyage as an opportunity to probe the subterranean secrets of our planet at a time when so much less about it was known.

Luigi did not remember the cabinet ever having been opened; it had been presented as a gift to the children long before he took up his post and he assumed the key was lost. Neither did he know where it might be now. There was so much confusion following the recent earthquakes, he said, and Amandola's primary school was evacuated for use by emergency workers, and later, engineers handling the deluge of applications for buildings to be repaired. Since then, some of its classrooms had been converted into temporary surgeries for local doctors evacuated from their usual premises. Its young pupils were transferred to Amandola's middle school where children were being taught in blended classes and much of its furniture was lost.

But, before we parted, Luigi mentioned something else. Had I been to the cemetery on the outskirts of Amandola, he asked. When he saw my quizzical look and hesitant nod, he suggested I might want to pay it another visit.

'Walk to the rear of the cemetery,' he said. 'There, in the oldest part, you'll find the family chapel where my Great-uncle Federico and others in the family are buried.'

The heat of the day was building as I parked my car beside the small wooden kiosk selling flowers at the entrance to Amandola's municipal cemetery the following morning. The walled enclosure was set back from a road leading into the mountains some way out of town. Ever since the Napoleonic edict of Saint-Cloud forbade burials within urban boundaries, most Italian *comuni* conformed to interring their dead in such places, often in multi-storeyed rows of stone vaults, a practice echoing that of the ancient Etruscans and early Christians. When the outer walls of Amandola's cemetery could no longer accommodate more of these high-rise tombs, underground chambers were excavated to provide space for further serried recesses.

Over the years, some families also commissioned miniature chapels as places of rest for the departed, each with an altar where flowers could be laid and candles lit. The newer section of this necropolis nearest to the entrance was now crowded with these elaborate dwelling places of the dead hewn from gleaming travertine. As I wound my way along the narrow pathway that led between them, I noticed some had flickering electric candles and appeared freshly swept.

But many of the family chapels to the rear of the cemetery seemed more like unkempt and gloomy caverns, with no one left alive or still resident in Amandola perhaps to tend them. Some of these were larger and outwardly more ornate than those that housed the recently deceased. They were more spaced out too and arranged around three terraced lawns. This is where Luigi had directed me to look.

One by one, I circled the grassy banks and peered into the chapels' dark interiors. As is the custom in many countries, certainly Italy, many of the tombs bore small round photographs of the faces of the departed encased in glass. In this older section, most of these were in black and white. Formal portraits of men and women who must have witnessed the consequences of the horrors of war in this place where they were born.

At first I studied the more modest chapels in this older section of Amandola's cemetery, believing these more in keeping with what I imagined to be the humble circumstances of the family of a parish priest. So I overlooked a flat-roofed structure of brick and stone that sat to the side of the lowest terrace. It must have been over twenty feet tall and was one of the most imposing in that corner of the city of the dead. It had an almost industrial look too – not the resting place of a priest, surely, I thought. But when I circled back and looked up, I saw the name 'CESARE BELLESI' carved in capitals on its facade. Above his name, two identical modernist-looking angels stood guard in stone relief, hands clasped in prayer, heads bent in unison to one side. Their wings were abstract, their faces mournful, their sculpted hair braided in the manner of ancient gods. The sanctuary over which they hovered had a symmetrical style that was typical of totalitarian architecture at the time of Mussolini, marking the period in which the chapel was likely built. Its wrought-iron gates were fashioned in the shape of a cross and, peering through the bars, I saw a narrow altar, bare but for a bunch of plastic flowers.

On either side of the altar were three vaults, each the length of an adult laid out to rest. There were six in all, one stacked on top of the other. Each vault bore a photograph. And so, for the first time, I looked into the eyes of those who had once lived in my house, all of them descendants of Amandola's one-time *inserviente comunale*, Cesare Bellesi.

I couldn't help but smile when I saw Cesare staring back at me. He wasn't at all what I expected. In my mind's eye I had pictured someone worn down by life, drained by hard toil and the strain of bringing up his children alone. Instead, he looked proud, upright and was dressed in a sharp suit, a round-collared white shirt and a raffish, bootlace-style tie. He had a tall brush of dark hair with a widow's peak, a thick grey moustache, protruding ears, a sharply pointed nose and deep-set eyes above which his bushy eyebrows were raised, as if surprised at having been found. From the inscription beneath Cesare's name, it was clear he was the first to take up residence in these final lodgings. He died, aged eighty-one, on Christmas Day in 1934, the year in which the last elections of any sort were held under Italy's Fascist rule.

Laid to rest beneath her father was Cesare's daughter Rosa, '*Rosina*', who, as a girl, wrote such rigorous instructions to her brother Federico about the scarf she was desperate for him to buy her to wear in church: one 'not too transparent' and most definitely 'without a fringe'. It was hard to reconcile the kindly looking elderly matron staring down from her tomb, grey hair in a bun, with the demanding teenager of the letters from my attic. From the inscription beneath her name, 5 April 1884–23 June 1983, it was clear she died just a few months short of her hundredth birthday. By the time the photograph was taken Rosa was perhaps already a widow; her husband, Gabriele Lombi, who lay opposite her, died twelve years earlier.

Gabriele was a distinguished looking man with round, metal-framed spectacles and a three-piece suit, whose inscription accorded him the distinction of '*Cav*', for *cavaliere*, gentleman. It also noted he held the position of *Segretario Comunale*, a municipal functionary, though it did not say where, and that he died in 1971 at the age of ninety.

Beneath their parents, the couple's two children, Licio and Ana, were laid to rest. Theirs were the only colour photographs. Licio, dressed in a sharp grey suit, white shirt and maroon tie, was deeply bronzed and had a thick moustache reminiscent of that of the actor Tom Selleck. His sister Ana, a firm-jawed woman with a dark bouffant and square, thick-rimmed glasses, was pictured wearing a chocolate-brown dress trimmed with gold braid. Both she and her brother, like their parents, enjoyed long lives. Licio died in 2001 at the age of eighty-eight. Ana died just a few months shy of her ninetieth birthday in 2003, the year before I bought what had once been the family home.

But of all the images of the dead in Amandola's final place of rest, it was the calm steady gaze of the figure dressed in a black jacket, dark shirt and white clerical collar that most captivated me. At last, after spending so many hours reading his personal correspondence and poems, his notes and exam grades as a young seminarian, his diary of stipends, books, magazines and music catalogues he collected, and official church records kept on him, closely guarded though they were. After marvelling at the beautiful, damaged canvases rolled away in the attic of the house that once belonged to his family and puzzling over the map of Sicily hidden beside the paintings for so long. After all this, I could, at last, put a face to the person to whom all this once belonged: Don Federico Bellesi.

And it had to be said it was a handsome face. The face of a man who retained something of his youth. With a broad, smooth, unwrinkled brow, a full head of dark wavy hair just beginning to silver at the temples, a refined nose, bow-shaped lips and a lightly dimpled chin.

Don Federico was laid to rest opposite his father Cesare and as I looked across again into Cesare's eyes, I felt his raised eyebrows more a reflection of startled sadness at seeing his son buried so soon after he was himself. For Don Federico was the only one of those six laid to rest in the family chapel who did not live into old age. He was just fifty-seven when he died in the spring of 1940. The inscription beneath his name confirmed the last position he held: '*Parroco Di Civitanova-Porto*'.

With a silent apology for the affront, I nudged my phone through the bars and captured the portrait of each member of the family in turn to study their features more closely. The more I stared at each one the more it felt as if the dead were returning to life. But of the six at rest there it was Don Federico who looked to me to be most at peace. His eyes were soft, focused slightly off to one side, and he appeared to me to be deep in thought. His was a kind and gentle face. The one that stared down at me from the wall of my study as I tried to piece together the vicissitudes and mysteries of his life.

Don Federico Bellesi

On my way back from the cemetery I passed Luisa's front door and rang her bell. After all the hours we had spent together deciphering Don Federico's letters and those sent to him by his sister Rosina and father Cesare, I wanted to show her their faces. Like me, she was pleased to finally be able to see what they had looked like. That afternoon she planned to take her usual walk up through *Pompeii*, she said, and asked if I wanted to join her. But I was tired. Another day, I replied, and carried on up our lane to check on my house.

Pompeii was what Luisa had taken to calling Amandola's near abandoned *centro storico* since all but a few of its houses had been evacuated. Far removed from any of Italy's still active volcanoes, there was clearly no danger of Amandola ever being buried in ash. But was it possible, I wondered, that this once vibrant community, one that had welcomed me so warmly, would never really recover? That its winding medieval alleys and cobbled pathways might continue to remain largely silent. That Amandola would one day join the roll call of Italian hill towns and villages slowly being reclaimed by the landscape. Yet another neglected treasure in the country's geography of loss.

Italy's rural hinterland, especially its mountainous regions, as in other parts of Europe and elsewhere in the world, has become peppered with such virtual ghost towns in the last fifty years. Two and half thousand such places were recorded throughout Italy as of 2016. Most of these have been depopulated as a result of poverty, mass emigration abroad and migration to urban centres elsewhere in the country. Or because of natural disasters such as flooding, landslides, volcanic eruptions and, of course, earthquakes.

Over the years, the mayors of a few such places have launched schemes that mix humour with desperation. A number have offered their small hamlets for sale on eBay, one of them listing its condition as 'used', while the mayor of another signed a decree outlawing death and illness among residents. Some small towns, such as Riace in Calabria and Sutera in Sicily, have thrown open their doors to welcome refugees, both as an act of humanity and self-preservation, pairing newcomers with local families to learn traditional crafts and skills in an effort to keep local cultures alive.

Other dying communities, such as Locana, a picturesque Alpine village surrounded by crumbling dairy farms and abandoned mills in Piedmont's Grand Paradiso mountain reserve, and Borgomezzavalle also in Piedmont, have resorted to financial incentives. Both offered thousands of euros to families with children willing to come and start a local business. While Sambuca in Sicily and Candela in Puglia are among those that have grabbed headlines by offering run-down prop-erties for sale for a pittance on the condition that new owners rebuild them within a few years. Some such offers succeeded in attracting both Italians and foreigners in search of a new way of life, many of them retirees or young professionals able to work remotely. To retain this influx of new blood, however, infrastructures need to be upgraded, and local services such as schools and medical facilities to be improved. For some communities this has proven a stumbling block.

I was only too aware that before the earthquakes I was blinded by the beauty of the place that became my second home and was too caught up in my own need for rest to notice that even then Amandola was struggling to maintain an economically viable population. But in the wake of the disaster, it was painfully obvious that this wounded community was desperately in need not only of financial support for reconstruction but also new employment opportunities and other means of restoring the spirit of those who remained and of drawing in young families to bring it new life. If this did not happen, not only would a unique cultural history be lost, but so too would something of central Italy's rich rural soul and authentic voice.

Perhaps it was that afternoon, as I stood in my garden waving to Luisa as she passed by on her way to *Pompeii*, that the idea took hold of travelling south to Sicily to discover what became of the small towns and villages marked on Don Federico's earthquake map of a hundred years ago. What remained of Messina too, the place that became known as the City of No Memory. How, I wondered, had such places survived the ravages of nature? Might their experiences, in some way, foreshadow Amandola's fate?

If I went, I knew the chance of finding any trace of Don Federico having visited the island a century earlier was remote. But as a jour-nalist you sometimes travel more in hope than expectation. Years before, I had set out for the Argentinian Andes to track down the Nazi war criminal Erich Priebke with few firm leads and found him in a ski resort in Patagonia. And some time later I journeyed north of the Arctic Circle for a promised assignation with a Russian admiral vowing to spill secrets about the sinking of the Kursk nuclear-powered submarine. After ordering a supper of smoked fish and beer for us both in our agreed meeting place, I waited for hours, looking out of the hotel window at a lone figure dropping his line through a hole in the ice of a frozen river in the hope of a catch until, finally, I had to accept the admiral was not going to show.

I was never one to allow scant odds to deter me from venturing forth once my mind was made up.

City of No Memory

'*Qui dove è quasi distrutta la storia, resta la poesia.*'
'Here where history is almost destroyed, poetry remains.'
Giovanni Pascoli, *Pensieri e discorsi* (1914)

Chapter 17

> Nowhere on earth is there a sight more beautiful than that of the Straits of Messina. High mountains line the horizon . . . From them descends a series of lower hills . . . terraced with olives to the sea. As we sailed into the bay, the tints of the Italian dawn made it a wonderland of green and blue and pink. It seemed a paradise.

So wrote a special correspondent of the *New York Times* in a dispatch from Sicily on 24 January 1909.

This narrow stretch of sea, less than two miles wide at the tip of the Italian boot, is the point at which the Mediterranean cleaves into the Tyrrhenian Sea to the north and the Ionian Sea to the south. A confluence that creates a natural whirlpool which can be treacherous. It is this watery passage that is famed in Homer's *Odyssey* as the domain of the twin monsters Scylla and Charybdis: dragon-like Scylla crouched on a rocky outcrop on the Calabrian coast, Charybdis deep below the surface, sucking in water to quench an insatiable thirst.

Here too that the Fata Morgana, named after the shape-shifting sorceress of Arthurian legend, are sometimes seen. These rapidly changing mirages form when warm air rises above the colder air closest to the currents of the straits and rays of light are strangely refracted to trick the eyes. Those who have seen the Fata Morgana in the straits describe phantasmagorical palaces with a thousand towering pilasters which suddenly lose height and bend into arcades, before morphing into the cornice of a castle, or a colonnade, or stand of cypresses and finally vanishing in a diaphanous veil.

The fortunes of Messina have always been linked to its strategic position as a port on the western shore of the straits. Founded in the eighth century BC by the Greeks, it was originally named Zankle, meaning scythe, due to the shape of its natural harbour. By the end of the First Punic War between Carthage and Rome it became a free city allied with the Roman Republic. When the Western Roman Empire fell, it was taken over by Goths, then became part of the Byzantine Empire before being ruled first by the Moors, then Normans and eventually becoming an important staging post for Western armies sailing east during the Crusades.

But it was under the domination of the Aragonese and, later, Spanish Bourbons that Messina became one of the ten greatest cities in Europe. Its renown spread so far and wide it became the setting for a number of notable works of literature including Shakespeare's *Much Ado About Nothing*, Molière's *The Bungler* and Schiller's *The Bride of Messina*. Its status as a free port and trade in spices, sugar cane and gold with the Levant, as well as its flourishing silk industry, with strong links to London, Antwerp, Lyons and other cities to the north, gave rise to wealthy merchant families.

Such affluence turned Messina into a thriving cosmopolitan metropolis that at one time coined its own currency and by the beginning of the twentieth century boasted seven daily and ten weekly newspapers. This was a place of gracious palazzo-lined boulevards and piazzas where the Messinese promenaded in their finery under palms and bougainvillea when the sun went down. Among the grandest buildings in the city was Messina's signature *Palazzata*, a sweeping amphitheatre of lofty colonnaded palaces hugging the great harbour where many of the city's wealthiest merchants and nobility lived. An edifice so improbably uniform and grand that, in the words of the British novelist Norman Douglas, it could be taken for a giant 'painted theatre decoration of cardboard through which some sportive behemoth might jump with frantic glee.'

Yet there was little of such grandeur to be seen when I sailed into Messina's deep natural harbour on a spacious passenger ferry at the height of summer. In place of the old palaces, the great watery arc was lined with multiple blocks of three-storey concrete apartment buildings painted gaudy lemon and pink. Hogging the quayside in front of them were prefabricated warehouses and customs offices with drooping necklaces of black rubber ship's buffers dangling down and slapping against the waves. Here and there, one or two church spires and a grand cupola stood tall above the sea of concrete. Beyond these, climbing the sides of hills once terraced with olives, rose a drab jungle of middle-rise buildings over which cranes loomed like giant, spindly-legged insects caught in the act of constructing ever taller nests.

When, a hundred years earlier, the *New York Times* correspondent rounded a headland from the straits and entered Messina's great bay, what he saw was so much worse. Standing on the deck of the former ocean liner SS *Nord America*, alongside doctors, nurses and a band of hastily assembled troops, he wrote:

'No one spoke. We stood staring like statues, except that, here and there, someone involuntarily raised a hand to shut out a sight that could hardly be borne.'

That unbearable sight was the almost total destruction of what had once been a burgeoning city of nearly one hundred and fifty thousand people.

It was just before 5.20 a.m. on 28 December 1908 when an ear-splitting howl emanating from the depths of the straits rose up and roared through the streets of Messina and into the hills and mountains beyond. Within seconds a vivid flash of lightning was followed by the most savage, murderous and seemingly interminable shaking of the ground on which the city stood.

Out to sea, far below the surface of the water, the great fault line separating the Euro-Asian and African tectonic plates had woken from its fitful slumber. The African plate had taken a sudden dive deeper beneath that of Euro-Asia and the latter had risen sharply by about ten feet. As a result of this colossal submarine shift, a force of energy more than forty times more powerful than that of the atomic bomb dropped on Hiroshima four decades later was unleashed. Just as the first violent shaking of the earth began to be felt, the sea gave a great heave and within minutes a monstrous thirty-foot wave thundered ashore and swept inland.

The twenty-eighth of December marks the Feast of the Slaughter of the Innocents in the Western Christian calendar; the day on which King Herod is said to have ordered the execution of all male children two years old and younger. The number of those slain by the earthquake and tsunami that December day in 1908 could never be accurately counted. For buried beneath the rubble, together with the majority of Messina's population, and across the straits that of Reggio Calabria, a city of forty thousand inhabitants, and that of countless surrounding towns and villages, were all municipal records.

Entire families, generations of families, were annihilated, leaving no one alive to testify to them ever having existed.

Given the level of destruction, the lowest estimated death toll of seventy-five thousand never made sense to me. Many historians agree it was twice that number, with some saying as many as two hundred thousand died. Even if the most conservative estimate were true, it would make the number of those who perished in southern Italy as a result of the Messina earthquake more than twenty times greater than the number who died in the Great Earthquake of San Francisco two years before. But while the Californian disaster of 1906 continues to hold a place in the collective imagination, not least because of its portrayal in films and literature over the years, knowledge of the suffering Sicily and Calabria endured in the aftermath of that 1908 earthquake, though front-page news around the world at the time, quickly faded.

Before travelling south to Sicily, I pored over reports from old journals and newspapers of the agonising hours, days and weeks that followed the quake. But it was accounts of the glittering evening enjoyed by some Messinese in the hours before the earthquake struck that were seared in my mind as we pulled towards the shore.

I thought of how the *gran corso* in front of the *Pallazata* had been thronged with chauffeured carriages waiting to convey bejewelled duchesses and counts in top hats to the Teatro Vittorio Emanuele for the highlight of Sicily's winter opera season. How that Sunday, 27 December marked the official end of the Christmas holidays and many wealthy families from Messina and Reggio Calabria had reserved seats for that evening's performance of Verdi's *Aida*, many travelling miles from their country estates to be able to attend the performance having arranged to then stay in the city overnight.

It was, by all accounts, a sparkling post-Christmas evening. 'A truly exceptional interpretation on the part of an excellent ensemble of artists,' was how the *Giornale di Sicilia* had described the performance of the opera which premiered a few days earlier. Then, just a few hours after the performers wiped their faces clean of make-up and the musicians packed away their instruments, the darkness of that night was pierced by the sound of a hundred thousand screams as what had once been a great city began to shudder and shake uncontrollably and its buildings began to crumple, then collapse, as if made of nothing more than sand.

Many of those asleep in their beds were, perhaps mercifully, killed within seconds. But many, many thousands more lay buried beneath the rubble in their nightclothes, unable to escape as their homes turned into death chambers. What terror they must have felt as they heard gas pipes burst and felt the heat of fires breaking out all around. When the sea gave a great heave and a tsunami swept inland. Those trapped at lower levels must have known their fate in the moments before they drowned: some sucked out to sea, others suffocating in mud the great wave left behind.

As dawn broke it started to rain hard and was bitterly cold. Those who survived wandered the streets half naked, hungry, deranged with grief. Millionaires became paupers. The population became ghosts. The city was reduced to a desolate wreck. Mothers sang to children they could not bear to believe were dead. Husbands dug through the rubble for missing wives. One pitiful report spoke of an engineer who scrambled home from another city and dug for days in search of his young bride only to find her buried in the arms of another man.

Survivors fought over scraps of food. Some dug through the rubble in search of statues of saints and, when they found them, carried them in procession, clad only in their nightclothes in the pouring rain. Many simply lost the will to live.

Amid this horror, there were surely countless acts of bravery. But there was depravity too. Rings and brooches were torn from the dead. Some who lay wounded and dying had fingers cut off or were strangled in order for them to be despoiled more quickly. In Calabria, where the death toll in the city of Reggio Calabria and places nearby was also catastrophic, five thousand beds were taken by looters from ransacked homes and carried up into the mountains.

Even allowing for the constraints of communication at the time, politicians in Rome were initially painfully and shockingly slow to send help. When the prime minister of the day Giovanni Giolitti was handed a telegram with news of the disaster while attending a state dinner on the evening of 28 December, he reputedly responded that it was most likely a 'typical Southern Italian exaggeration'. A case of someone confusing 'the destruction of a few houses with the arrival of Doomsday'. When a special commissioner was finally appointed to co-ordinate the efforts of the Italian military, its commanding general is said to have dispatched his men to first secure all the safes in the ruins of the Bank of Italy before attending to the rescue of the wounded and recovery of the dead.

Many other countries, however, did respond to the Messina earthquake with an overwhelming show of solidarity. Even though it was just six years before the outbreak of the First World War, and the mood on the international stage was tense, Russian, French, British and American warships on manoeuvres in the Mediterranean were swiftly diverted to Sicily and Calabria and their crews sent ashore to dig for survivors. The absence of any significant help from Austria in the wake of the disaster was said to have been a contributing factor in the rise of Italy's anti-Austrian sentiment as the shadow of the Great War drew nearer.

In the weeks that followed, cargo ships and requisitioned passenger liners crowded into the bay of Messina too. Smaller crafts ferried medical staff and other emergency workers and supplies ashore then carried the injured back on board to be transported to cities elsewhere in Sicily and the Italian mainland. In these weeks, the sheltered bay into which my ferry had quietly sailed must have borne some resemblance to the armada of small ships assembled off the northern coast of France decades later when mounting the evacuation of Allied troops from Dunkirk.

But those who went ashore in the aftermath of the earthquake spoke of what was left of Messina as a 'vision of the Apocalypse'. A labyrinth of death with a pervasive, unbearable stench. When soldiers were promised a hundred-lire reward for reporting anyone buried alive, some cared little whether the poor wretch was able to be recovered or not before scrambling on further amid the rubble. Meanwhile gravediggers went on strike and demanded a pay rise.

Rumours that the Italian navy was planning to bombard the ruined city and cover it in quicklime to prevent the spread of disease were swiftly quashed. 'It would be uselessly cruel and ugly. Like shooting a dead body,' one minister said.

For those who survived, Messina became a place where individual psychology shattered, where collective shock splintered people's nerves. In the months that followed, both the Italian and international press were full of descriptions of the ruined city as a 'vast tomb', 'a mortuary landscape', 'an immense labyrinth of death'.

Yet there were increasing calls too for Messina to be reborn. Many regarded it as an 'historical duty'. Italy at the time was still a young and fragile nation, and rebuilding the city was seen as an act of patriotism. Metal boxes draped in the Italian *Tricolore* flag were set up in every *comune* throughout the country for citizens to make a contribution and sign books of condolence. Such a box must have sat under the shelter of the colonnade in Amandola's main square, bitter winds sweeping down from the snowy slopes of the Sibillini, as Amandolesi queued up outside the town hall to offer whatever they could. There were collections in every church and the disaster must surely have been the subject of private prayer behind the bleak walls of the seminary in Fermo where Don Federico was just then entering his final year. Dressed in his dark clerical robes, with only the few coins in his pocket his father Cesare could send him to cover *le piccole spese*, I imagined him slipping these into the box and retreating to the seminary's high dormitory or its roof overlooking the sea. His thoughts must surely have been with the poor souls three hundred miles to the south. Preoccupied with their torment, but with the ferment then coming to a head in the seminary too. With spies everywhere and severe restrictions imposed on what he and others were allowed to read, I could imagine the seed of an idea to travel to Sicily being sown at this time as a way to pursue his fascination with the frailties of our planet as well as those who inhabit it.

Some Catholic commentators were quick to explain the catastrophe at the time as an admonishment to the people of Messina for their lack of devotion. Some even saw the earthquake as fulfilment of the prophecy of San Francesco da Paola, a humble fifteenth-century friar much revered as one of Sicily's patron saints, who was said to have miraculously crossed the Straits of Messina using the cloak of his wool habit as a sail while declaring:

'*Dove ora sorge Messina, passeranno le navi e diranno: hic fuit Trinacria*' – Where Messina now stands, ships will (one day) pass and say: here once was Trinacria (the ancient three-legged symbol of Sicily).

The disaster certainly brought to the fore deep divisions within Italian society between the Church and anti-clerical politicians. One of the fiercest debates that quickly emerged was over the upbringing of the many thousands of children who lost their mothers and fathers under the rubble. A subject I imagined touched Don Federico's heart, having lost his own mother so young. Mistrust of the ability of Italian state institutions to deal with the aftermath of the earthquake was fuelled by rumours that vast sums of money contributed by foreign nations were going astray. In the absence of a well co-ordinated government response, a pontifical committee was convened to oversee relief efforts by Catholic organisations and priests began to travel from all over Italy to help.

In among Don Federico's personal papers was an anonymous card sent to him ten months after the Messina quake, on 31 October 1909, to mark the occasion of his first celebration of mass as a fully ordained priest in the church of Saint Augustine in Amandola's main square. Within a few months of this Don Federico would take up his first post as chaplain in the small village of Monte San Pietrangeli and so there would have been little opportunity for him to travel to Messina so soon after the earthquake. The outbreak of the First World War just a few years later meant the enormous task of resurrecting the city from the ashes did not begin in earnest in any case until after the war ended.

But what of the once great city today? As I stepped ashore, I had little idea what to expect. I knew that Messina had become known not only as the City of No Memory but also *Città dei Morti*, the City of the Dead. That its streets and houses now sit several metres higher than they did more than a hundred years ago. That it was eventually rebuilt on the bodies of the tens of thousands of Messinese the rescue workers were never able to recover.

Many of those who survived left their ruined city for good in the wake of the disaster and many who were evacuated elsewhere never came back. But not all. What memories there were of the earthquake and Messina's painful road to recovery marked forever the lives of those who did return and were handed down through the years to their descendants.

I was to meet one of them. The granddaughter of a musician who played in the orchestra of the Teatro Vittorio Emanuele for the performance of *Aida* on the night of 27 December 1908, after which the theatre fell dark for over seventy years.

Chapter 18

The three figures that loom over the facade of the Teatro Vittorio Emanuele, close to the grand sweep of Messina's natural harbour, were hewn out of marble fifty years before the 1908 earthquake. The winged and bearded figure of Time holding an hourglass. The half-naked nubile figure of Truth carrying a torch. And turned towards Time and Truth, as if drawn by the light of the encounter, the crowned goddess Messina, her hands outstretched.

While ninety per cent of Messina's buildings were destroyed or damaged beyond repair on that fateful December night, the perimeter walls of the theatre and these three statues that mount its facade remained standing. To the poor souls who wandered through the wreckage of their city overcome with grief this must have seemed like a miracle or perhaps a cruel joke; whatever wisdom the goddess Messina was granted in her encounter with Truth and Time was lost when so many under her protection perished.

As I stood looking up at those three statues, I thought briefly of Luisa walking through the deserted streets of Amandola's *centro storico* as if through Pompeii and that ancient city in the shadow of Mount Vesuvius came to mind. But unlike Pompeii, preserved under layers of ash for nearly two thousand years before the intimate secrets of its inhabitants were revealed – lovers embracing, mothers cradling infants, precious artwork exposed – Messina became a vast necropolis. Only a small proportion of the bodies of those who died were ever recovered and most were buried in mass graves.

When the city was levelled to begin anew, one of the few churches to survive the earthquake was the Chiesa dei Catalani, a little way south of the theatre. It is only here, peering down into the pit in which the old Norman structure nestles, that a sense of the scale of the city's destruction begins to dawn. The entrance to the church once stood at street level and now it lies at the bottom of a flight of thirteen steep steps, four more steps than the circles in Dante's imagined *Inferno*. Yet some of the scenes that played out at the level of the last step in the hours, weeks and months after the 1908 earthquake must have rivalled some the Florentine poet conjured up six centuries earlier in his vision of Hell. Looking up from the bottom of the pit, the uniform layers of ashlar stones in the surrounding walls appeared to me like the rings of a core sample drilled through rock or ice, even a piece of human bone, to determine its age. But instead of these layers of masonry speaking of solid matter, I had the chilling sensation that bricked up on all sides were the suffering spirits of those who had perished, and in that moment Messina truly felt like a city of ghosts.

A short walk from the church, Saveria Campo sat in a quiet corner of the city's Mondadori bookstore surrounded by scores of academic volumes on the history of the disaster. Saveria's daughter Eleonora Iannelli, a journalist and author of a moving book about the earthquake, had generously offered to help in whatever way she could and had arranged to meet me with her mother at the family's country house a few miles south of Messina on the coast. But strong, hot sirocco winds blowing across the Mediterranean from Africa made her widowed mother nervous that day, so she preferred to remain in the city, and I arranged to meet Eleonora the following week in Palermo.

Saveria, an elegant woman in pearl earrings and necklace, greeted me with a warm embrace as if we knew each other of old and began to speak quietly about the past. Her hands were neatly clasped in her lap and her posture upright, but I quickly sensed she had a very sensitive nature and she became flustered when she forgot some detail or date and started to apologise. 'I'm sorry. I get anxious and nervous and become too quickly agitated,' she said. 'It's a bad characteristic.' Yet it was I who felt I should be apologising for asking her to revisit a painful chapter in the family's history.

Throughout the years I spent talking with victims of tragedies elsewhere in the world I was aware that asking someone to speak of a painful episode in the past risked unsettling or, worse still, re-traumatising, them. Most expressed relief that their voices were finally being heard, but I remembered too the faces and trembling words of those who told me I was the first person to whom they had confessed some awful, buried wound. A hundred years had passed since the city of Saveria's grandfather was reduced to dust. But the trauma of that momentous tragedy had been passed down through the generations, she explained. Memories of the earthquake '*sono troppo vive*', they are very alive in the soul of survivors' descendants, she said.

Yet there was also unmistakable joy and pride in her voice when she began to speak about her beloved grandparents. Her mother's family were from Florence and of noble descent and after they moved to Messina they cherished ambitions that their son Cesare would enter the city's naval academy, she continued. '*Ma lui teneva sempre il pallino della musica*,' he was always crazy about music, she said with a broad smile. When Cesare refused to comply with his family's wishes, they punished him by sending him to work as a watchmaker's apprentice. Bent over a bench in the watchmaker's workshop Cesare rebelled. He acted out his defiance by scratching musical notes onto the casings of watches he was given to repair. Horrified, the horologist dispatched the boy back to his family and they finally gave in, allowing their son to begin studies to become a professional musician.

Cesare was just twenty years old when the conductor of Messina's finest orchestra raised his baton to the upbeat on the night of 27 December 1908 and the first tender violin notes of Verdi's *Aida* drifted up to the gods. Verdi had died less than eight years earlier and the theatre was packed for the performance of what was considered to be one of the composer's greatest works. Cesare had only to wait a few minutes into the overture before the conductor waved him in to play the double bass cradled between his knees.

The performance finished well after midnight. But many theatre-goers and performers lingered longer on the streets outside, marvelling at the strange light pooling on the pavements around them. That Christmas, Messina's old gas lamps had been replaced by electric lighting and, looking out across the straits, they saw similar bright beacons reflecting off the water as Reggio Calabria too made the transition to the same artificial lighting that very night. Cesare was among those who marvelled at the new illuminations as he made his way home in the early hours. He crept quietly into the house so as not to disturb his sleeping parents and sister and fell into bed exhausted. There was to be another performance the following evening, so he left his double bass in the orchestra pit to save himself the trouble of carrying the heavy instrument back and forth.

Saveria fell silent for a few moments as her recollection of what her grandfather told her about these last glittering hours in the life of the once world-famous city faded. It was hard for her to speak of the hell that broke loose in the hours that followed and she briefly lifted her eyes to the heavens to give thanks that her grandfather's family were spared.

Cesare lay under the rubble for all of the day and night following the earthquake. His parents and sister Graziella were trapped close by. Before going to bed, Graziella had loosened and brushed her long blond hair and, as the family home crumbled around them, her hair became entangled with the headboard of the bed. Rescuers had almost to scalp her to free her. Cesare and his parents were eventually dug from the rubble too and her grandfather's thoughts quickly turned to his double bass. 'It was his great companion in life,' Saveria explained. 'He had to find it.'

It is impossible to imagine the true scale of the horror that confronted him as he tried to do so, stumbling back through the wreckage of the fallen city to what was left of its once magnificent Teatro Vittorio Emanuele. While the walls of the theatre remained upright, the entire structure had been ravaged by fire. Cesare wandered through the ruins of the building, half crazed, for many hours but was never able to find his beloved instrument.

Others who survived lost their minds and never recovered. One wealthy woman became so deranged after the earthquake she insisted servants suspend her outside the window of her ruined house in a basket attached to a rope and there she stayed as they attempted to feed her. Others ran into the hills and carried on running for days.

After much persuasion, Cesare was convinced by his parents to leave the city while his sister stayed behind to look after them until the family could be reunited. Like thousands of others, he clambered into one of the small boats of the rag-tag rescue fleet assembled to ferry survivors from the quayside, then awash with corpses, out into the bay and one of the larger ships bound for Naples.

Scenes of pandemonium greeted Cesare and others as these ships drew into the port of what was once capital of the Kingdom of the Two Sicilies. Relatives frantic for news broke through police cordons and stormed the ships' gangplanks. Some were told their loved ones had not lasted the journey; deranged with grief at all they had lost, a small number threw themselves overboard.

When Cesare read in a Neapolitan newspaper some weeks later that the Giolitti government had ordered wooden barracks, *baracche*, be erected as temporary housing for survivors in Messina, he sailed back to Sicily and was reunited with his parents in the two-room shack with shared open latrines the family was assigned. Within a year he returned briefly to Naples after receiving news that a cousin had also survived and was in hospital there, recovering from the amputation of a leg. Cousin Giuseppe had lost every single member of his immediate family and that he was rescued from the rubble was little short of a miracle. Giuseppe, 'Peppino', had wanted to spend Christmas with his family and had only just returned from America where he worked as the manager of a large hotel. He was well educated, well travelled and spoke four languages.

When his family home collapsed, Peppino's leg was crushed and he was trapped, but was near enough to a crack in a broken pipe that he could just reach with the tip of his tongue. These drops of water kept him alive, barely, for eleven days. Pinned down and unable to free himself, he would surely have heard the last words, the last breaths of his parents and siblings trapped close by. But on the eleventh day, he also heard, far above him, distant voices speaking in Russian, of which he knew a few words, and with the last thread of his voice was able to call out. His faint cry was picked up by Russian sailors who worked for hours to dig him free. 'Those Russians were strong and brave,' said Saveria. 'It was the Russians who were first to help in Messina.' A kindness few Messinese who survived ever forgot.

Peppino's recovery was slow and painful, but after he returned with Cesare to Messina, he eventually found work as a school adminis-trator, while Cesare went to work in the army's conscription office. The two cousins went on to marry, and years later it was Peppino's grandson Bruno who Cesare's granddaughter Saveria wed.

'So much of what we heard came directly from the mouths of those who survived,' said Saveria, a tired look in her eyes. 'We felt their anxiety. We lived it. We were, and still are, somehow *coinvolti*,' she said – involved, implicated, affected by the trauma they experienced. Even now, when the windows of her house rattle in a strong wind she looks up, she explained, to see if the lamps are swaying and the earth itself is on the move. It is a reflex those who have lived through earthquakes anywhere in the world will recognise. Something I have done myself.

A friend of Saveria's, a professor of geography who came to join us in the bookshop, spoke of how her father had been born under an orange tree in the province of Catanzaro in Calabria just hours after the 1908 quake. Her grandmother had gone into labour with shock and delivered her baby herself, biting the umbilical cord with her teeth. Her son, the professor's father, lived to the age of one hundred and three. 'But it is as if we are all still tied by an umbilical cord to that fateful day,' said the professor. 'We grew up with mothers, fathers, grandmothers who kept bags of clothes and documents always ready by the door.'

Both Saveria and the professor believe such memories will be lost almost entirely when their generation passes away. 'The young people of today do not want to know any of this,' they agreed. 'They are distracted by too many things. They don't want to live with the anxiety we have, which is understandable. But it means they refuse to acknowledge the reality that Messina is built on *terra ballerina*,' Saveria concluded, echoing once again the phrase those in the Sibillini use to speak of the earth that dances beneath their feet. 'This, it can be very dangerous to forget.'

Before we parted with a hugged goodbye Saveria rummaged in her handbag for a small gift she had brought me, a pamphlet of her own poetry entitled *Voli*, Flights. On its cover was a delicate pen and ink sketch of seagulls flying up over the clouds, a symbol perhaps of how Saveria and many Messinese preferred to soar above memories that were difficult to recall.

For a while afterwards I sat in the shade of an olive tree nearby and read Saveria's poems. The title of one '*Fragilità dell'Essere*', the Fragility of Being, transported me back to the gathering dusk in the Sibillini mountains when the words of the Sicilian-born author, Alessandro D'Avenia, were read out as a way of consoling traumatised Amandolesi. The words of Saveria's poem were a little less uplifting as they read:

> Indulgent accomplice,
> calm tonight my troubled thoughts . . .
> Cast me into another dimension.
> Take me away from earthly worries
> that brutalise the spirit . . .

Despite all the promises in the immediate aftermath of the earthquake that Messina would rise from the ashes and be reborn, little was achieved before the city was dealt the *coup de grâce* of two world wars. When grand plans for reconstruction were eventually drawn up, and speculators moved in with dynamite to flatten entire areas and realise their projects, most of these were to favour the rich. The struggling majority who survived the tragedy continued to live for decades in the wooden *baracche*, intended as provisional housing, but which one Italian writer later described as 'old, soaking wet shanties . . . very much worse than the doghouses a hunter with even the minimum amount of respect for his hounds might possess.'

The initial response of the Giolitti government and army was shambolic. Italian soldiers shot those scavenging for food. Crates of meat sent from France and shiploads of clothing and shoes sent from America and Japan were boxed up and diverted to the mainland. As were countless paintings, jewels and other valuables recovered from the rubble. In the face of chronic mismanagement and rampant corruption, the role of the Church in the eventual reconstruction of the city became increasingly important. In the 1920s, the newly appointed archbishop of Messina, Angelo Paino, oversaw the rebuilding of the city's churches, schools and libraries and quickly became known as the Bricklayer of Christ. It was during these years that Don Federico forsook his beloved Sibillini mountains and moved to the Adriatic coast, to the parish of Civitanova Porto fifty miles to the north-east of Amandola, where reports of Paino's work would surely have reached him, perhaps prompting him to take action too.

But these were the years when Mussolini was tightening his grip on power, and he seized on the reconstruction of Messina as a mark of personal prowess. Grainy newsreel from 1937 shows him leaping from a heavily armed launch onto the city's quayside in a flamboyant white suit, chin jutting, arm raised, chest puffed out, to be greeted by crowds crushed onto the balconies of those lucky, or wealthy, enough to have seen their houses rebuilt. Next *Il Duce* is seen wielding a pickaxe at what remained of the city's grand old railway station with the promise it would be resurrected within two years. Which it was, with a large mural showing him, *Il Fondatore dell'Impero*, on the prow of a ship, medals across his chest, surrounded by helmeted troops and bare-chested labourers, all resolutely staring ahead.

While much early reconstruction adhered to anti-seismic guidelines that buildings be kept low and widely spaced apart, Anglo-American bombing raids on the port in the Second World War reduced much of the city once again to dust. In the post-war years, unregulated development mushroomed. Streets were narrowed. Buildings grew in height. Streams and river tributaries were tarmacked over to make way for roads, rendering the land underneath waterlogged and doubly unstable.

Knowing this did little to steady my nerves when I discovered the small studio which I had booked for my stay was on the top floor of a high apartment block which was so close to a similar block on the other side of the street that, when I opened a window, I could almost follow the conversation of the people in the room opposite.

As has happened in the aftermath of many earthquakes in Italy since the 1950s, which was when the Mafia began to infiltrate the construction industry and the country's many natural disasters became, in the words of Roberto Saviano, a 'paradise of profit' for criminal networks, some of this later reconstruction in Messina was of a dangerously poor standard. And while such building work boomed, the city's cultural life and entrepreneurial spirit stultified. As Saveria's daughter Eleonora writes in her book, the mentality of the *baracche*, the wooden shack, that of welfare, clientelism, political corruption and stagnation, prevailed.

A culture of denial and superstition prevailed too, as I discovered before leaving Messina, when I met historian Angelo Sindoni, an avuncular professor with square glasses and ferocious eyebrows, to talk about Messina's past. But it was something that happened more recently, when a meeting of eminent historians was convened to discuss how best to mark the centenary of the 1908 earthquake, that struck me most about our conversation. Sindoni told me how, at that meeting, he proposed a conference be held to discuss the disasters and earthquakes that had occurred throughout Italian history and the lessons that might be learnt. Not only was his idea quickly squashed, he said, but he noticed several of his esteemed colleagues, '*fare la corna*', fold their middle and ring fingers inwards under the table to make the sign of the horns, the Italian equivalent of touching wood. 'They told me it's better not to discuss this because it might be tempting fate,' he said, raising his hands in exasperation. '*Siamo scaramantici*,' – We are a superstitious people.

When I mentioned why I had come to Messina to younger people I met in the city, they didn't want to talk about the earthquake either. Some just shrugged. None seemed aware that, as Professor Sindoni described, every year at twenty past five on the morning of 28 December, church bells are rung to commemorate the countless souls who perished before dawn on that terrible day a century earlier. Some Messinese, like Eleonora, have worked hard to ensure the memory of the city is kept alive. While her great-grandfather was never able to recover his beloved double bass, the baton that waved Cesare and fellow musicians into the Overture of *Aida* that fateful December did survive, as did the conductor. One hundred and ten years later, in the winter of 2019, the same baton was raised once again in a concert to commemorate the one hundred and eleven musicians and other artists from that night's performance who did not.

As I walked through Messina's largely characterless streets, I saw few official reminders of the events that once destroyed the city. In one quiet square I came across a statue erected half a century after the earthquake to the memory of Queen Elena, eulogised for briefly tending to the injured when she visited the stricken city. Elsewhere I found a marble tribute in memory of Nicolai II Alexandrovich Romanov '*Zar di Tutte le Russie*' for immediately sending Russian warships to aid the afflicted. But it was a plaque on the wall of an old abandoned building near the port that captured my imagination:

Starting from this place, many went in search of *l'America*, whether out of necessity or desire. One tragic December dawn multiplied their number. They left for overseas with one last sad image that only a few were ever able to erase, by returning.

Marcello Saija *scripsit*

3 December 2018

As I read these words I thought of Donato Bellesi's voyage to America and his despondent verdict, when writing to his cousin Don Federico from Boston on New Year's Day 1906, that 'America is not America any more.' If a couple who sailed the Atlantic full of hope and energy had struggled, how much more formidable it must have been for those who made the journey three years later, utterly broken by the total collapse of everything they held dear.

What, I wondered, standing on that street corner in the cool night air, the sound of birds' wings fluttering against the glass roof of the abandoned customs building, would have been the fate of these destitute Messinese fleeing their stricken city?

Forgetting and Remembering

'*Memoria est thesaurus omnium rerum e custos.*'
'Memory is the treasury and guardian of all things.'

Cicero, *De Oratore* (55 BC)

Chapter 19

North-west of Messina, in the cobalt-blue waters of the Tyrrhenian Sea, there is an arc of volcanic islands that serve as a further reminder of the volatility of the splinter of the earth's surface on which Italy rests. At the end of the arc of seven islands lies one of our rifting planet's most active volcanoes, Stromboli, that has erupted so frequently over the past two thousand years that its fountains of fiery lava seen from afar have led it to become known as the Lighthouse of the Mediterranean.

At the centre point of the arc lies its second-largest and more tranquil island, Salina, comprised of several volcanic cones now considered to be extinct. But while the island itself may be more physically stable than its volatile neighbour, there is one building on the island that bears witness to the precarious fate of many of those who were born not only here in Sicily but elsewhere in Italy too: a small museum that pays tribute to the many millions of Italians who, over more than a century, have faced uncertain futures abroad.

This *Museo Eoliano dell'Emigrazione* was founded by Marcello Saija, the man whose words are inscribed on the wall of the abandoned customs building in Messina where he lives for much of the year. Saija is a professor of history at Palermo University whose own family suffered the dire consequences of Messina's 1908 quake.

Ever since the discovery of the *Marchigiana* magazine in my attic, which spoke so scathingly of Italian politicians acting like spineless 'molluscs' for ignoring the problem of so many of their countrymen leaving Italy, I had wondered how many Amandolesi were seduced by the promise of *l'America*, as Donato and Rosa had been. The answer to this lay closer to home than Salina: in the birthplace of the poet Giacomo Leopardi, forty miles north of Amandola, in a series of underground chambers filled with battered suitcases, wicker baskets, bundles of rags and other exhibits that spoke of the emigrants' harsh journeys abroad. There in Recanati, in another small museum beneath rooms full of paintings portraying the poet in life and in death, lies a written tally of how the small community of Amandola alone lost nearly one thousand sons and daughters to the American dream in the first decade of the last century. This is a small fraction of the 700,000 Marchigiani who left Le Marche, today a region of little over a million, between the end of the nineteenth century and the early twentieth century for new lives further north in Europe and overseas. While many of these emigrated to South America and Argentina in particular, the figures for Amandola show the overwhelming majority were bound for the United States.

Part of the reason for this mass exodus from Le Marche and other rural areas was a crippling increase in taxation at the end of the nineteenth century which reduced many already struggling sharecroppers to utter poverty. This provided fertile ground for agents working on commission for shipping companies intent on packing as many emigrants as possible below decks on their transatlantic steamers. Agents who toured the countryside distributed flyers and postcards peddling false promises of cities paved with gold and luxury sea passages on which meat would be served every day, an unimaginable extravagance for those reduced to grinding acorns to make bread.

On display on one wall of this *Museo Emigrazione Marchigiana* was an intriguing collection of misshapen felt hats with small tickets discreetly tucked in their brim. These tickets acted as coded signals to unlicensed agents waiting in Italian ports and train stations that those who wore them were *clandestini*, or so-called illegals intent on circumventing new laws that had been introduced to regulate the flood of people leaving the country. The laws were meant to prevent overcrowding and unhygienic conditions on ships by requiring licensed agents to register passengers and so limit their number. But tickets sold by licensed agents were more expensive than those sold to *clandestini*, who were herded onto ships with few controls. So, for many, emigrating illegally was their only option.

Beside the display of misshapen hats was evidence of an even more pernicious practice: a record of the system of *prepagato* tickets, pre-paid by labour bosses in the United States who guaranteed loans with American banks to cover the cost of the fares. This was on condition that the emigrants accepted loan contracts they often had no way of understanding, many of which would bind them to virtual slave labour on arrival.

No matter what type of ticket emigrants possessed, however, all faced similar fears as they set off across the Atlantic. If the weather was bad, crossings could take up to a month and were spent in open dormitories where diseases such as cholera quickly took hold. Some did not survive. Fear of importing epidemics led to laws being introduced in the United States to curb overcrowding on board by requiring a certain amount of space for each ship's passenger. These laws were circumvented, however, by ships packed with human cargo sailing into southern ports such as New Orleans where few controls were carried out and even fewer records kept.

The cost of the loan Donato and Rosa took out for their transatlantic passage indicated they had travelled legally; this was confirmed when I found their arrival in the United Sates registered in the meticulous records kept by the Ellis Island Foundation. These noted that the couple disembarked on Ellis Island from the SS *Princess Irene*, a two-funnel German steamship, on 5 July 1905.

But it was not until one of my closest neighbours in Amandola died some time after the 2016 earthquakes that I learnt the full story behind their decision to return to Italy. Eva and her husband Lucio had lived in the house on the other side of the lane from mine for more than fifty years. But the main entrance to their home opened into the piazza, and in all the years I had lived in Amandola I had rarely seen them out and about. They had no children and seemed to prefer to keep to themselves. But Lucio was Donato's first grandchild, the boy born out of wedlock to his eldest daughter Filomena, and when Lucio passed away at nearly one hundred years old, Eva was lonely and invited me in one day to talk. She was ninety-two years old then and so frail it seemed a gust of mountain air might sweep her off her feet. Her dyed hair was like a wisp of spun sugar coiffed into a halo, and her giggle so high-pitched and frequent that, if you closed your eyes, you could mistake her for a young girl. But her memory was sharp and the few details about Donato and Rosa she let slip, in between reminiscing about her long and happy marriage to Lucio, touched on some of the hardships faced by emigrants crossing the Atlantic.

I already knew something of the couple's voyage to the New World from the records kept on the SS *Prinzess Irene* when it docked in

New York in the summer of 1905. The ship's manifest revealed that the couple were not alone when they left their home in the Sibillini mountains. They were joined by ten other Amandolesi when they boarded the German steamship in Genoa on 11 June and descended into steerage quarters along with nearly two thousand others. Like Donato, then twenty-nine, and Rosa, twenty-five, all ten were in their twenties or thirties, so better able perhaps to withstand the privations of the voyage. But Eva had heard them once say there was such a serious outbreak of disease on board that the ship's passengers were forced to languish in quarantine in New York harbour for some time within sight of Lady Liberty, by no means sure they would enjoy the rights she promised, before finally being allowed to disembark.

When they were eventually herded through the cattle-pen-like corridors of Ellis Island's cavernous immigration hall and stood before a uniformed officer, whose language they did not understand, the papers of all ten were stamped with the words 'North Italian race'. A distinction that would have weighed in their favour at a time when those from southern Italy faced even more severe discrimination than most new arrivals. All but two were literate, the records noted. And none was found to have any kind of mental or physical deformity, reason enough for a chalk cross to be scored on an immigrant's clothes signalling the wearer should be immediately deported. As many were. Hence the reason Ellis Island became known by Italians at the time as *l'isola delle lacrime e speranza*, the island of hope and tears. All ten Amandolesi declared they were bound for Boston, Massachusetts. Six, apparently unrelated, for the same address, a boarding house perhaps, in the neighbourhood of North End. But Donato and Rosa, who it was noted had just $8.36 in their pockets, were to make their way to a different address in the city – no. 71 Down Street – though it was not clear from the records why.

Eva took up the story from here. The couple had gone to stay with Donato's younger sister Vincenza, a renowned beauty who she said had been lured across the Atlantic some years earlier at the tender age of sixteen by a wealthy Italian-American businessman with links to Amandola. After marrying his young bride, however, he became increasingly jealous of the attention paid to her by other men, said Eva. So much so, she continued, that he eventually banished her to a mental asylum where she was left to die. Perhaps it was because she bore witness to her brother-in-law's jealous rages that Rosa became increasingly anxious and determined to leave Boston and return in haste to Amandola, said Eva. Perhaps it was this that made her fearful of the consequences of her own husband's jealousy if he found out that the owner of the factory where they both worked had tried to seduce her.

As if to demonstrate the reason for Donato's jealousy, when she told me this Eva had sprung up from her chair with the lightness of a sprite to fetch a photograph of her grandmother-in-law she kept hanging on the wall of the long stone staircase that led up from the main entrance to her house. The black and white image showed a woman I judged to be in her thirties with soft eyes, a full mouth and delicate nose in a perfectly proportioned oval face. She was dressed in a black blouse buttoned up to the neck with a small brooch ensuring it remained closed, her thick dark hair piled into a tight top knot. A portrait of someone determined, it seemed to me, to dispel any hint of impropriety.

Rosa Bellesi

Eva did not know anything about the factory in which the couple had worked or whether they remained living with Donato's unfortunate sister throughout the years they lived in Boston. But the year after they arrived, 1906, the year Donato wrote to Don Federico of sparrows settling like snow on the city's trees, the population of North End was said to be roughly 27,000 of whom around 22,000 were Italian immigrants.

I could only imagine the wretched circumstances in which many must have found themselves, crowded into this patch of land measuring little more than a third of a square mile on the banks of Boston's Charles and Mystic rivers. But part of Marcello Saija's life work in building his museum of emigration on Salina had been to record the conditions that drove so many of his countrymen abroad and those they found on their arrival. It was this, and the prospect of learning more about the fate of those who fled Messina after the earthquake, that drew me to the small volcanic island where his family had lived for generations.

The crossing to the Aeolian islands was rough. As our ferry pulled north through the Straits of Messina, it was easy to imagine Homer's Charybdis churning the currents from below. Out in the open waters of the Tyrrhenian Sea, ash-grey clouds raced overhead, pummelling the sides of the boat with strong gusts and showers so that what should have been a journey of two and half hours took more than four.

Most passengers sat hunched over newspapers or lurching screens. But I kept my face pressed close to a lower deck window and, between the spray, caught glimpses of Calabria's steep cliffs clothed in emerald forests plunging directly down into the ocean's depths. Then, slowly, the silhouettes of the volcanic islands of Lipari, Salina and Stromboli emerged one after another through the mist. Each still and silent, as if caught in a great game of grandmother's footsteps. The height of the waves did not allow our first docking and by the time I stepped ashore in Santa Marina di Salina I was late for our meeting.

But Marcello was gracious in unlocking the small museum he had created beyond its opening hours. Ushering me into the cool vaulted interior, he motioned me first to the display of exhibits of which he was most proud. Ones that spoke of Salina's former wealth and the achievements of those who had emigrated from the island to the United States and found good fortune. Among them a senior judge who became an advisor to both JFK and Bobby Kennedy.

Further back in time, Salina's fertile volcanic soil nourished vineyards so famous for the production of white Malvasia wine that families who grew rich from its exportation sailed across the Atlantic in first class, wearing fine suits and furs. Some who then chose to settle in the United States set up successful businesses selling fruit in Brooklyn and downtown Manhattan, and continued to flourish.

But as in much of Europe, a plague of the insect pest phylloxera decimated Salina's vineyards in the second half of the nineteenth century. Those who sailed for America in its wake, did so in drastically reduced circumstances. Like those driven abroad by poverty in Le Marche, these later emigrants fell victim to unscrupulous agents preying on their desperation.

Just one of the hardships they faced when they arrived was brutally clear from a notice on a wall on the upper floor of the museum. A crude drawing of a skull and crossbones beneath which the following stark warning had been daubed in black paint. Some of its words were marred by dark splotches where whoever scrawled them had presumably hesitated over spellings:

Bewar!! (*sic*) we are desperut! (*sic*)
Mister Angelo we must have $1000
Give it to us or we will take your Maria
And Blow up your shop!
BLACK HAND

Underneath this warning was a photograph of women and children staring at the imprint of a hand dipped in black paint and pressed against the shop's window. The photograph was taken on Mulberry Street, Lower Manhattan, in the last years of the nineteenth century. Beside it was a note written by a local resident at the time saying: 'Whoever wanted work in America had to pay them . . . If you were not to pay . . . mmmamma mia!'

The Black Hand was an extortion racket which originated in Calabria and Sicily and was exported to the United States at the time when mass emigration started in the latter half of the nineteenth century. Those who belonged to it demanded protection money from Italians, not just in New York, but in many places throughout United States, Marcello explained. That evening he invited me to share a drink on the roof terrace of his small family hotel where he offered to tell me further tales of the Mafia and the fate of many Messinese who fled Sicily after the 1908 quake.

There was not a cloud in the sky by that evening. The sea was mirror calm, with waves gently lapping Salina's pebble shore where *Il Postino*, the humble postman in Michael Radford's film of the same name, stooped to record the sound of seawater to send to his hero, the Chilean poet Pablo Neruda. But there was still a cone of white vapour billowing up from the neck of Stromboli, which a few weeks earlier had exploded in a sudden paroxysm, spewing a three-mile-high column of ash and lava into the air – the largest eruption for a hundred years. And as Marcello talked, with jazz playing softly in the background, this reminder of nature's brute force remained firmly in my line of sight.

Marcello began by correcting the popular belief that the Mafia was born of poverty. On the contrary, he explained, it was born of the enormous wealth of Sicily's citrus industry in the middle of the nineteenth century. In these years, when the nation of Italy was born, there was little law and order in many corners of the fledgling state and the Mafia's power base lay in providing protection for the wealthy landowners and farmers who cultivated vast lemon and orange groves in the vicinity of Palermo. At that time Sicily's citrus orchards were the most profitable agricultural land in Europe. They exported millions of cases of oranges and lemons every year to the United States, principally to New York, but also via New Orleans. In order to ensure their paymasters' interests were protected on the other side of the Atlantic, Mafia bosses followed these trade routes to the US and, once there, eventually developed their own independent criminal networks.

After the citrus industry began to flourish in Florida and trade with Sicily dwindled, the Mafia was forced to look for other business opportunities. The end of the American Civil War presented them with just that. When the need for cheap labour to replace newly emancipated slaves in southern states became clear the Mafia substituted citrus bound for New Orleans with human cargo. Sicilians, impoverished by crippling taxes, queued up for *prepagato* tickets guaranteed by Mafia bosses and whole villages slowly emptied of able-bodied men.

But the back-breaking work the new arrivals faced on plantations was coupled with increasing hostility towards them. When eleven Sicilian immigrants accused and later acquitted of killing the police chief of New Orleans in 1891 were nevertheless publicly lynched, alarm among Italian immigrants in the south grew. Those who could, freed themselves from Mafia control by fleeing north, most of them bound for New York and already established Italian communities elsewhere. Some were eventually able to buy small parcels of land close to railway lines and began cultivating their own crops such as strawberries and other soft fruits. After toiling for years in the American South, the majority of those from the small village of Gesso, north-west of Messina, which lost half of its population to emigration in the last decades of the nineteenth century, eventually settled in the New Jersey town of Hammonton which later became known as the 'Blueberry Capital of the World'.

When the seabed beneath the Straits of Messina convulsed in December 1908, however, a fresh trail of human misery followed the human-trafficking route already established between Sicily and New Orleans. By Marcello's estimation, around 35,000 Messinese fled to the United States in the wake of the earthquake, the majority of them packed onto overcrowded ships headed for unregulated ports in the southern states of Louisiana and Mississippi. Like so many Sicilians before them, those who could also made their way north by whatever means possible to seek shelter with *paesani* already settled in places like Hammonton and elsewhere in New Jersey, Lower Manhattan, Brooklyn and Boston.

Whether Donato would have come into contact with some of Messina's survivors in Boston's tightly knit Italian enclave before returning to the Sibillini is a matter of conjecture. But I choose to think he did and that once back in Amandola he told his cousin Don Federico of the utter misery they endured when their world fell apart.

Marcello was unable to throw any light on whether such a meeting might have taken place in Boston. Instead, he ordered more drinks and went to fetch two photographs from his private quarters that spoke of the tragedy his own family endured as a result of the 1908 earthquake. One sepia image showed a young woman with abundant fair curls piled into a loose bun and such translucent eyes I imagined them to be of the palest blue or green. The other was of two young children with hair cut in identical short bobs that glistened as if freshly washed. These, Marcello explained, were the first wife and children of his paternal grandfather. All three were buried in the ruins of Messina.

His grandfather, a ship's captain, was away at sea the night of the earthquake. But news of it reached him before his ship docked in Savona on the northern coast of Liguria two days later. Marcello's grandmother, a newlywed, also lost her first husband in the disaster. When she and Marcello's grandfather met and married, both still grief stricken, they buried their pain so deeply it was never spoken of in the family. But as a young boy, Marcello remembers slipping into his grandmother's bedroom to try to steal a look inside a suitcase he knew she kept hidden under her bed. 'Every time I went to my grandmother's house I checked to see if it was there. Then one day I discovered it was full of gold jewellery and silver cutlery,' he said. 'I never asked about it and no one ever talked about it. But my grandmother never left the house because she never wanted to be parted from that suitcase.'

As he grew older, Marcello said he came to understand that this was her 'earthquake suitcase' which she kept close in case she needed to flee her home quickly in the event of another quake. This was, he said, *'inquietante, molto inquietante,'* – very, very disturbing. 'Often, when I go to bed, even now, I think of that suitcase and ask myself, if another earthquake comes, what will I do? But I don't talk about it. Nobody does,' he sighed. 'Everyone in Messina has inside of them the problem of the earthquake. We know our city is built on a *faglia assassina*, a killer fault, but nobody wants to talk about it.'

The following night, my last in Messina, I could not sleep. I felt a deep sense of unease. It felt as if everyone in the city was playing a game of collective Russian roulette, banking on unseen forces continuing to slumber.

Chapter 20

There was a strange colour to the sky as the sun began to rise above Mount Etna five years after Messina was razed to the ground. A rare spectrum of greyish-orange light that, in more northern climes, might presage the onset of snow. But since the early hours on that warm spring day in May 1914 dogs had been barking, and roosters, even hens, crowing almost constantly and this continued for many hours.

This was a time when those who worked the land lived by nature's rhythms, rising with the sun, sleeping at dusk, labouring in the fields for a pittance. All the men and women of working age had been up since dawn on that day and were out readying crops for the season ahead, tending the vines that flourish on Etna's mineral-rich volcanic soil. So only the young and old were left at home when a prolonged roar rose up from the mouth of the volcano, followed by an explosion of vapour and dark ash and a tremendous trembling and shaking of the earth below.

There are many kinds of earthquakes, both physical and metaphorical. And in Sicily, where besides Stromboli in the Aeolian arc, Etna, another of the world's most active volcanoes, dominates much of the north of the island, there are triggers for those of the physical kind which are more unusual but also devastating in their consequences. And on that Friday, 8 May 1914, a vast subterranean cavern deep below Etna collapsed, causing fault lines already weakened by the Messina quake to quiver and then fracture so that the earth convulsed. And in the next few seconds, the lives of those in a cluster of villages on the volcano's north-eastern slope were wrecked.

Those out in the fields saw a great cloud of dust rising up on the horizon and ran towards it and the homes where that morning they had kissed their children as they lay asleep. Most of their homes were simple single-storey stone dwellings which eased the escape of those they had left behind. And though thousands were gravely injured and made homeless, the number who lost their lives was counted in dozens rather than hundreds. What was left, however, after the dust settled, was a desolate and gloomy scene caught in the sad light of the Moon. Some who lay entombed called out for help until their voices grew fainter then ceased altogether. Some who survived sat among the rubble holding the cold hands of those who did not. One grandmother in her eighties stumbled out of her ruined home the sole survivor of a family of eighteen, with the baby of a neighbour still alive in her arms. After handing the infant to another she clambered back into the wreckage, telling her neighbours it was worth risking one old life if only she could rescue her grandchildren. Immediately afterwards there was a crash of falling masonry and she was interred.

With roads destroyed and the one railway line connecting the villages to the coast left dangling into an abyss, the first to set out to help, including a local bishop and an entourage of priests and nuns, walked by moonlight to reach those stricken. As dawn broke the next day, and the principal aqueduct to the small town of Linera at the centre of the disaster area was found to have ruptured, survivors and rescue workers alike began to suffer a terrible thirst.

Black and white photographs of the earthquake show villages that look as if they have been bombed, just as those further north in the Sibillini would do a century later. They show collapsed houses with skeletal beams sticking out of the rubble like the ribs of a dry carcass, and men in flat caps, bearing away stretchers draped in cloth that conceal the onset of rigor mortis. Rescue workers so caked in dust they resemble marble statues. Survivors hunched on the ground staring blankly at the camera. Women kneeling in prayer.

One photograph shows a group of priests in floor-length black robes huddled in front of a wrecked church with rescued paintings at their feet. When I saw this, I examined it closely to see if any of the men might resemble Don Federico. For the names of Linera and its surrounding villages – Zafferana Etnea, Cosentino, Fleri, Santa Maria dei Malati, Passo Pomo, Beata Vergine della Catena and others – are those marked on Don Federico's 1914 earthquake map recovered from my attic. The fault lines drawn across it in red and black ink indicate those that ruptured, causing havoc and heartache on that spring day.

But all the clerics in the photograph wore the distinctive *cappello romano* or *saturno* hats, the wide, ring-like brims of which were cocked at angles that cast infuriating shadows on the men's faces so it was impossible to see them clearly. And most of my attempts to track down Sicilians who might help unravel the mystery of my hidden map had resulted in silence or polite suggestions that I enquire elsewhere.

There was one person, however, who said he was both happy to help and *molto interessato* to know how the map came to be among the private papers of a parish priest so far away in Le Marche. His name was Giovanni Mammino and he was *vicario generale*, vicar general, of the nearby coastal city of Acireale. Not only that, but Don Giovanni was born in Cosentino, one of the small communities worst hit by the quake and he offered to accompany me there.

The road south from Messina to Acireale offers a spectacular view of Mount Etna and, as this colossus gradually fills the horizon, it is easy to see why so many myths have surrounded it through the ages. The Greeks believed it to be the place where Hephaestus forged thunderbolts and swords in its flames, while the Romans deemed it the smithy of Vulcan, god of fire. And medieval writers saw it as Avalon, the place to which Morgan le Fay brought King Arthur after his final battle.

Today, most of those who revere Etna see it as a powerful symbol of the unpredictable force of nature. And on the clear July day I drove south towards it and saw silvery clouds of ash billowing up from one of the volcano's lopsided craters, it looked as if nature was scheming to once again flex her muscles.

On Christmas Eve, the year before I travelled to Sicily, Etna had erupted and unleashed a torrent of lava that flowed in a fiery molten river towards the sea. Two days later, a ring of towns and villages on Etna's eastern flank was shaken by an earthquake measuring 4.9 on the Richter scale, the largest seismic event close to Etna in three centuries. Houses collapsed. Pavements and roads buckled. The walls and bell towers of churches crumbled. Several dozen were injured and in the small hamlet of Pennisi a statue of Saint Emidio, protector against earthquakes, toppled over in the main square.

As I passed Etna's lower flanks and drove into Acireale, it reminded me of a neglected house where someone had forgotten to cover the furniture in dust sheets. Everything was coated with a fine, grey film of volcanic ash: roofs of cars, window ledges, empty benches, even the leaves on the city's trees. Everything, it seemed, but the curia building attached to the city's splendid honey-coloured cathedral. Part baroque, part neo-Gothic, with its two imposing campaniles and great colourful rose window it looks down on the Piazza Duomo.

It was here that I had arranged to meet Don Giovanni Mammino, whose title had suggested to me a prelate of advanced years. But as he held out his hand to greet me, I guessed from his boyish good looks, smooth round face and widow's peak only just beginning to recede, he was not long out of his thirties.

As we set off for Cosentino, and Don Giovanni navigated his car through Acireale's narrow streets, I could feel the heat beginning to seep up from the dark lava cobblestones with which much of the city is paved. Once we reached the outskirts and Etna once again loomed into view, I asked how people felt living in the shadow of such an active volcano and found Don Giovanni's reply unexpectedly graphic.

'We are not afraid. She is like a mother with lava inside her womb. When she goes into labour and her lava flows out it enriches our soil. Most of the time there are warning signs that this is about to happen, so we have time to get out of the way,' he explained. 'But with earthquakes it is different.'

As he drove, Don Giovanni recalled sitting at his grandmother's knee and hearing her talk of the day in May 1914 when her young world was shaken and the lives of others fell apart. 'I'll never forgot the fear in her voice,' he said. 'My grandmother was just a girl at the time. She was out in the fields collecting fruit when she heard a great roar from the mouth of the volcano and then saw a gigantic cloud of dust rising up from the village.'

Don Giovanni's family lived on the outskirts of Cosentino, close to the land they worked, so their home suffered less damage than many others nearer to the main square. Most of these were ruined and the bell tower of the village church there, that of Maria del Rosario dedicated to the memory of five sisters who became nuns, teetered on the edge of collapse. So, when Don Giovanni pulled his car up in front of this church I was taken aback.

Tucked in my bag I had a copy of an old document I had traced through a network of senior geologists in Rome that included a photograph of the church with a makeshift tent pitched in front of its great wooden doors in the wake of the 1914 earthquake. The report was drawn up shortly after the quake by a government commission chaired by one of the most eminent geologists of the day, Venturino Sabatini. It was to a copy of this report that the geologists in Rome were certain the map from my attic would once have been attached. Photographs of Sabatini at the time show him posing on an outcrop of undulating bare rock, dressed in a three-piece suit and fedora of the kind a Victorian gentleman on the grand tour might have worn. But Sabatini's mission was deadly serious. He was sent to Sicily to identify areas close to Etna where all new construction should, in future, be strictly forbidden. And beneath the photograph of the Chiesa Maria del Rosario in his report he delivered the following bleak, but utterly unequivocal verdict:

'As for existing churches, they should all be demolished regardless of protests of any kind.'

Yet here the church was, and not only was it still standing, but it was clear it had been enlarged. In place of its once simple square stone bell tower, the church now had an elaborate facade embellished with narrow pillars and topped with four pointed turrets, painted cream and white like the decorations on an iced cake – one that might topple calamitously if shaken.

In the years following the earthquake, Don Giovanni said the church had been strengthened, though apparently not enough. 'Come, let me show you something,' he said, beckoning me to follow him inside, to a tall narrow staircase with steep steps climbing up to the belfry. I hesitated. I don't have much of a head for heights. Not only that; there were cracks in the walls of the cramped dark stairwell and there was broken masonry strewn across the steps. Maria del Rosario church had suffered some damage more recently, in the previous December quake, Don Giovanni explained as he forged ahead and began climbing, his voice echoing down from above as I hugged myself close to the wall and followed warily behind.

Once we reached the belfry, Don Giovanni picked his way across the floor of the narrow turret, crunching broken plaster from its roof and walls underfoot. This is where he had been a bell ringer as a boy, he said, motioning me to stand back as took hold of a thick faded rope that dangled from one of five great bells yoked to a metal beam in the roof.

'*Questa è la campana delle ore*,' – this is the bell of hours, he said, as he gave the rope a gentle tug so as not to confuse the villagers. The metal clapper barely brushed the lip of the bell. But its deep, clear toll rang out across the lush landscape towards the smoking Cyclops in the distance.

'E questa la campana dei quarti,' he said, hitching up his drooping trousers as he stretched up to grasp a rope attached to a smaller bell. As the mellow, higher pitch of the bell of quarter-hours sounded, a broad smile spread across Don Giovanni's youthful face and in that moment it was as if he became the boy he had once been. A boy whose feet might have lifted into the air as he tugged on the ropes of the heavy bells. The boy who sat at his grandmother's knee, listening transfixed as she spoke of the day the earth shuddered and broke apart.

As the sound of the bells continued to reverberate, I thought of the huddle of priests who once gathered in the shadow of this very belfry in the aftermath of that May day a hundred years earlier. Salvaged paintings lay before them in the dust as they urgently discussed what they could do to help their flock. But, as in Messina, it would be many years before those in these small struggling communities would see their lives and homes rebuilt. And for much the same reason. It was the eve of the First World War and many men had left to fight. So, as in the once-great seaport forty miles to the north, reconstruction after what became known as the Linera earthquake did not begin in earnest until after the end of the war, in the early 1920s.

At that time, a relatively young prelate by the name of Fernando Cento, had just been appointed bishop of Acireale, Don Giovanni explained. Just thirty-nine years old, Cento was considered so dynamic and charismatic he became known as *il vescovo fascinatore*, which might be translated roughly as Cento the Charmer. In the four years in which the charming Cento held the office of bishop, before being dispatched as papal nuncio to South America and then becoming a cardinal, it was he who was the driving force behind reconstruction efforts in this devastated area close to Etna. And Cento, it transpired, was originally from Le Marche, born in the small town of Pollenza, just twenty miles or so north of Amandola. He and Don Federico were the same age and attended seminaries not far apart – Don Federico in Fermo and Don Fernando in Macerata, close to his childhood *paese*. It was quite possible, then, that the two men knew each other and might have been friends and that Don Federico came to Sicily at Cento's invitation. At least this is what Don Giovanni Mammino led me to believe.

For any visit at this time would have been during the years that Cento was deeply involved in raising funds for rebuilding the damaged communities within his diocese. As such, he would almost certainly have had, and regarded with contempt, a copy of Sabatini's harsh report sentencing all damaged churches to demolition regardless of protest. The very report to which my mysterious map was once attached. So, it was quite possible that it was Cento who gave the map to Don Federico, knowing he had an interest in such things. Or perhaps he had an ulterior motive.

One stinging telegram sent by Cento to the ministry of finance at that time complains bitterly that if the ministry is not prepared to provide him with financial support for rebuilding damaged churches and destroyed communities, then they should immediately return the plans he sent them for the work to be undertaken so that he can get on with the job of trying to raise the funds himself. This was just one message among many letters and documents Don Giovanni unearthed in diocesan archives on my behalf that bore testimony to the lengths church elders went in trying to raise the money in the wake of these disasters.

Some were curt replies to what must have been nothing short of begging letters. One from the estate of the Duke of Norfolk, an aristocratic family of longstanding Catholic faith, expressed deep regret that, owing to the 'great pressure of claims upon him', the duke was only able to send a donation of £2 'as a small mark of sympathy.' In stark contrast to this, another elaborately handwritten note sent on behalf of the congregation of St Joseph's Church in Niagara Falls, in the state of New York, accompanied a donation roughly three times that amount.

Despite many hours of searching, however, Don Giovanni could find no trace of Don Federico Bellesi in any of the old records. But when I told him something Amandola's parish priest Don Paolo De Angelis had once mentioned to me it piqued his interest. For he had heard that during Don Federico's later years spent in Civitanova Porto, he had become very friendly with one of the city's wealthiest industrialists, a factory owner named Adriano Cecchetti whose machine plant became a major manufacturer of war materials during the First World War and in the years that followed. Don Giovanni did not find this surprising. At that time, he explained, the three most important figures in any community would have been the mayor, the doctor and the priest and often it would have been priests who recommended workers to local landowners and factory bosses. Perhaps Bellesi was good at persuading wealthy *padroni* to give their money to good causes, Don Giovanni mused. Perhaps, encouraged by Cento, he persuaded Cecchetti to help contribute financially to relief efforts after the earthquakes.

Finally settling the ropes to each bell in the belfry of Maria del Rosario between his palms, Don Giovanni went on to stress that the heart would have gone out of communities such as Cosentino if their churches had been torn down. No matter how the funds to repair them were raised, the fact remained that Sabatini's advice was ignored, and people stayed.

As I approached the edge of the bell tower, careful not to look down, I could hear the voices of children playing in the small square below. Stretching off into the distance, I saw a sprawl of newer houses fanning out from the cluster of lower, older dwellings which too had been rebuilt and wondered if it was possible that in decades to come stricken communities in the Sibillini might also be similarly revived. That piazzas in places like Amandola, Arquata and Amatrice would once again be filled with the laughter and chatter of children, the music and excitement of festivals and the bustle of everyday life as much as they had in times gone by. For not only had Cosentini survived, it appeared to have thrived and grown. In the intervening years it had become largely a dormitory settlement for workers commuting to Acireale and Catania fifteen miles to the south, Don Giovanni explained. Especially those with families who preferred the pace of life and sense of community such a place offered their children.

But it wasn't just funding for reconstruction to which clergy have contributed in the aftermath of Italy's many earthquakes. Some academics speak of post-seismic reconstructions having been carried out on nearly five thousand separate occasions throughout the Italian peninsula and its islands since the Middle Ages. Little wonder, then, that the study of modern seismology was born in this land of such fragile beauty. Little wonder too that those drawn to the mysteries of life, to the subtleties of the spirit that underpin the human experience, to the unseen, have also been drawn to probing the mysterious inner workings of our planet.

For priests have played a central role through the ages in furthering our knowledge about forces at work deep underground. Some have paid a heavy price for this. As I was to discover before leaving Sicily.

Chapter 21

Leafing through Don Federico's missionary almanac one day before travelling to Sicily I came across an interesting story. In among the reports of Catholic converts in places as far away as Patagonia, Nagasaki, Tahiti and Baghdad was a curious account of a Catholic nun working in a leper colony in Burma.

'While those in Europe are still laboriously researching the nature of earthquakes, uncertain about their cause, and that of volcanoes, underground caverns and the equilibrium of the earth,' it began, 'Burmese seismologists have long since managed to solve the problem for themselves.' The mistake of the Europeans, it continued, was that they fundamentally misunderstood the way our planet is held in the universe. The Burmese belief was that the Earth is balanced on the backs of four devils and that the weight of it is so great they have sometimes to roll their shoulders to ease the strain. If they do so carefully then it results in only slight tremors, the veiled sister explained. But if the devils move simultaneously and *senza garbo*, impolitely, it causes the most disastrous earthquakes.

This belief that supernatural forces were at work echoed those held throughout the ages in other parts of the world. But in Don Federico's day seismologists in the West had also yet to understand that such telluric forces were the result of the movement of colossal tectonic plates. One widely held theory at the time of the Messina earthquake was laid out succinctly by an English professor expressing his condolences on the suffering of the Sicilian people in a letter printed in the British press. These terrible quakes, he wrote, were caused by the surface of the earth wrinkling and cracking 'like the skin of an old man.' The professor's comment stemmed from the view of our planet as a homogeneous ball which is gradually shrinking as its molten core cools. This contraction causes the earth's outer crust to slowly pucker like the skin on a cooling custard, so the belief went, which over aeons creates mountains and valleys and sometimes, within seconds, can lead to sudden, devastating earthquakes.

Both the nun's account and the professor's letter, both written at the start of the last century, served to underline how far our understanding of the dynamics by which our planet is shaped has evolved in the last one hundred years, to the point that we now accept it is the result of plate tectonics. But while great progress has been made in such understanding, and oracle bones have long since been replaced by computerised models drawing on vast pools of global geological data, far less has been achieved in the field of predicting sudden, catastrophic seismic events. As was in evidence as I stood surrounded by some of the most advanced seismic technology of the modern age in a place where such activity is monitored around the clock.

The Etna Observatory, or National Institute of Geophysics and Volcanology as it is more properly known, is housed in a grand palazzo on the outskirts of Catania less than ten miles south of Acireale. I had been invited there by a senior seismologist and expert in historical earthquakes keen to see my old map. When we met in the foyer of the palazzo, Raffaele Azzaro greeted me warmly before leading me up to a rabbit warren of rooms on an upper floor. As he did so we passed through a great hall lined with glass display cases exhibiting an array of seismic measuring equipment through the ages with bells, wires, coils and trigger mechanisms that looked like something out of a sci-fi movie. Most were relatively recent contraptions and had none of the beauty of inventions from further back in time.

As far back as the Han dynasty in the first millennium there were descriptions of rudimentary but ingenious devices used to monitor earthquakes. One of the most imaginative of these was a porcelain sphere containing a pendulum attached to eight miniature dragons, each facing different points of the compass and with a small ball cupped in its lower jaw. When the earth shook, one or other of the dragons would pitch forward and drop its ball into the open mouth of one of eight small frogs squatting below and so indicate the direction in which an earthquake wave was likely to travel.

It would be more than a thousand years before experiments with simple pendulums to record ground movement were carried out in the West, said Raffaele as we began to climb the stairs. Some of the earliest were done in Italy and undertaken by men of the cloth. One of these was a Benedictine monk from Perugia, Father Andreas Bina, who fashioned the first embryonic seismoscope in the middle of the eighteenth century by suspending a heavy stone, tipped with a metal spike, above a bed of sand to trace the movement of the earth when it shook.

The monk's work preceded by a few years the great earthquake that destroyed the city of Lisbon on All Saints Day in 1755, costing an estimated sixty thousand lives. But for many the Lisbon quake marked the beginning of a more systematic attempt to understand and quantify what happens when the earth shakes. It also provoked a heated debate between the two great philosophers of the day, Voltaire and Rousseau, which highlighted a change in the way mankind had begun to regard natural disasters. Voltaire's rationalist questioning of divine intervention marked the start of a widespread shift away from religious explanations of misfortune.

Yet some were still persecuted for their pursuit of knowledge. Among them was a brilliant young inventor from Naples, a layman named Asciano Filomarino, who in 1795 devised the first modern seismoscope, a mechanism attaching bells and a timepiece to a pendulum to record the amplitude of seismic activity close to Mount Vesuvius. Derided by those who believed his experiments challenged the workings of the divine, Filomarino was set upon and killed by an angry mob and his workshop on the slopes of the volcano was burnt to the ground.

Such prejudice and maltreatment persisted into the early years of the twentieth century. Most notorious is the case of one of the giants of science, fellow Italian Giuseppe Mercalli, who achieved world renown at the turn of the last century for developing a scale to measure the intensity of earthquakes – a scale still widely used in a modified form today. Mercalli was a respected volcanologist who spent years observing and photographing eruptions of Vesuvius and Stromboli. He was also a Catholic priest and professor of natural sciences in a seminary in Milan. But like the young seminarians who studied with Don Federico and were threatened with excommunication, Mercalli too was persecuted by the Church. He was dismissed from his post in Milan for harbouring liberal ideas and went on to teach in universities in Catania and Naples before being appointed director of the Vesuvius Observatory, a position he held until he died in suspicious circumstances in the spring of 1914. The official report on Mercalli's death concluded that he upset a paraffin lamp on himself and burnt to death. But further investigations suggested he had been strangled and his body doused in petrol.

News of Mercalli's death made global headlines. As I considered this, I thought of Don Federico reading it in a newspaper. Or perhaps word of it reached him in his parish in the mountains and it weighed on him as he stooped to collect fossils and rock samples of the kind he later donated in a glass cabinet to the local schoolchildren.

As I spread the old earthquake map of Sicily across Raffaele's desk, he reminded me that it was priests who made some of the world's first scientific observations in the fields of astronomy, mathematics and the natural sciences. Particularly the Jesuits, who through their missionary activities in poor countries liable to earthquakes, were often the first to set up seismographic stations. So much so that by the middle of the nineteenth century they had created and were running about forty geophysical observatories around the world, as far afield as China and the Philippines, and some began referring to seismology as 'the Jesuit science'. And it was not only Jesuits but also parish priests in Italy who kept records of local earth tremors and contributed their observations to specialist journals, he added, eyes glowing as he held my old map up to the light. Perhaps Don Federico had done so too while in his monastery chapel in the mountains, surrounded by paintings of angels and saints, bent low over his desk making notes by candlelight.

After checking the records in his office, Raffaele agreed that the map had almost certainly once been attached to Sabatini's report. This meant there were likely other similar copies made though he had never seen one before and was pleased I had brought it to show him. Folding the map carefully he then led me along a corridor to the control room of the observatory where all the latest technology was on display.

At first glance the scene there seemed more an expression of art than science. An entire wall was covered with monitors displaying a series of moving images in vivid fluorescent colours slowly morphing into different shapes, rather like a sluggish sixties lava lamp, the first a pale yellow and lime-green bulge tipped with scarlet. The next a turquoise dune with a skyline above seeping from indigo to pink then a deep crushed orange – a surreal spectacle of thermal images transmitting fluctuating temperatures above and below Mount Etna. Beside them was a dizzying array of screens covered with numbers, maps and graphs. All this was under close scrutiny by the small team of expert seismologists on duty who waved a brief greeting before returning their attention to the task at hand, constantly scanning the torrent of data for any sign that the volcano was on the move or that the earth was trembling elsewhere in Sicily or further north in the Italian boot.

I had not been following the news regularly since arriving in Sicily and when I spotted a red bull's eye pulsing urgently in the very centre of a map of Italy my heart skipped a beat. The throbbing target looked perilously close to the area of the Sibillini mountains and I turned to Raffaele with alarm. He pointed to the rolling ticker beneath the map. This recorded a 2.2 magnitude quake close to Amatrice that morning. It was a negligible tremor, but still the most significant anywhere in Italy so far that day. Unlike the alarm signals that thermal monitoring of Etna can offer, however, even these most sophisticated instruments measuring activity the Burmese once believed was caused by restless devils, offer little in the way of advance warning.

'Nowhere in the world are we yet able to predict exactly when or where the next earthquake will occur,' said Raffaele. 'It is a fundamental problem still to be solved.'

As I drove away from Catania en route to Palermo I found myself navigating one narrow vertiginous bridge after another, crossing deep valleys that cut into the last vertebrae of the Apennines before they disappeared beneath the sea. As I did so, I couldn't help thinking how the many feats of recent gravity-defying engineering – these bridges and skyscrapers and above all nuclear reactors – have greatly increased the risks posed by our shaking earth.

At the time of the central Italian earthquakes, I took some comfort in the seismologists' assessment that the sequence of quakes released so much pent-up seismic energy that another major shock beneath the portion of the Sibillini mountains where Amandola nestles was unlikely for decades, if not a century or more. The same could not be said for Messina or other major cities precariously perched above fault lines around the world. But I also realised I had never before given much thought to matters such as probability, or prediction, or the way each of us assesses risk. In my work, I had become used to a certain amount of jeopardy in some of the places from which I reported. Though I never considered myself reckless; I had a daughter who relied on me and who I loved beyond measure. But looking back, I wondered if the almost visceral drive to get a story might sometimes have clouded my judgement.

There were certainly times when I had felt distinctly nervous. When reporting on the mass murder and disappearance of women in a poor barrio in Guatemala and confronted by a pack of heavily tattooed *pandilleros*, notorious gang members, near railway tracks where the headless corpse of a woman had just been found. Elsewhere, in the Middle East, at the sound of Israeli drones buzzing overhead in the Jenin refugee camp when interviewing the head of the al-Aqsa Martyrs' Brigade, a man on Israel's list of most-wanted terrorist suspects with a 9mm Smith & Wesson tucked in his belt. Or while on the trail of the wanted war criminal Radovan Karadžić on a remote logging track in the mountains of Montenegro, when relatives of the Butcher of Bosnia surrounded me with threats that anyone who betrayed their hero would be made to 'eat their own bones'.

I am certainly not physically brave or a thrill-seeker. I could never jump out of a plane with a parachute, scale a sheer rock face or go deep-sea diving. But perhaps the biggest risk many of us ever take in life is in matters of the heart. And, at the time I bought my Italian home, seeking a sanctuary from the harsh realities of my working life, my heart yearned for the peace and beauty I found in Amandola. Had I understood more about the potential seismic risk in the area would I have bought it anyway? I believe I would. I might have paid more attention to the structure of the house, asked more questions about its ability to withstand strong tremors. I knew I was fortunate that the bedrock on which it stood was more stable than softer strata underlying others in the countryside. And that, despite damage to the top-floor vault, the basic structure of the house itself was found by engineers to be sound and was being made safer still.

Whether consciously or unconsciously, most of the decisions we make are driven by emotion not calculation. Our minds do not operate like actuaries, carefully weighing up costs and benefits. As the Harvard professor of psychology Daniel Gilbert puts it, 'our brain is essentially a get-out-of-the-way machine' – good at reacting quickly to imminent danger, far less adept at judging long-term threat. We may be a world away from the days when the predictions of oracles like the Apennine Sibyl were sought. But no matter how sophisticated technology becomes, it is hard to imagine it replicating the complexity of the human mind in anticipating what risks any one person is prepared to live with. Were this to become possible one day it seems to me our world would be an infinitely more arid and less extraordinary place.

As my time in Messina underlined, endlessly anticipating danger – be it an earthquake or any other potential threat – is stressful. It can paralyse. Something the entire global population would experience soon enough. After a while, people switch off, eager to get on with life. As Nobel prize-winners Daniel Kahneman and Amos Tversky famously recognised, we all tend to weight our assessment of risk towards what we can most readily recollect, that which remains most vivid in our minds. At what point a Pollyanna attitude tips into denial is quite another matter.

As my route took me west, within sight of the barren peaks of central Sicily's Madonie mountains, I thought of the paralysis gripping those I once visited in another more lush and remote mountain range on the northern fringe of the Colombian Andes. Those who lived at the end of the heat-buckled road I rattled over for hours with a photographer on one side and a doctor on the other, pistol poking from the hip of the passenger in front. That road had led to an isolated cluster of towns and villages north of Medellín terrorised for decades by drug traffickers, Marxist guerrillas and a ruthless gang of right-wing paramilitaries known as the Twelve Apostles. But it was another threat stalking those who lived in these villages I had set out to investigate. A form of premature death robbing generation after generation of all memory long before they perished.

For centuries the disease ravaging the population there was known simply as *la bobera*, or idiocy, a condition locals believed caused by a curse or contact with a poisoned tree. Their affliction mirrored that of villagers in Gabriel García Márquez's *One Hundred Years of Solitude*, but while in the novel the villagers' health is eventually restored by a gypsy's magic potion, for those we were about to meet there was no known cure. Nearly half of the members of some families there were born with a rare inherited form of early-onset Alzheimer's which, by the age of forty, reduced many to mute and motionless ghosts. In recent years those afflicted have been found to be carriers of a gene mutation traced back to Spanish settlers in the eighteenth century. Its prevalence is the result of repeated intermarriage in hostile terrain that offered few options when it came to finding partners.

I remembered feeling a sense of foreboding as we stepped over the threshold of one simple dwelling where the shadow of a man in his fifties sat upright in a cot being spoon-fed by his slender son. As the doctor examined the man, I began to speak quietly with the son, his soulful eyes searching mine as he recounted his family story. How his father's six siblings also suffered with the disease and three had already died of it, one at the age of thirty-eight. In a nearby house, a young mother, whose husband lay lifeless, drew me aside and revealed her own mother, grandmother, five aunts and uncles, brother and sister had already succumbed to the disease.

The further on we drove, the more army units patrolling the area thinned, until they vanished altogether. Proof that state security forces had finally abandoned the area. Here, as the hour grew late and my notebook filled, I remembered the guilt I felt as I gently prised the frail fingers from my arm of a man who begged us not to leave as our driver insisted we must after being warned a paramilitary raid was imminent.

The doctor's work was far from done. He was struggling to find volunteers for clinical trials to identify those with the mutant gene as part of an international research effort to detect Alzheimer's early on in the hope of finding better treatment and eventually a cure. But few young enough to be unaffected wanted to know if they were carriers, believing it tantamount to being handed a death sentence. Was this denial? Or simply a desire to live as fully as possible in the present until the inevitable happened?

I understood both. I had felt both myself. While in no way comparable to those suffering in that forsaken place, I too found myself sometimes wishing I could have remained ignorant of an underlying health condition, and this thought nagged away at me too as I drove on through the Sicilian mountains. For just a few months before travelling to Messina, during a routine medical check-up, my GP picked up a heart murmur and further tests confirmed that sooner or later, and I fervently hoped later, surgery would be needed. The delicate operation they proposed was a procedure that would partially involve repairing my *cordae tendinae*, quite literally my damaged heart strings. An operation that would one day leave me with my very own, carefully sewn, *kintsugi* scar. Coming, as the diagnosis did, in the wake of the earthquakes, it felt as if my visceral tectonic plates had shifted. That I now had an underlying physical fault line just as surely as did the cloud-making mountain, Monte Vettore, close to my battered Amandola home.

Of all our body's vital organs it is the heart that we invest with so much more meaning than its purely mechanical function. Some cultures speak of the heart as a microcosm for the entire universe. Others view it as a mirror, or a treasure chest, or place of shelter for the soul. The thought that this too would need shoring up one day provoked a painful contemplation on the nature of mortality and, once again, the ground beneath me began to shake. There were times after that when I wished I had not been told and could have enjoyed far greater peace of mind. I knew this was a form of sticking my head in the sand and was grateful for the regular monitoring that followed. Yet I understood those who preferred to remain ignorant of potential existential threat. Such thoughts continued to play on my mind as the road dipped away from the Madonie mountains and followed the crystal blue of the Tyrrhenian Sea before climbing inland again.

My final destination before leaving Sicily was a valley to the west of the island where I had heard the ruins of an entire town had been encased in concrete following an earthquake in 1968. The colossal undertaking in the Belice valley was the brainchild of one of Italy's most important post-war artists, Alberto Burri. His intention was to create a vast art installation, now known as *Il Grande Cretto di Gibellina*, or simply Burri's *Cretto*, or 'cracked surface', as a memorial to all those who lost their lives.

But was this how those who survived the earthquake saw it, I wondered. Or was it viewed by some as an attempt to cover up, forget or ignore reality, as villagers in the Colombian Andes chose to do, rather than confront an unbearable truth?

Before leaving Sicily I made one last detour to find out.

Chapter 22

'They say you can see *Il Grande Cretto* from the Moon,' my guide Rosario said, as we rounded a bend in the Belice valley and a hillside came into view, gleaming white. It looked strangely out of place in the early morning sunshine. As if a winter sky had hovered over this one patch of Sicily and covered it with snow while pastures all around basked in warmth. From a distance, the hillside appeared to be a smooth, unbroken, icy cloak. But as we drew nearer, I could see it was riven by deep skeletal cuts, like the carapace some monstrous creature sloughed off and abandoned as it sloped away.

I parked the car and we approached on foot. The site appeared utterly deserted. There was a gentle breeze and a faint distant hum of wind turbines on the crest of the hill above. The light reflecting off the white concrete installation was almost blinding and the sheer size of it invited silence. Rosario and I went in different directions without speaking.

Burri's *Grande Cretto* – Great Fissure – covers an area of more than twenty acres, roughly the size of twenty football fields. Its giant concrete slabs have been cut to form channels and walkways, most of them little more than the width of arms outstretched, that mirror where streets in the stricken town once stood. Each slab is roughly shoulder height, so that, unlike in a maze, it is possible to see in all directions.

Many have hailed the *Cretto* as both beautiful and sublime. But its starkness and sense of desolation instilled in me a feeling of labyrinthine wretchedness.

Il Grande Cretto di Gibellina by Alberto Burri

The *Cretto* was constructed when all that was left of the small town of Gibellina after two earthquakes struck in the winter of 1968 was dynamited and then bulldozed. One reason given for such drastic action was to prevent looting and stop survivors from returning to the unsafe wreckages of their homes to recover personal belongings. Some also argued that what remained of Gibellina had to be obliterated in order for it to be commemorated. But years of neglect followed, until Alberto Burri proposed his post-minimalist vision to cover the ruins in a concrete shroud. His *Cretto* has since become one of the world's largest works of land art. But as I stood there in the ghostly silence of that bleak, bleached monument, Burri's *Cretto* felt to me more like a veil that concealed rather than memorialised what happened in the hours before dawn that 15 January.

'I think so too,' said Rosario when he rejoined me at the heart of the maze. If I wanted to know the truth, he said, then we should walk further down the valley to a small museum that told the full story.

I had been introduced to Rosario by a local journalist and he proved an ideal person to accompany me that day. He was a retired architect, had time on his hands and a good memory. Born in the nearby town of Poggioreale, he was only eleven years old when it too was devastated. The official death toll of the '68 quakes, one at lunchtime on 14 January and a second, stronger one, before dawn the following day, was 231. But some estimate it was much higher.

For in the biting cold of that winter, disease took hold among those who survived and more perished. Many of the one hundred thousand rendered homeless, including Rosario's family, were relegated to living in what were meant to be temporary barracks, as in Messina. Some languished there for decades.

The once vibrant life of the community was reflected in the faces that lined the walls of an old church some distance from the *Cretto* where the museum was housed. Black and white images capturing a wedding party walking through the streets, the bride in a billowing veil. Neatly dressed women with lace collars sitting ankles crossed for a portrait of their sewing class. Farmers in cloth caps beside trucks laden with grain, gathering to talk. Children playing ball. A crowd following a priest in procession along tree-lined streets.

Alongside these images of Gibellina, fully alive, were those of its destruction, together with an account of the chaotic rescue operation and bureaucratic mismanagement that followed. Emergency workers not arriving for many hours, in some cases, days. Survivors left to fend for themselves in the bitter winter weather. Children and the elderly suffering from exposure. Families eventually herded into Nissen-style metal huts.

'My family lived in those huts for ten years, others for twenty years or more,' said Rosario, propping his wire-rimmed glasses above his high-cropped, Caesar-like grey fringe. 'In the summer, the metal heated up like an oven. In winter, it was like a fridge. There was a big problem with mud. And with rats.'

Some of those who survived were offered money and passports to leave Sicily by local authorities who saw this as an easy solution to the problem of rehousing the homeless. And so another wave of emigrants left the island.

As I stood studying the photographs, I overheard Rosario talking to a younger man who had come to the museum to learn more about the destruction of his parents' home town. Both men lamented the area's dramatic decline in population, a familiar story from the mountains further north. But they also spoke of the political infighting that followed the disaster. How for years afterwards, mayors of neighbouring towns vied with each other to attract the most avant-garde artists and architects to draw up plans for their reconstruction. Some urged those in authority to pool the resources of their struggling communities by uniting three previously independent towns,

Poggiorèale, Gibellina and Salaparuta, into one *comune*. 'It would have been far better for people to have been united. To have one big school, one strong *comune*,' said the younger man, again repeating a narrative one sometimes hears in the central Italian earthquake zone.

'Yes, but then the rows started,' Rosario sighed. 'Each *comune* wanted to know who would be mayor. No one was willing to lose power.'

When they lowered their voices and began discussing the infiltration of the Mafia into the reconstruction projects their stories of sabotage and kidnappings became so convoluted I struggled to follow. But both agreed that what happened in the Belice valley was unique to those times. While it was the rupture of fault lines deep beneath Sicilian soil that wrought havoc here at the start of 1968, by the year's end, the world itself was in tumult. A spirit of rebellion prevailed. Uprisings occurred simultaneously across the globe. Societies began to spontaneously combust. Politicians were assassinated. Students were in open revolt. Conventions of fashion, music, art and architecture were overturned.

The result of this seismic shift in cultural norms was not only the creation of Burri's *Cretto* but the eventual relocation of the remaining populations of Gibellina and Poggioreale to new towns several miles from their original location. Places that served as open-air laboratories for radical art and experimental architecture.

I had little idea what to expect when Rosario directed us along quiet back roads to see first one new town and then the other. He said little as we drove through their largely deserted streets, but Rosario's despair was palpable. Gibellina Nuova had the feel of a futuristic, abandoned museum, its wide, empty streets dotted with gargantuan multicoloured sculptures. Its geometric grid offered few clues to the location of any central piazza, the usual social hub of Italian communities. The piazza proved to be a windswept open space so vast one corner had been commandeered by teenagers as a makeshift football pitch. Sitting in the shade behind the youngsters a group of old men were slamming playing cards onto a plastic table. The men looked up suspiciously as we approached. When I explained I had come from the area hit by more recent earthquakes they showed little interest. When I asked what they thought of their new town and Burri's *Cretto*, they muttered among themselves and went back to their game. All but one, a man with dark circles under his eyes and a deep scar running from his cheek to his upper lip.

'The politicians and builders just made money here and then left,' the man scoffed. 'Tell the people of central Italy they will be waiting forty years for help.'

What was certain, said Rosario as we walked back to the car, was that Belice, like Messina and the small communities around Etna, suffered additional neglect because they were in Sicily and so had to endure the political apathy and underinvestment that have long blighted the central government's attitude to the island, and much of the rest of southern Italy – the so-called Mezzogiorno, or land of intense midday sun.

When Rosario led me on to the new town of Poggioreale it was as if we had strayed into a foreign land. Built three miles from the site of the old settlement, on land once scorned as malarial, it was dominated by concrete and cement. One housing complex, a grey monstrosity squatting like a mutant insect with petrified legs, showed no sign of life in any of its windows. Further on Rosario pointed to a colossal raised cement walkway encircling the town 'on which not a soul ever places a foot'.

The new town was built to accommodate up to ten thousand people, he explained, even though Poggioreale's population before the earthquake was less than half that and in the last fifty years had dropped by half again. 'What they built here was not a Sicilian town. Look around. They built houses but there were no jobs. So many left and never came back,' said Rosario, who also left as a young man and only returned in recent years.

'If you had come last week, you would have seen this place full of strangers, but just for a few days,' he said, explaining that emergency workers sometimes came to the area from different parts of the world to learn the lessons of the disaster. To show me how, and where, he directed us back out of town on a road that wound its way further up the valley. After a few miles, Rosario instructed me to pull over and we got out of the car. The sun was blinding and all I could hear was the buzzing of flies, the distant bleating of sheep and the sound of bells tinkling as they grazed.

'Look,' Rosario said, waving towards the horizon. At first, it seemed he was pointing towards an archaeological dig, the remains of an ancient settlement half exhumed. But as I strained my eyes, I realised that rather than the huddle of stones in the distance being reclaimed from the earth, they were instead sinking back into it. 'This,' said Rosario, 'is the Poggioreale of my childhood.'

Turning away and retreating into the shade of an old olive tree, he then told me what he remembered of the day the first earthquake struck. It was a Sunday. But his father was out working in the fields and his mother was busy with the laundry, so he had gone to his grandmother's for lunch and was seated at her kitchen table waiting for her to ladle pasta onto his outstretched plate. He remembered there were church bells ringing and the sound of the latest football news drifting into the kitchen from houses nearby when he felt his plate fly back into his face and his chair topple. Half blinded by the scalding sauce he staggered screaming into the street, calling out for his mother, but found it filled with falling masonry, thick clouds of dust and the screams of terrified neighbours stumbling from their own crumbling homes.

Rosario did not see the horseman galloping up behind him, grab the back of his collar and swing him across the saddle. Once clear of the town, the rider set him down and turned back, leaving the petrified boy by the side of the road. In the hours that followed, the road we had driven down filled with bedraggled survivors hunched against the biting wind. It was not until nightfall that Rosario was reunited with his family who had also escaped. 'I never knew who the horseman was. Sometimes I think it was a dream,' said Rosario. 'I owe him my life. But our lives were never the same again.'

Listening to him speak it was hard to imagine this scorching hillside swept by bitter weather. But as Giuseppe Tomasi di Lampedusa writes in *Il Gattopardo*, The Leopard, his chronicle of Sicilian life at the time of the Risorgimento, it is 'the violence in the landscape' here, the extremes of weather and 'continual tension in everything', that has formed the Sicilian character. It was exactly ten years after his novel was posthumously published that the Belice earthquake destroyed the grand Palazzo Filangeri-Cutò, the fictional *Donnafugata*, where he spent his youth and set some of the novel's most memorable scenes, less than ten miles from where Rosario and I stood talking.

As we approached the ruins of Rosario's childhood home on foot the only sign of life were a few stray dogs that followed us as we picked our way over weed-covered rubble, a pungent smell of rotting fruit from wild fig trees hanging heavy in the air. What appeared from a distance to be little more than a pile of stones was clearly once a community of some standing. The shells of a number of palazzos with wrought-iron balconies and stone porches looked virtually untouched, and glancing up through their gaping windows I could see traces of elaborate frescoes. Further along, we passed the remains of an imposing columned church, a post office with a mural of an old weighing machine on its wall and the wreckage of a school where pupils' scribblings were, remarkably, still faintly visible on the blackboard.

Much of the wealth in these western highlands once came from rich seams of sulphur-bearing rock, Rosario explained. At one time Sicily had a virtual global monopoly on the mineral. But it was rich farming land too. 'This street where we are now used to be the main thoroughfare for farmers leading their mules out into the fields. But after the earthquakes farmers had nowhere to keep their beasts. They sold them to slaughterhouses. Eventually, some with a little money saved and bought tractors. But people no longer lived with their fingers in the soil and the culture completely changed. We have an expression: *la terra fa la casa, la casa non fa la terra*,' – it is the land that creates a home, not vice versa, he concluded. 'Here the connection to the land was lost. We lost our roots. Our history. Look at this place. It is a *paese fantasma*.' A ghost town.

It was as he spoke that I noticed some buildings had strange, coded symbols painted on their walls. This was all that remained of the international emergency exercise held in the ruins a few days earlier, Rosario explained. Just one of the exercises held here for a week or so every few years when this ghost town is used as a test site for civil protection experts to practise strategies for rescuing survivors and recovering bodies in the aftermath of major disasters. The week before, teams had come from England, France, Morocco and Israel, and prior to this from as far afield as Iran and the United States to spend days lugging ladders, cutting equipment and dummies strapped to stretchers through the deserted streets.

Ironically, a month earlier, the mayor of Poggioreale had travelled to the US to try to re-establish links with *Poggiorealesi* emigrants and their descendants – an estimated eight thousand now living in Texas and Louisiana – in the hope of persuading some of the diaspora to return to their roots. Two years before that a mayor had flown to Australia with a similar aim, though there were few signs so far that the missions had borne fruit. But I couldn't help wondering if Amandola and other afflicted communities in central Italy, their populations slowly bleeding away, might seek salvation through such forays abroad at some point in the future.

*

The heat of the day was subsiding as I left Rosario and the ruins of Poggioreale behind to continue on to Palermo. The road that climbed out of the Belice valley led through the rugged western highlands before descending to the coast. Here barren escarpments loomed over hardscrabble terrain.

Twenty miles or so from Poggioreale I passed a turn-off for the town of Corleone, home to some of the most brutal Mafia mobsters of modern times, the 'jackals and hyenas' Lampedusa's fictional Prince Don Fabrizio prophesied would one day take the place of the leopards and lions of Sicily's past. The most savage of these was Salvatore 'Toto' Riina, *capo dei capi* of the infamous *Corleonesi* clan who ordered the murder of anti-Mafia prosecutors Giovanni Falcone and Paolo Borsellino in the 1990s along with countless more cold-blooded killings. After witnessing so much devastation wrought by nature, I had little appetite for experiencing any lingering sense of man-made misery and drove on.

I knew I had bypassed many of the splendours of Sicily on my earthquake tour of the island. That my search for answers to how communities here handled natural disasters in the past had led me to forgo many sites where Sicily's rich history is nurtured instead of forgotten. Places such as Noto, itself devastated by an earthquake in 1693 and rebuilt in baroque grandeur by Sicily's former Spanish rulers as a demonstration of their power and wealth. Agrigento's Valley of Temples and Syracuse, once the largest city of the ancient world.

But once I reached Palermo I was finally able to meet Saveria's daughter Eleonora and with her enjoy something of the beauty the city has to offer. The grand Corso Vittorio Emanuele and Palazzo dei Normanni, the former seat of the kings of Sicily with its shimmering golden mosaicked Cappella Palatina that speaks of the island's former glory. I declined her invitation to climb onto the high crenellated ramparts of the cathedral to take in a bird's eye view. But I delighted in the secluded cloisters of the former convent of Santa Caterina, filled with the aroma of cinnamon and nutmeg, where elaborate sweets and pastries once made by Dominican nuns are still sold.

In recent years, Palermo has undergone a significant revival. In the wake of the bloody Mafia wars of the early 1990s which brought the city to its knees, its erudite mayor, Leoluca Orlando, rode a wave of public anti-Mafia protests to enforce tough laws against Mafia bosses, who over decades tore down entire neighbourhoods of graceful villas and neoclassical buildings, sometimes in the middle of the night, to make way for brutalist tower blocks. The tide was turned on the city's decline, culminating in its nomination as Italy's capital of culture in 2018.

After our tour of the city, Eleonora invited me to lunch with her husband Fabio at their home in the historical heart of downtown. Over a delicious lunch of grilled swordfish with capers the couple spoke of their hopes that Palermo would continue to flourish despite its troubled past. Too many of their countrymen and women had become resigned to the Mafia, said Eleonora, a vivacious woman with an infectious laugh. 'In Sicily there is a prevailing sense of fatalism,' she said. 'Perhaps it comes from our Arab heritage.'

In passing, she mentioned that there is no clear future tense, nor one of the immediate past, in the Sicilian dialect. Whether this indicated a desire to forget what had gone before and a lack of faith in what lay ahead, or simply a determination to savour the present moment, remained unclear. Similar ambiguity surrounded a popular Sicilian saying which Eleonora wrote out for me in bold letters: '*Comu finisci si cunta*'. Our lunch grew cold on our plates as we batted its meaning back and forth. But a rough literal translation of the phrase seemed to me to be 'when it ends it is told'.

I was still turning this over in my mind as my plane took off from Falcone Borsellino airport later that night and the lights of Palermo dwindled to a glittering tapestry skirting the sea far below. Eleonora had quoted the saying as an example of Sicilian fatalism. Another way of saying *che sarà sarà*. A recognition that we control very little in our lives. What will be will be.

Perhaps, I thought, it might also mean it is only at a journey's end that its true purpose is understood. An echo of T.S. Eliot's wisdom that, in the end, we arrive back in the place from which we started and only then grasp the meaning of all our ceaseless exploring in life.

Chapter 23

Preparations for autumn festivals were underway on my return to Amandola at the end of summer 2019. This is the time of year in the Sibillini mountains when the heat begins to subside, but days are still long and sunny. When the mountain slopes are burnt pale by the sun. Fields below are shorn of crops and ears of wheat freckle the cobbles in the piazza, remnants of the *Canestrelle* harvest festival held every August to honour the town's patron saint Beato Antonio.

When I first settled in Amandola, the town had come alive with music, fairs and feasts throughout the year. The *Befana* in January, carnival the following month, sports and food festivals in the spring and summer and, in the autumn, the two festivals I loved most: the chestnut *Castagnata*, and *Diamanti a Tavola* truffle festival that drew visitors from all over Italy and beyond. Following the earthquakes these festivals were either cancelled or reduced to shadows of their former selves, the *Castagnata* consigned to a few braziers near the main square.

But unlike the aftermath of the disastrous quake three centuries earlier, when all festivities in the town were suspended for ten years and citizens were forbidden from wearing flamboyant clothing, by the end of the third summer there were tentative signs of recovery. Plans were underway to once again bedeck the lower part of the *centro storico* with pennants for the two popular autumn festivals in an effort to lift people's spirits. The silence that fell across this mountain community in the aftermath of the more recent quakes was slowly replaced by the low chatter of visitors trickling back, some drawn by the efforts of performing artists who organised open-air concerts and classical recitals in the high meadows of the Sibillini.

With the church of Saint Augustine in the piazza secured, each passing hour was once again marked by the tolling of its great bell.

And, here and there, the voices of builders and the sound of construction machinery could be heard. Thanks to Francesca's diligence and the fact that my house had suffered lighter damage, the project for repairing my own home had also been approved and once work had begun it progressed relatively quickly. More than a decade after I first brought the house back to life, it was once again enveloped in scaffolding with the roof removed. This time there would be no hidden treasures retrieved. The purpose was instead to secrete within the structure of the building materials and mechanisms using the most up-to-date engineering techniques to repair and strengthen it, while at the same time keeping alterations discreet to ensure its historical integrity.

For several months the top floor once again resembled a building site. Internal walls were stripped back to bare brick then encased in reinforced mesh before being replastered. Steel girders the size of railway tracks were embedded in the floor and walls of one bedroom to act as a brace, then boxed in and re-covered so they were invisible. Architraves were repaired or replaced, and another steel brace was embedded under the eaves, like a girdle, with the bridle-like metal harness attached to secure the roof beams. Once the work was complete and steel rods inserted to tie outer to inner walls, it was as if my home had been tied together like a parcel and returned to me as a gift.

As Francesca led me up the staircase, and from the middle to top floor, I marvelled at the way each intervention employed to strengthen its structure was almost entirely hidden from view. In addition to the exterior having been repainted the colour of ripe corn that reflected the midday sun, every room had also been given several fresh coats of calming white. And in the bedroom with the vaulted ceiling overlooking the garden, part of which was now encircled with a hefty, but invisible, steel brace, the floor had been re-covered with warm maple wood. After Francesca handed me back my keys and we sealed our goodbyes with a hug, I wandered from room to room, whispering a silent prayer of thanks, and wondered what Don Federico would have made of it all.

When the mayor's office finally declared my house habitable again, I celebrated with friends on the terrace and, as night settled, gazed out of my bedroom window at the mantle of stars above the Sibillini, thankful that my sanctuary was once again safe.

Tens of thousands elsewhere in The Crater were not so lucky. By the end of that summer of 2019, more than fifty thousand people had still not been able to return to their homes. Some had been transferred to emergency housing units, wooden *baracche* of the kind Messinese endured for more than a hundred years. Others got by as best they could in the temporary accommodation they found themselves. But more than a thousand remained lodged in hotel rooms requisitioned by the government close to the Adriatic.

As time passed it became increasingly clear that this largely rural heart of Italy had been consigned to the political back burner. '*Qui ci sono pochi voti da pescare,*' – here there are few votes to fish – was a popular refrain as remaining residents watched those at a national level turn their backs on the multiple problems the earthquakes had created. Special commissioners in charge of reconstruction came and went. Bureaucracy entangling rebuilding efforts became ever more complicated. The number of ordinances issued to correct perceived errors in ones issued just months before mushroomed; three years on there were eighty-eight separate statutes on the books, the following year there would be more than a hundred.

There was no sign of a rush of architects and artists wanting to prove their mettle by building futuristic monuments and model towns to house the homeless, as there had been in the Belice valley. All the grandstanding and promises that places would be rebuilt with all possible haste appeared forgotten. In Amatrice, where so many lost their lives, soldiers in armoured vehicles continued to stand guard. One road cleared through the devastated town centre, and bordered on either side with tall wooden barriers, shielded the ruins of what remained from public view. But it also hid the fact that almost nothing had been done to begin rebuilding this historic heart of the town since it was razed. Just visible above the barrier was the tip of one medieval bell tower that miraculously survived, with the hands on its clock face frozen at the moment the first August earthquake struck. Three years on it seemed more of a taunt that time since then had remained at a virtual standstill.

In places like Ùssita, where the mayor wailed that he saw a vision of hell when the earthquake struck, and Pieve Torina, where the home of the family who invited me to spend Christmas with them lay buried, it was as if barely a stone had been disturbed. Compared to such places, Amandola's prospects seemed more encouraging. Yet here too, there were still hundreds of displaced *terremotati*. Vincenza, Primetta and her son Adriano continued to eke out each day in the prefab containers near the sports stadium – Primetta by then ninety-three, Vincenza in her late seventies. And with little sign of progress on their condemned homes being rebuilt, the slow trickle of people leaving their makeshift lodgings to live elsewhere continued.

Uppermost in the minds of many who remained, however, was the future of Amandola's mountain hospital which had been evacuated within hours of the first August earthquake. But for a small emergency room on the ground floor close to the entrance, it remained largely boarded up. For centuries the hospital had been a central focus of the town. Not only vital to the health of communities throughout the Sibillini, but an important employer and one that drove other businesses catering to those who came for treatment.

Amandola's tradition as a place of sanctuary and healing was born even before the town itself came into being. From the Early Middle Ages to the beginning of the Renaissance there are thought to have been ten infirmaries and hospices known as *senodòchi*, or places of friendship for strangers, within its territory. All were run by monks, nuns, friars and priests who could offer little more than shelter, basic sustenance and liniment. But as time passed, what became the town's principal hospital, Vittorio Emanuele II, evolved into a sophisticated medical facility with a hundred beds and forty employees on duty at any one time. As late as 1910 the hospital also offered facilities for Amandolesi to take a hot bath there for a payment of one lira, or a cold one for half the price. Since the hospital was just a short walk from my house and I found only sinks in the corner of two bedrooms when I bought it, it seems likely Don Federico's father Cesare would once have taken his son and daughter Rosina to bathe there; perhaps Donato and his wife took their children there too.

Over the years, however, there had been cutbacks. Some of the hospital's facilities had dwindled as various departments such as obstetrics and gynaecology were closed, with patients referred to larger hospitals near the coast. But when I first arrived in Amandola, people still talked with pride of specialisations such as ophthalmology that continued to be offered there. And it was always possible to tell the timing of busy shifts ending by the number of doctors in white coats climbing into their cars along the side of the road leading from the hospital to the main square.

One of the hospital's former chief administrators, Nicola Kardos, who spent nearly thirty years within what he called its 'beloved walls' and meticulously researched its history, spoke about the place as a beacon of hope and pride to those far and wide throughout the mountains. Now his eyes fell to the floor when asked about the fate of the hospital as time passed and it remained boarded up. '*Lascialo*,' – leave it, was all he would say, his shoulders slumping.

Some in the town had even filed a *denuncia*, a formal legal complaint, against the *comune* for failing to repair and reopen the hospital as quickly as possible. But the authorities argued it stood on unstable land. They were pinning their hopes instead on building a brand-new eighty-bed facility on lower ground on the southern edge of town, part of which would be funded by a considerable donation from a Russian oil company recently allocated to the project. The donation was for five million euros and came from the state-controlled Russian oil giant Rosneft. While other nations and private companies also made significant gifts towards reconstruction projects in The Crater, this was, as far as I knew, one of the largest.

Within months of news that President Vladimir Putin had offered such a large sum to Italy's then Prime Minister, Paolo Gentiloni, and that this money was being allotted by the regional government of Le Marche for the building of a new mountain hospital, dark rumours started to circulate about the donation. Some spoke of a possible link to undefined plans for a natural gas pipeline that might one day run beneath a central portion of the Apennines, some way to the north of Amandola. But, for the first time, I noticed usually garrulous Amandolesi nervous of openly voicing their opinions.

The total cost of building the new hospital was estimated at nearly nineteen million euros, with thirteen million coming from the Italian government and nearly a million from contributions by private individuals. Building work was projected to start in the spring of 2020 and be completed within two years. For a civil engineer like the mayor Adolfo Marinangeli, the opportunity to build a new hospital in Amandola from scratch was 'a dream come true,' he enthused to me one day. 'A perfect example of hope and opportunity being wrested from adversity.'

But for older Amandolesi, it felt like a cherished institution with roots far back in time was being shuttered. That yet another chapter in the history of the town was closing, all the intimate memories contained within its walls forgotten.

A short walk from the old hospital, another Amandola landmark, albeit a more recent one, also continued to teeter on the brink of ruin. For Oreste, it seemed, had become resigned to the near certainty that his beloved Hotel Paradiso was beyond salvation and would have to be torn down. As a way of keeping the family's hope alive, he had painstakingly converted the old palazzo in the grounds of the Paradiso where they were living into a five-room boutique hotel he named Villa delle Rose, though its rooms had yet to receive any guests. As he ushered me from one room to another one morning, proudly pointing to the delicate paintings of flowers and butterflies now decorating some of the rooms' ceilings, it was clear the prospect of a wrecking ball erasing his parents' life work hung heavy on his shoulders. 'I grew up in the Hotel Paradiso. I remember its history and how hard my mother and father worked to make it a success,' he said, as we sat looking out at the mountains.

The rise and fall in the fortunes of the Paradiso closely mirrored those of Amandola itself in the years after the Second World War. The Liberty-style palazzo that became Villa delle Rose had been commissioned in the 1920s by a marquess of Amandolesi nobility known locally as *La Madame* and sold thirty years later to Oreste's great-uncle, after whom he was named. During the Second World War Great-uncle Oreste ran a pharmacy in Amandola's main square. But he spent much of his time in Rome and kept an eye open for other business opportunities. At a time when land on the outskirts of Rome was cheap, he bought a number of large plots where he grew fruit and vegetables to be sold in the capital's ancient Campo dei Fiori market. As business flourished, he bought a bus company operating routes across the mountains.

After the bodies of Mussolini and his mistress were strung from the girder of a petrol station in Milan in April 1945 and remaining German forces in the north surrendered to the Allies, Italians went to the polls and voted to depose the House of Savoy in favour of Italy becoming a republic. With much of the country left in ruins and political turmoil, however, Italy struggled to recover after the war. Economic reconstruction was slow and painful, especially in the south. The injection of over a billion dollars of aid under the Marshall Plan in the late 1940s and early 1950s boosted industrialisation and urban areas began to expand. Though the Rome of Fellini's *La Dolce Vita* was still some years away, the value of the land Oreste's great-uncle had bought on the capital's periphery increased significantly. When he sold part of it, he bought the villa of *La Madame*, together with a large plot of wooded land surrounding it that stretched almost as far as my back garden.

But this was not enough. His great-uncle was *orgoglioso*, a proud man who wanted to show off his wealth, said Oreste. In the past, Amandola's noble families had funded many buildings in the town and his great-uncle wanted to make his mark too. So, in the late 1950s, land alongside his villa on the crest of Castel Leone was cleared and construction of the Hotel Paradiso began. It was an ambitious building project which included a large banqueting room and it became one of the first hotels in Le Marche to have a lift – a polished wooden booth I recalled clattering and wheezing from floor to floor in its open metal shaft. Unfortunately Oreste's great-uncle died in 1966, before the hotel could be completed, and left behind a mountain of unpaid bills. He had no children, but his brother Giovanni, Oreste's grandfather, whose financial circumstances were a great deal more humble, had eleven sons and daughters with children of their own and it was left to Oreste's father and cousins to take out loans to clear the debts.

Oreste's father, who like Don Federico was sent to the seminary in Fermo to receive a good education, went on to train as a *geometra*, a surveyor, and it was he who oversaw the completion of the hotel. As car ownership in Italy rose and people began to have more leisure time the hotel flourished and soon became an important destination for tourism in the Sibillini mountains.

The late 1960s through to the 1980s was not only a golden age for the hotel where Oreste grew up, but for Amandola too. During those years he remembers its *centro storico* full of life. Its narrow streets were lined with food stores and artisan workshops: carpenters, seamstresses and small enterprises making shoes. In the 1990s, however, the number of guests coming from other parts of Italy to stay in the Hotel Paradiso began to dwindle as the hotel's regular clientele aged. By the first decade of the twenty-first century, when I became a regular guest during the years my house was first being restored, I remembered its dining room dotted with elderly widows who continued to come each year 'to take the air', each seated at separate tables in the dining room, drawing deeply on cigarettes.

It was once the Sibillini mountains were given protected status, with the formation of the *Parco Nazionale dei Monti Sibillini* in the early 1990s, after which Le Marche's subtle charm became more widely known abroad, that the Hotel Paradiso began to attract an increasingly international clientele. But, as became clear in the aftermath of the earthquakes, there was a downside to Amandola's one-time status as a wealthy community where the nobility chose to live. For the wealth accrued by rich Amandolesi over centuries came largely from their extensive lands worked by generations of *mezzadri* sharecroppers. Even as the post-war world began to change and land reforms were introduced, these, often absentee, landowners were convinced their interests were best served by continuing to rely on farming returns. When the state-financed *Cassa per il Mezzogiorno*, Fund for the South, was set up in the 1950s to stimulate economic development and promote industrialisation in neglected parts of central and southern Italy, while neighbouring communities were deemed eligible for funding, Amandola missed out.

As I understood it, pressure was brought to bear by powerful Amandolesi who exerted influence in Rome to ensure their substantial territory was not included in the zone qualifying for the scheme. Their fear was that industrial development in the vicinity would draw workers from the land and leave them short of manpower. But industrialisation along the coast proved too great a pull for struggling sharecroppers and they abandoned the land anyway. As more and more began to move away, Amandola's population went into decline.

'It was a missed opportunity,' was all Oreste would say. 'A time when jobs could have been created locally that would have given new life to this town.' I did not press him further, recognising that we were veering into sensitive territory. I had long ago made a decision to keep my distance from local politics. After so many years spent untangling complicated power plays in areas of violent conflict, I knew those in the smallest of communities can sometimes be the most fraught. Besides, it was to the future that Oreste now wanted to look. His hope was to eventually be able to build a new hotel on the site of the old Paradiso. One that incorporated all the latest seismic safety standards with fewer rooms and improved facilities to cater to a more sophisticated clientele. 'We have to adapt. We have to be better prepared. We have to learn to live with earthquakes in a better way if we are to move forward,' he concluded.

'People who come here now from different parts of the world are *colti*, cultured. They want a different experience. They sometimes know even more about this mountain area than I do,' he said, with a smile. 'They come here to enjoy the beauty, the clean environment. They come to find things that have been lost in other places.'

Hidden Beauty

'*Forma bonum fragile est.*'
'Beauty is fragile.'

Ovid, *Ars amatoria*, Book II (AD 2)

Chapter 24

There is one often-quoted line in Fyodor Dostoevsky's classic *The Idiot* which the Russian writer poses as a question to the novel's ailing protagonist Prince Myshkin. 'Is it true, Prince, that you once said, "It is beauty that will save the world?"' A century after the novel was published his fellow Russian and Nobel laureate Alexander Solzhenitsyn scoffed at the notion that there was any redemptive power in beauty.

'When in bloodthirsty history did beauty ever save anyone from anything?' he raged, after suffering years of political persecution at the hands of Josef Stalin. 'Ennobled, uplifted, yes – but whom has it saved?' It was only later in life, Solzhenitsyn conceded, that he came to realise his countryman's enigmatic remark was 'not a careless phrase but a prophecy'.

Of all those who took to the podium in the cloisters of Jesus College, Cambridge, when the fate of Amandola took centre stage in the wake of the earthquakes, it was the Italian culture ministry's chief inspector for artistic heritage in Le Marche who left the deepest impression on me when he summoned Dostoevsky's immortal words, before adding his own heartfelt plea.

'Beauty *will* save the world,' the silver-haired Pierluigi Moriconi declared, before stepping away from the lectern that day. '*Ma la bellezza, chi la salvera?*' But who will save the beauty?

As the years following the earthquakes passed, it became increasingly clear that Amandola was pinning great hope on the beauty of its setting in the Sibillini proving to be its salvation. A long-term guarantor that it would not find itself gradually reclaimed by the landscape as so many of Italy's rural communities have been. Of it not becoming a virtual ghost town or, as Luisa would have it, a latter-day Pompeii.

But the beauty Pierluigi spoke of that day was beauty crafted by man rather than the powerful forces of nature it takes to form such mighty mountain ranges. His concern was the fate of the region's unique architectural and artistic heritage. For while Le Marche may not have the abundance of grand museums of Florence, Venice or Rome, the vast majority of artworks here are still found in the places for which they were originally commissioned. Often these are small churches in rural or mountain communities like Amandola, Amatrice, Arquata and Pescara del Tronto, where they are both venerated and treasured as integral to local identity. But they are also acutely vulnerable to the vicissitudes of nature.

So much so, that when Pescara, for instance, was razed by the earthquakes, those who survived, though utterly traumatised by the loss of so many lives, still begged rescue workers to dig through the rubble to retrieve an ancient processional cross from the ruins of their village church. This cross, thought to be one of the oldest in Le Marche, is believed to have been brought back from the Crusades by an unknown Knight of Jerusalem from the crusading order of the Knights Hospitaller who tended to the needs of sick pilgrims travelling to the Holy Land. When it was retrieved, it was all that remained of Pescara's Chiesa di Santa Croce. Ground to dust and buried beneath the rubble of the church was a series of fifteenth-century frescoes portraying seven widows dressed in black and seven virgins dressed in white, all praying for divine intervention to save the village from disaster. Though the frescoes and the village itself were lost, the cross was saved and brought comfort and a glimmer of hope to survivors.

Pierluigi has made it his life work to safeguard such treasures for future generations, his task nothing less than preserving ties with the immortal. Never was this task more vital, challenging and swiftly executed than in the wake of the disasters that befell central Italy in the summer and winter of 2016. For within forty-eight hours of the first August quake, he had gathered a crisis unit of art historians, architects and archaeologists to join forces with an elite team of *carabinieri* intent on recovering as much of the region's cultural legacy as possible from the ruins. This elite corps, known as the *Caschi Blu per la Cultura*, or cultural blue helmets, had only been established six months earlier, under the aegis of the United Nations. Born of a conviction by Italy's culture ministry that precious heritage sites around the world were as deserving of international protection as the people of countries torn apart by conflict and war, one of the corps' first deployments was expected to be to the ruins of Palmyra, then under assault by Isis. But instead of being dispatched to that far corner of the former Roman Empire, the art experts found themselves less than a hundred miles from its one-time seat of power.

Within a year, the *Caschi Blu* rescued more than fifteen thousand paintings, statues, altarpieces, bells and other precious objects, together with many thousands of antique books and documents from devastated communities throughout The Crater. Through the rain and snow of the first harsh winter they worked against the clock, performing a kind of cultural triage amid the rubble. Objects in need of urgent attention were classified 'code red' and prioritised for recovery. Those less exposed or damaged were coded yellow or green and left *in situ* until the spring. Many deemed too dangerous to access simply had to be abandoned, the work of countless craftsmen and artists through the ages left to crumble to dust.

Most of what could be rescued was bundled off to secret storage depots close to the earthquake zone to await the ministrations of experts. There, in the cold and dark of vast warehouses and underground bunkers, works of great beauty would languish for years. Where possible, salvaged church bells were returned to be hung in the bell towers of temporary wooden chapels erected beside the *baracche* built for the displaced, their time-worn tolling marking each long day for the *terremotati*. But in the autumn of the third year after the earthquakes a number of artistic jewels were brought out from their dark hiding places, some having been restored, others simply stabilised to prevent them from deteriorating further. All were brought together for a collection of wounded or recently healed masterpieces as a plea to the public not to forget the cultural crisis continuing to grip the heart of Italy.

On a raw November day, as a mist swirled around the ramparts of the fortress Malatesta on a riverbank in the ancient city of Ascoli Piceno, a throng huddled by its drawbridge waiting for the *Rinascimento Marchigiano*, Marche Renaissance, exhibition to open. Once inside, the chatter of the crowd quietened to a murmur as onlookers shuffled along narrow stone passageways, entering one chamber after another, clustering in whispered awe before the most spectacular pieces.

One of these was a tall, exquisite painting in tempera and ground gold of the Madonna and child flanked by angels playing lutes by the Renaissance master Vittore Crivelli, who, together with his brother Carlo, spent most of his life working in Le Marche. As I stood before the glimmering masterpiece, I thought of the magnificent polyptych by the same artist that once graced the altar of Amandola's Saint Francis's church before its panels were unceremoniously dismantled in the aftermath of the Napoleonic invasion. One now hangs in the El Paso Museum of Art in Texas, another in Nashville's Vanderbilt University in Tennessee. The whereabouts of others are still unknown.

Another of the most striking pieces that attracted the attention of the crowd was a towering oval canvas, as tall as two men, of a host of angels, one cradling a lamb, attributed to one of the most prominent Baroque artists of his day in Le Marche, Filippo Ricci. Few stood for long before a small red and blue painted wooden statue tucked away to the side of a winding stone staircase. A sixteenth-century Madonna, her hooded eyes downcast as if contemplating the space where her palms once met in prayer, hands shorn away in the earthquake by falling masonry. Yet for me this forlorn amputee was one of the most compelling treasures on display. For her very existence had only recently come to light because of the earthquake that severed her hands. The niche where she once stood had long been concealed behind a wardrobe in a church in the ruined town of Arquata del Tronto and her presence was only revealed when the wardrobe toppled to the ground in the quake. This haphazard unveiling of the small painted Madonna was just one of many such discoveries: hidden beauty revealed as a consequence of the convulsions of the earth.

Further north, in a church in the devastated town of Camerino, a heavy bundle was discovered in a secret compartment of an old oak cupboard which the priests had known nothing about. There, wrapped in folds of blue satin, they found a rare fifteenth-century statue of the Black Madonna of Loreto dressed in a golden robe, holding an infant Christ in her arms.

'My jaw dropped when I saw it because not many such things exist. 'È particolarissima, una chicca,' – a most particular and special gem, Pierluigi told me when we met in Cambridge. 'For all the terrible destruction wrought by the earthquakes, these are true gifts, concealed for centuries, that might otherwise never have come to light.'

In Amandola too, during an earlier earthquake, a number of fifteenth-century frescoes had emerged from behind the crumbling plaster of the now crippled church of Saint Francis where Crivelli's altarpiece once hung, he said. And in neighbouring Monte San Martino, when a confessional box toppled over in the same quake and the plaster behind it crumbled, it exposed a sixteenth-century fresco of *The Crucifixion* painted by Vincenzo Pagani, a student of Renaissance master Raphael.

While all earthquakes led to destruction others could lead to something being reborn. A constant cycle of endings and new beginnings. So, as the crowd surged past the Madonna with missing hands, barely giving her a glance that day in Ascoli, I thought again of my own hidden treasures. The paintings that had lain unseen in my attic for a hundred years and, after that, been all but ignored as they stood wrapped in a cylinder behind my study door in London for a further decade.

Over the years I had shown photographs of the paintings to those I thought might help me understand more about them. When I discovered a connection to Sicily in the painting of the Madonna and the Moon, I wondered if it was in some way linked to the map that had been hidden beside it for so long. To a time when Don Federico had some association with the island in the wake of its disastrous earthquakes. For the dark-robed figure that was revealed when the canvas had been cleaned, was, I later learnt, San Francesco da Paola, patron saint of seafarers. A humble friar greatly venerated by Sicilians for the miracle he is said to have performed crossing the Straits of Messina using his cloak as a sail – a story later set to music by Franz Liszt in his *Deux legends*. The same friar who foresaw Messina would one day lie in ruins.

But it was only as my interest in everything else hidden away in the attic and in the lives of those who once lived in my house grew, that I resolved to bring the paintings back to their rightful home. With a determination to find out what I could about their origin, who had painted them, and why they had been concealed and then forgotten.

After the crowd in Ascoli's great fortress thinned, I caught up with Pierluigi Moriconi again and, as we had arranged, took out the photographs I had brought to show him of my own hidden gems.

'*Fabuloso! Bellissimo!*' he exclaimed, leaning in to examine them more closely, before turning to ask how and where they had come into my possession. When I told him the story of my house, of Don Federico and his legacy, Pierluigi listened carefully, then led me back to one of the paintings that had drawn the attention of most visitors that day.

Without saying a word, he held up my photograph and then gestured for me to take a closer look at both it and the painting by Filippo Ricci that towered above us on the wall. At first, my untrained eye failed to grasp his meaning. But then I saw it. Its central figure, the dark-robed friar with a wooden staff at his feet and an angel close by, gently cradling a lamb, was very similar to the one with his hand outstretched in supplication to the Virgin Mary in my painting of the Madonna and the Moon. Both were of the venerated saint San Francesco da Paola.

Filippo Ricci, Pierluigi explained, was a pupil both of Donato Creti, whose work forms part of the collection of London's National Gallery, and Corrado Giaquinto, court painter to King Ferdinand VI of Spain. While he could not be sure without seeing the originals, Pierluigi believed at least one of my paintings, that of Saint Anthony, could be the work of the same artist.

This was quite possible, he said, for Filippo Ricci was the scion of an artistic dynasty that dominated art throughout much of Le Marche from the mid-1600s for nearly one hundred and fifty years: Ubaldo and his brother Natale in the latter years of the seventeenth century; Natale's son Filippo and Filippo's son Alessandro for much of the eighteenth century. Three generations of painters whose *bottega*, or atelier, lay in the heart of Fermo, not far from the old seminary where Don Federico trained. Not only were the Riccis prolific, but almost all of their work depicted biblical scenes typical of Baroque art with its emphasis on compositions intended to evoke religious fervour and encourage piety. Throughout much of the time they were creating their art the tribunals of the Roman Inquisition held great sway. These tribunals, set up to tighten discipline in the Roman Catholic Church and counter the challenge of the Protestant Reformation, might have been less onerous in other parts of Italy, but in the Papal States such as Le Marche, discipline would have been rigorous.

Before we parted, Pierluigi led me into a side room and showed me two books his exhibition partner Professor Stefano Papetti had curated a decade earlier about the Ricci artistic dynasty: five hundred pages of coloured plates and text depicting many of their sumptuous works in oils. Professor Papetti was the director of Ascoli Piceno's municipal museum and art gallery, its celebrated *Pinacoteca Civica*, and he would surely be able to tell me more, Pierluigi said as he bade me farewell. Was it really possible that one or other of my paintings might be the work of such a celebrated artist, I asked myself, feeling both stunned and suddenly guilty at the thought that I might have continued to neglect the paintings were it not for the earthquakes.

As I passed under the great stone portal of the Forte Malatesta and walked back over the 'devil's bridge' that spans Ascoli's Castellano river, I once again gave silent thanks to Don Federico for all he had bequeathed me, unknowingly, and for all it was leading me to discover.

Chapter 25

Once described by a leading Italian art critic as 'the most beautiful museum in the country', Ascoli's *pinacoteca* is spread over two floors with fifteen exhibition rooms, each decorated with sparkling Murano chandeliers, pink marble floors, red and gold velvet curtains, Venetian mirrors and lacquered consoles covered with gold leaf. It was here, surrounded by the work of Renaissance masters such as Titian and Carlo Crivelli and those of Bernardo Bellotto, student and nephew of Canaletto, that Professor Papetti invited me to unfurl my paintings on a long, leather-covered table.

The professor, a tall, calm, elegant figure, dressed formally in dark suit and tie, had to stoop to look at the canvases and took his time adjusting his gaze from one to the other. It was the first time I had subjected the originals to such scrutiny and waited nervously for him to pronounce judgement. Like me, his eye seemed drawn first to the portrayal of Saint Anthony with its warm ochre colours and the tenderness of the scene: the gentle gesture of the saint's hands, the delicacy of the lily frond clutched in the Christ child's tiny fist, the expression on the cherubs' faces and fold of their wings. Although the more damaged of the two canvases, it was, he mused as if talking to himself, '*simpatico, meno eccentrico*', more pleasing and less eccentric than the second painting.

Then, standing straight, crossing his arms, and slowly turning to face me, he declared it was indeed likely that this portrayal of the patron saint of all that is lost and hopes to be found was the work of the well-known artistic dynasty from Fermo, the Ricci family. More specifically that it was most likely one of the last in its line, as Pierluigi Moriconi had thought, that of the painter Filippo Ricci born in 1715. It was impossible to be certain of this, said the professor, as much of Filippo Ricci's work was left unsigned, as was my painting.

But to his expert eye it carried many hallmarks of the artist within its classically devotional scene, its warmth and the sensitivity with which it had been painted.

Oil painting of Saint Anthony recovered from the attic. It is believed to be the work of prominent Baroque artist Filippo Ricci

'Filippo Ricci had a great reverence for sacred art in the tradition of Carlo Maratta,' one of Rome's leading artists in the 1600s, he continued. 'Much of his work was commissioned by private patrons, wealthy individuals, the nobility and clergy of Le Marche, particularly those in the vicinity of Fermo,' where the Ricci family had their studio.

The series of holes around the plain border at the edge of the canvas confirmed that it must once have been stretched over an oval frame, perhaps to hang in the home of a wealthy patron or beside a church altar, he explained. As far as I had been able to establish, none of the Riccis were commissioned to paint works for Amandola's many churches. But their work, he said, does hang in churches in Monte San Pietrangeli and Montefortino, both places where Don Federico once served. Had the painting belonged to a wealthy family, it might have been given to him out of gratitude for his care or left to him as a bequest in their will. If so, surely Don Federico would have recognised it was a precious work of art and hung it carefully on a wall to whisper a prayer before it from time to time. Why then had the painting been treated so harshly, folded twice, and stashed out of sight in its dark hiding place? That spoke to me of desperation. This sense of mystery I came to feel enveloped both paintings deepened further when the professor turned his attention to the second canvas.

For so long I had thought of this painting as that of the Madonna and the Moon or the pregnant Madonna. Even now I can't explain why as the figure of Mary is not obviously with child. But to the professor the symbolism of the image was immediately clear. The painting, he explained, was a depiction of the *Immacolata*, the Virgin Mary from the Book of Revelation, the final book of the Bible which forewarns of an Apocalypse. It is a scene from a vision in which the Woman of the Apocalypse, as she is sometimes known, appeared to John the Apostle on the island of Patmos in the first century – the word apocalypse being derived from the Greek *apokaluptein*, meaning to uncover or reveal. A vision in which she appeared to be bathed by the Sun, with the Moon at her feet beneath which a dragon or serpent lay in wait, ready to devour her unborn child.

It is in this last book of the Bible that the Four Horsemen of the Apocalypse appear: the first riding a white horse of pestilence, the second a red horse of war, the third a black horse of famine and the fourth a pallid horse of death. It is an allegory of the end of the world as we know it: one filled with fantastical imagery of flashes of lighting, deafening thunder and a great earthquake 'unlike any mankind has known' after which 'cities and nations collapsed', 'islands fled away' and 'mountains could not be found'.

As the significance of this painting began to dawn, I thought of the times the cardboard cylinder containing the two canvases had toppled to the floor of my study in London. What if I had paid them more attention long before and understood something of their meaning? I doubt I would have sensed they carried some kind of warning, but the very thought of it was unsettling. I mentioned nothing of this to the professor as I stood beside him in the museum that day, but the nagging thought took hold. Instead, I listened carefully as he explained that he believed the second painting bore the mark of a different artist, one working in the same period as Filippo Ricci or possibly a little later at the time of his son Alessandro, around the middle of the eighteenth century. 'Look, you see the way the Madonna's garments are caught by the wind. This kind of flourish was more typical of Rococo than Baroque art,' he said, pointing to her billowing blue robe and veil.

The professor believed this painting to be the work of an artist named Antonio Liozzi, a native of Penna San Giovanni, a small *comune* ten miles or so from Amandola. 'This is also a fine work. But it is more . . . particular,' he continued, hesitating, as if looking for the right word. 'The Madonna's face is a little unusual. She has a long *nasetto alla francese*,' a slightly upturned French nose, the professor called it, which made me smile since I too had found her expression rather strange.

'*Ma guarda qui!*' – But look here! the professor then said in a firmer voice, beckoning me to his side and bending down towards the canvas again. Running his finger around its edge, he pointed to the way the paint reached the very limits of the linen cloth, something I had never noticed. And also to how the figure of San Francesco da Paola, the saint with his hand raised in supplication, looked as if he had been amputated at the knee. The same was true of the cherub offering up the flaming heart. Most telling of all however, said the professor, was that the painting was totally out of perspective for its size. Had he not said so, I would not have realised it, but now I saw what he meant.

'What this means,' he continued, 'is that it has most definitely been cut from a larger canvas.'

I was astonished. Why would anyone do such a thing, I asked?

'This was quite common practice when a painting was stolen,' he replied. 'Thieves who stole paintings from churches almost always cut them up into smaller pieces to make them easier to sell.'

This was even more disturbing. Could it mean Don Federico had unknowingly, or worse still knowingly, taken possession of a stolen painting? Not necessarily, said the professor. It was quite possible that the painting of the Madonna had been cut to fit the shape and size of the one of Saint Anthony and both had been presented to

Don Federico, framed, as gifts. Whoever might have done this, he believed, would almost certainly have felt a special devotion for Saint Anthony and San Francesco da Paola, both humble Franciscan friars, or would have known Don Federico did.

It was important to remember too, he said, how much art was stripped from Italy's churches, especially those in Le Marche, by invading forces over the centuries. And as he spoke of this, I reflected again on how it is not just the instability of the land at the heart of Italy that poses a threat to such beauty; human greed has long played its part. There was nothing new in the looting of art, of course: the Romans sacked the city states of Greece; Crusader armies looted Byzantium; Spanish conquistadors looted gold from the Aztecs; the British oversaw widespread looting in pursuit of empire. And Le Marche has offered rich pickings over the centuries. In one letter Napoleon wrote to one of his generals in 1796, which Pierluigi Moriconi cited when speaking in Cambridge about the fragility of the region's artistic heritage, the military commander described central Italy as 'an open-air museum' ripe for pillage.

As Napoleon's armies advanced through Italy in the closing years of the eighteenth century and the start of the century that followed, his troops were trailed by art experts with instructions to confiscate all the best works. Paintings by Michelangelo, Raphael, da Vinci, Titian, Correggio and others were loaded onto carts and transported north, many destined for the Musée Napoleon, as the Paris Louvre was then known. After Napoleon appointed Eugène de Beauharnais – his stepson by Empress Joséphine – as Viceroy of Italy, much looted art was also sent to Milan's *Pinacoteca di Brera*, which de Beauharnais aspired to turn into a second Louvre.

Written proof of how the invaders considered such booty theirs by right is contained in another letter held in Amandola's town archives: a curt missive, dated 9 November 1810, instructing *Il Signore Podestà*, as mayors were once known, not to obstruct in any way the efforts of two of Napoleon's *abili Soggetti*, able subjects, appointed to confiscate the town's most precious books and paintings. The Amandolesi staged what resistance they could to the invading forces and, in retribution, soldiers ransacked the town. Some of Amandola's most treasured artworks disappeared in the years that followed. The most significant of these were the panels of Vittore Crivelli's magnificent polyptych which once hung above the altar of Saint Francis's church.

The disappearance of such astonishing beauty helped explain the determination of Amandola's mayor Adolfo Marinangeli to stop any works of art being removed from the town in the wake of the 2016–17 earthquakes as they were in so many places throughout The Crater, albeit for their own safekeeping. To this end he fought hard for a conservation laboratory to be established on the upper floor of a former church building in the *centro storico*. There each damaged piece could be worked on *in situ* by restoration experts under the watchful gaze of Amandola's most treasured cultural symbol: a towering statue, known as *Cristo Trionfante*, believed to be one of the most significant wooden sculptures in all of Italy. This roughly hewn bearded figure with long braided hair and widespread arms is now understood to be a representation of the transformation of the eighth-century Holy Roman Emperor Charlemagne to resemble Christ on the cross.

Another treasure lost at the time of the Napoleonic invasion, however, was a ten-foot-high canvas entitled *La Madonna col Bambino e Quattro Santi* by Pietro da Cortona, a leading Italian Baroque painter of his day, confiscated from the Capuchin monastery that my house overlooks. This still hangs in Milan's Brera gallery today. Curiously, in among Don Federico's papers, I found a calling card printed with the address via Brera, N. 16, Milan and the name CH. Lorilleux & Cia., a Parisian purveyor of fine ink, oils and watercolours with a shop close to the Brera gallery. On the reverse of the card was a pencil sketch of what looked like the folds of the sumptuous, fringed curtain that framed da Cortona's painting. Whether Don Federico had once taken the train north from Amandola to Milan to visit the gallery and stood admiring the vibrant colours of da Cortona's Madonna in her sumptuous blue gown and Saint Catherine of Alexandria in gold and crimson robes, sketching this small detail as a simple memento, I would never know. One of my neighbours had once told me that the deaf, mute son of Don Federico's sister Rosina, named Licio, became an accomplished artist in later life, commissioned, for instance, to restore paintings in Orvieto cathedral. Perhaps his uncle had visited the premises of Charles Lorilleux to furnish his nephew with art supplies.

What was certain was that while the *Pinacoteca di Brera* burgeoned as a depository for works of art stolen on the orders of Napoleon, many of its priceless paintings were uprooted again when the maelstrom of war and terrors of the Third Reich engulfed Europe a century later. Hitler's ambition to create a *Führermuseum* housing the world's greatest masterpieces in his home town of Linz in Austria saw countless works of art plundered from territories he invaded, annexed and occupied. And in Italy, where Mussolini was more interested in his own grandiose building schemes than protecting his country's cultural patrimony, once reportedly declaring 'Italy has too much art and too few babies', *Il Duce* put up little resistance to the *Führer* and his kleptomaniac henchman Hermann Göring at first buying and then stealing art on an industrial scale.

The extraordinary lengths a small team of art scholars and experts serving with the Allied forces went to in their efforts to rescue Italian works of art from destruction and Nazi plunder following the liberation of Sicily and removal of Mussolini from power in 1943, have been exhaustively documented. Not least, in recent years, by the American author Robert M. Edsel in *The Monuments Men*, on which a Hollywood film of the same name was loosely based. Far less well known, at least beyond the confines of Le Marche, is the vital role one man, a passionate young Italian art historian named Pasquale Rotondi, played in preventing tens of thousands of precious works of art falling into the hands of the Nazis. Without his efforts much of the later work of the so-called monuments men would have been impossible. I had heard mention of Rotondi over the years. But it was not until Pierluigi Moriconi spoke to me of him in the wake of the earthquakes that I delved further into the past and his extraordinary story unfolded.

Rotondi, I learnt, was Le Marche's newly appointed *soprinten-dente* of fine art for Le Marche in 1939, a similar position to the one Pierluigi was to hold eighty years later. But Rotondi was barely thirty when he received secret instructions of the utmost urgency from the Italian ministry of education to carry out a mission that would decide the fate of some of Italy's greatest cultural treasures. It was September 1939, just days after Hitler ordered the German war machine to begin its invasion of Poland. The telegram Rotondi received was an order to immediately begin scouring Le Marche for a remote location where the country's greatest artworks could be hidden in the event that Italy once again became engulfed in war – a task that became increasingly urgent as German troops made rapid advances through western Europe the following spring.

Le Marche's mountainous terrain provided the perfect topography in which a place of secret safekeeping could be found, the country's cultural experts concluded. They were right. By the time Mussolini declared war on the Allies from the balcony of Rome's Palazzo Venezia on 10 June 1940, Rotondi had found just the place. The small Renaissance-style fort of Rocca Ubaldinesca, perched on a rocky outcrop above the town of Sassocorvaro in the province of Urbino, was chosen as an ideal remote location for hidden art.

Within days, with the help of his personal driver and a handful of trusted volunteers, Rotondi began loading his black Fiat 508 Balilla with prized paintings, tapestries, ceramics, religious artefacts and original musical scores such as those of Puccini, and transported them under cover of darkness in multiple journeys to the Apennine fortress that became known as the Ark of Art. First to arrive were treasures from churches, museums and galleries within Le Marche itself: nearly three hundred and fifty pieces in all, including artworks by Crivelli, Titian, Bellini, Rubens, Signorelli and Piero della Francesca. Next to be brought to safety were seventy crates of paintings, sculptures and other rare artefacts from Venice, including the glorious gold and silver Byzantine altarpiece, the *Pala d'Oro*, encrusted with emeralds, sapphires, rubies and other gems, from Saint Mark's cathedral. When Sassocorvaro could hold no more, three further depositories in the Apennines were found to receive the overflow.

Over the next three years an underground network of Italian art connoisseurs co-ordinated by Rotondi conveyed nearly seven thousand boxes and crates of artwork and other cherished objects to these hiding places from galleries and churches all over Italy, including from Rome's Borghese gallery and the Brera gallery in Milan.

After the fall of Mussolini, Italy's change of alliance and the influx of German troops into Italy in the autumn of 1943, Rotondi went to even greater lengths to safeguard the treasures under his protection. Some he hid behind false walls in the fortress at Sassocorvaro. One, *The Tempest* by Giorgione, he stashed under a bed where his wife lay feigning illness to deter searches by suspicious Nazi officials. When German forces were pushed back northwards by the Allies the following year, Sassocorvaro and the other secret depositories stood in the direct line of fire: close to Germany's final defensive positions along the ferociously contested Gothic Line that snaked across the treacherous summits of the northern Apennines where some of the fiercest fighting of the war in Italy raged.

With countless artistic treasures once again in great peril, Rotondi gathered his volunteers and oversaw a series of clandestine journeys across rugged bomb-cratered mountain roads to transport some of the most precious works in his care for safekeeping in the Vatican. But much of the hidden art remained under his protection in secret sanctuaries in Le Marche until the end of the war when it could be returned. While these perilous operations were mounted to safeguard the art of some of Italy's greatest cultural cities, in smaller towns and villages it was up to individuals to try to save whatever they held dear from Nazi looting. As elsewhere in Italy, the Amandolesi took to hiding anything, and anyone, they could that was likely to be seized in house-to-house searches by German soldiers either billeted in their towns or staging a retreat: guns, food, family heirlooms, partisans, escaped prisoners of war and, surely, some treasured works of art too.

Was it possible, then, that the paintings of the Madonna and Saint Anthony might have been hidden in my attic to keep them from falling into the hands of the Nazis, I asked Professor Papetti that day in Ascoli.

'*Certo*,' certainly, said the professor, 'It's quite possible that the priest or his family hid them away to protect them or prevent them from being stolen.'

Given the history of wholesale looting and plunder in Amandola's past, it was easy to imagine the concern Don Federico might have felt for the safety of his own paintings as storm clouds of war gathered over Europe once more. Perhaps he had chosen to hide them along with the religious statues and other personal belongings on a brief return visit to the town from the coast – unpinning them from their frames and clambering under the rafters to find a dark corner where they would be safe. Or, perhaps, he sent instructions for his nephew Licio, by then a young man and passionate artist, to do so on his behalf.

Both fascinated and chastened by everything the professor and Pierluigi Moriconi told me, I could not bear to return the two canvases to the cardboard tube in which they had sat forlornly behind my study door in London for more than a decade. After being hidden away in a dark attic for nearly a century before that, I knew they deserved to be appreciated once again. Not only to honour the artistry of the men who created them, but because of the symbolism in the scenes I now knew they portrayed. So, in the months that followed, I had the painting of Saint Anthony relined to stabilise the damaged canvas and prevent it from deteriorating any further. I then asked for it to be partially restored and framed by a father and daughter in Fermo with experience of working with pieces of art by the Ricci dynasty. When I finally brought it back to my Amandola home, I hung it at the top of the wide stone staircase leading up from the front door. A reminder of all that was lost, and then found, not only in the earthquakes, but also further back in time.

The faint blemishes that remained in the canvas also acted as reminders too of the years it had been hidden away in the attic and the voyage of discovery I had taken in the footsteps of the long-dead priest to whom it once belonged. Of all this journey had taught me about the rich heritage of his birthplace and everything the people of Amandola and Italy have had to overcome.

At first, I planned to restore and hang the second painting back in the house too. I dreamt of taking it to the top floor where, on clear starry nights, moonlight floods in through the windows and I imagined it falling on the pale crescent beneath the Madonna's right foot. I saw a synergy in this. For it is when the Moon wanes that a bright arc of rocky peaks on its surface to the south-east of the Sea of Rains, *Mare Imbrium*, can be seen most clearly. These are the lunar Apennines. In the Bible, the Moon is sometimes seen as a reference to the ephemeral nature of life. No further reminder of this is needed than all that has happened in the mountains outside those windows in the aftermath of the 2016–17 earthquakes. But it is the cycles of the Moon that determine cycles of life on Earth and the creation of life itself. Its constant waxing and waning symbolise change. For many, therefore, a waning crescent Moon, the slender sickle that hangs in the sky before the start of a new lunar cycle, is a sign of imminent rebirth. It is a symbol of hope.

In the aftermath of the earthquakes so many living within the area of central Italy designated The Crater lost hope of being able to return to their homes for many years, if ever, and I counted myself immensely fortunate to have been able to return to my own. In light of all this, I began to see that the second painting might, perhaps, offer a glimmer of comfort, even hope, where it was more needed. And so I asked Pierluigi, the culture ministry's representative in Le Marche, to consider where it might best find a new home.

Wherever the painting hangs one day, be it in Amandola or another beleaguered community in the Sibillini, I know I can always call to mind its strange beauty: the Madonna with her halo of stars, the saint said to have sailed across the Straits of Messina with only the wind in his cloak, and the cherub offering up a flaming heart.

Chapter 26

Aside from my own hidden treasures and the plaque on his tomb, there is one lasting trace of Don Federico's time on earth that no traveller along Italy's eastern shore at a certain point can miss: the place on the map where the calf of the Italian boot bulges into the blue-green waters of the Adriatic. There, just south of the sheer white cliffs of the Conero peninsula with its sheltered coves that remind me of the Welsh coastline where I was born, a distinctive silhouette can be seen jutting up from the skyline. A tall circular tower with a conical steeple surrounded by a broad balcony that, from a distance, looks something like a witch's hat.

Those who approach this stretch of coastline by boat, at night, find their watchful gaze drawn to the periodic flashes of light radiating from a lantern at the top of this tower. First, a blink lasting one second. Then another blink lasting two. Followed immediately by the same one- and two-second flashes and after this a pause before the pattern is repeated. These are the visual *dits* and *dahs* that signal the letter C in Morse code. When a thick mist or fog descends, and the lights can no longer be seen, a low bellowing can be heard through the murk from a foghorn that once sat by the side of the lantern on the brim of the witch's hat, but which is now situated on a man-made spur stretching out to sea.

Far from an exercise in any kind of dark arts, the source of the beams of light that reach out through the night as far as ten nautical miles, can be found on the balcony of the bell tower of what is now the principal church of the busy port of Civitanova Marche. Hence night-time signalling to sailors of the letter C. While there are many churches in Italy dedicated to the souls of those at sea, this red-brick belfry and blue-green copper spire of the Chiesa di Cristo Re is the only one, as far as I am aware, that offers both spiritual and navigational guidance to those who may find themselves lost.

The Italian navy designates Cristo Re's lantern a *faro votivo*, a votive light. This is to distinguish it from larger beacons operated by lighthouses throughout the Italian peninsula and many of Italy's four hundred and fifty islands. Who knows how many seafarers Cristo Re's blinking vigil and deep warning wails have helped steer to safety? How many lives might otherwise have been lost.

I must have driven along this coastline at least a hundred times en route to and from Amandola and the strange silhouette had often caught my eye. But it was not until my search for answers about the last years of Don Federico's life led me from the mountains to the coast that I realised neither the church of Cristo Re nor its beacon of light would have existed but for him. In one last attempt to unravel the mystery surrounding the century-old earthquake map of Sicily that had intrigued me for so long, I remembered the words of the prelate Don Giovanni Mammino as he tugged on the bells of the church in the shadow of Mount Etna: 'Perhaps Bellesi was good at persuading wealthy *padroni* to give their money to good causes,' he said of Don Federico's friendship with Civitanova's richest industrialist of the day Adriano Cecchetti.

Gusts of wind rattled the shutters and thunderclaps heralded heavy rain to come as I sat in the kitchen of a medieval townhouse in the oldest part of the coastal city, Civitanova Alta, talking about the map with one of the busy port's most enthusiastic local historians, Alvise Manni, a local schoolteacher. Alvise's father Giuseppe had been managing director of the Cecchetti factory for nearly thirty years from the early 1960s, by which time it had shifted from production of war materials to the manufacture of railway carriages, and he and his sister Enrica had made a documentary of the factory's one-hundred-year history. Over time we became friends and he helped me unravel something of Don Federico's last years.

Adriano Cecchetti, it transpired, had been a fiery radical and idealist in his youth. At a time when much of Italy was beset by intense social unrest in the 1920s, Cecchetti had built a residential neighbourhood in Civitanova to house his workforce and their families. This was a model village with allotments where workers could grow vegetables and keep chickens, a subsidised general store, a social club, a free canteen for children and free medical treatment when families fell on hard times. Cecchetti's factory and home were less than five hundred yards from the imposing neoclassical church of San Pietro where Don Federico became *parroco*, parish priest, in 1922.

Alvise didn't believe Cecchetti was a regular churchgoer, but many of his workers' families would have been. And if Don Federico had been chaplain to the factory, as he almost certainly would have been, the two men would have known each other well. Given his early idealism and wealth, it was quite possible, said Alvise, that Cecchetti donated funds or collected clothing and furniture to help those caught up in Sicily's devastating earthquakes. Quite possible too that he entrusted these funds to Don Federico, who travelled south to distribute them where needed. We could find no proof of this, however, and it seemed destined to remain speculation. The mystery of how and why the earthquake map of Sicily came to be in my attic, and beside it the paintings, remained unsolved. I finally had to accept that I would likely never know.

The only certainty that did emerge in Civitanova was Don Federico's involvement with Cristo Re and the fact that it was he who secured land close to the seafront where it could be built. It was he who travelled to Rome to lobby the Vatican and the culture ministry for initial funds for the project after convincing the local archbishop that the expanding port needed a new church, the same archbishop he once praised so fulsomely in a newspaper article. But these funds ran out after foundations for the building were laid. So Don Federico did not live to see his vision realised.

As soon as the Second World War broke out, plans for the Gothic-style church he envisaged were mothballed. After German troops flooded into northern and central Italy three years later, the strategic port of Ancona, and with it Civitanova, came under heavy aerial bombardment by Allied war planes. It was not until the 1950s that construction of a more modern church on the site Don Federico had secured began again. This time money was raised by levying a tax on the proceeds of fish caught by local fishermen. In return, the design of Cristo Re was amended to incorporate a beacon at the top of its bell tower so it could double as a lighthouse.

All this was contained in a brief account Alvise found after searching through old records. Despite the passage of time, he felt it possible there might be others who knew more and invited me one evening to address a small gathering in Civitanova's town hall organised for the launch of a local history book he had edited. It was the first time I had been invited to speak in public in Italian and when the time came I was nervous and did not speak for long. But when I mentioned the founding of the church of Cristo Re was due to the efforts of Don Federico, I heard muttering in the audience and noticed someone shaking their head. I stopped for a moment to give whoever it was a chance to speak out. No one did. At the end of the evening, I tried to find the person I thought had raised his voice, but he had left. It felt as if a ghost had slipped from the room.

Some time later, a member of the audience and dedicated collector of old photos and postcards contacted me to say he had discovered a card connected to Civitanova bearing Don Federico's name for sale on eBay. He made a bid on my behalf, and I waited weeks for it to arrive through the post, hoping it might shed some light, however small, on the last years of Don Federico's life. But rather than being a further piece of personal correspondence, as I had hoped, it turned out to be a small prayer card with his name and position, *Parroco F. Bellesi*, printed at the bottom. The prayer was a plea to the Virgin Mary for the safe return of those who made their living at sea. On the front of the card, alongside a sepia image of the *Madre di Misericordia*, Mother of Mercy, its edges stained with what I presumed to be seawater, three words had been scrawled in pencil in a shaky hand: *ricordo di Mamma*, a memory of Mum. It was a token of love, no doubt tucked in a sailor's pocket in the hope that his next voyage would not be his last.

Perhaps Don Federico had eventually come to love the coast as much as he did the mountains. Perhaps his love of nature and fascination with the forces that shape our planet had led in later years to a fascination with and respect for the power of the sea.

From all Alvise told me, it was clear Don Federico did not live to see the second horseman of the Apocalypse trample his coastal parish of Civitanova underfoot. His body was brought back to Amandola and laid to rest beside that of his father in the summer of 1940, three months before Italy entered the Second World War. His death was sudden and unexpected. This, I learnt, finally, in a long-distance phone call to a small town on the palm-fringed northern coast of the Dominican Republic.

My friend and neighbour Cesare, a jeweller with a workshop in the same lane as my house, had an old telephone number for Don

Federico's great-nephew, also called Federico, who had gone to live on the island many years before. The two men were friends but had not spoken in a while, so Cesare doubted the number was up to date. But when I called one evening a male voice answered in Spanish laced with an Italian lilt. It was strange to think I was speaking with someone surrounded by the warm lapping waters of the Caribbean about the ending of a life so deeply rooted far away in the Italian mountains. And yet, after I explained who I was, Federico told me we had met once, on the terrace of the Hotel Paradiso years earlier, long before the story of his family took hold of me.

I had entirely forgotten the brief encounter, but it must have been shortly after I bought the house he inherited from his mother Ana, the daughter of Don Federico's sister Rosina. Before I discovered its hidden treasures. The young policeman, who I had met with his mother while signing the purchase papers in the notary's office, was his son. I had a sense that family relations were complicated and tense, but Federico relaxed when we began speaking of his *zio prete*, uncle priest.

A retired accountant and avid Beatles fan, Federico was named after his great-uncle, he explained, though he never knew him since he was born eight years after Don Federico died. But he had grown up hearing his grandmother Rosina speak of her brother with great affection. 'She always told me how well educated he was. How he loved writing and how, above all, *soprattutto*, he loved the mountains *molto, moltissimo*,' very, very much, he recalled.

'She used to say he was always *in azione*,' that he liked to be doing things all the time, he continued, and remembered his grandmother describing her brother as *molto pignolo, molto preciso*, very pernickety and precise. 'He wanted everything to be done properly, just so,' he recalled, saying Rosina was just the same. But above all, Federico remembered how often his grandmother spoke of her brother's untimely death and how she would repeat the same phrase over and over: '*Non doveva morire, non doveva morire!*' he didn't have to die! 'It was a simple operation. A problem with his bladder. He was admitted to hospital in Macerata and should have been home in a few days. But something went wrong. It was an enormous shock for *Nonna*. She was devastated. She never really got over it,' Federico said of Rosina, who outlived her elder brother by more than thirty years.

He knew nothing about anything being hidden away in the attic and showed little interest when I mentioned the letters and paintings. When I asked if he had any photographs of his great-uncle, he said no, that most family photos had been lost in various house moves. That there was really nothing more he could tell me. But that if his small pension allowed him to visit Amandola again one day he would call me so we could meet.

As I put down the phone it felt as if I had come to the end of the line. Perhaps it was Rosina who hid Don Federico's belongings in the attic after all. I thought of her trudging, grief-stricken after his funeral, up the narrow, cobbled lane to the house and, unable to bear seeing anything in the old family home that reminded her of her beloved brother, handing everything of his she could find up to her husband Gabriele crouched in the loft.

How the house must have echoed with Rosina's sorrow after her brother was lost. The thought of it made me shiver. And yet she had returned for the few following summers and sat knitting and gossiping with Attilio's mother in the shade of the arbour while Attilio played nearby. The thought of Attilio's childish babbling and the sound of him playing hide and seek with friends in the garden was more of a comfort. But the fact remained, the house was eventually abandoned and its shutters firmly barred. Until I threw them open, drunk at the sight of the Sibillini mountains, all those years later.

The last voyage any of us makes is one that takes us into the unknown, its timing and manner the ultimate uncertainty we all face. While our mortal remains may be buried or scattered to the wind, I belong to the school of thought that believes something of what some call our spirit lingers long after we have gone. It was this belief that drew me back to the Bellesi family chapel once again.

In contrast to the summer heat of my earlier visit, the cemetery was exposed to icy blasts from the mountains that late January day, *un giorno della merla*, or blackbird day as Italians would say, traditionally the coldest time of year when, according to legend, even blackbirds, once feathered white, sought shelter in chimneys and emerged covered in soot. The wooden kiosk selling flowers at the entrance was shut and I didn't see a soul as I wound my way through the maze of more recent tombs to those from another age towards the rear. Pulling the collar of my coat close to my ears, I took in the long span of years that all six who lay in the chapel had spent on this earth. All, that is, but Don Federico.

I wondered how his life might have unfolded had it not been cut short by what sounded like medical negligence. Would he, with his love of nature, walking, poetry, writing and, above all, his devotion to the Sibillini, have returned in later years to once again serve a quiet rural parish in the mountains? Might he have written more books? Had he lived in the present day would he have devoted his life to studying the natural world rather than the mysteries of faith in a world beyond? Become a scientist instead of a priest? Dedicated himself to examining the wonders and fragility of nature rather than attending to the frailties of his flock?

After returning to my Amandola home following the earthquakes, I sometimes felt Don Federico's presence there more strongly than I had before. Not in a morbid way, but in recognition that the house held traces of his life and memories and, more intangibly, his dreams and secret longings. I felt it that day in the cemetery too. So, as I stood looking up at the small, round, black and white portrait of him in the family vault, his kind face and wistful eyes gazing off into the distance, I silently asked for his forgiveness.

'Forgiveness for what?' he might have asked, were he to address me from behind the fretted screen of a confessional box.

'For reading your letters. Laying your life, or what I have understood of it at least, bare to others.'

I knew this imagined dialogue with the past was a little foolish. Not having been raised a Catholic, I had never formally sought any kind of spiritual absolution. But I felt, if not guilt, then a sense of responsibility, and so another question formed in my mind.

'Do you mind that I have written everything I have about you?'

'It depends on why you have done it,' he might have answered, 'What did you hope to achieve with all your searching and delving into my past?'

The only answer I could give Don Federico that day was my hope that what I had written might make some readers care more about his beloved birthplace with its rich history stretching back a thousand years, and about what the future might hold, not only for Amandola, but for other struggling communities in the Italian mountains.

But there was more to it than this, I realised. Another more personal reason. For me, the uncovering of everything he left behind was not only a journey into Amandola's past; it was part of a quest I had begun long before. A way of finding a light to follow through the darkness. A way of understanding how to accept impermanence and uncertainty and how to stay balanced when the earth beneath us begins to dance, wherever and in whatever way that might be.

The strange voyage of discovery I took in his company taught me something else that my previous wanderings had not. Counter to my journalistic instincts, it taught me greater patience in living with ambiguity and the unknown. What the great Romantic poet John Keats once called negative capability: a way of being with 'uncertainties, Mysteries and doubts, without any irritable reaching after fact and reason'.

Moonlight

'It is a beautiful and delightful sight to behold the body of the Moon.'

Galileo Galilei, *Sidereus Nuncius* (1610)

Chapter 27

On the day the great Renaissance master Raphael breathed his last, the earth beneath the Eternal City of Rome shuddered with a fleeting earthquake. Small cracks are said to have appeared on the cheeks of angels he painted on the walls of the Vatican Palace, as if nature mourned his passing. The words inscribed on his sarcophagus in the Pantheon read: 'Here lies Raphael by whom, while he lived, Mother Nature feared to be defeated and when he died, feared she would die too.'

Five hundred years after his death in 1520, at the age of just thirty-seven, his extraordinary brief life and work were to be the focus of global celebrations. Tens of thousands of people were expected to visit an unprecedented exhibition of his paintings in Rome's Scuderie palace. Countless more events were arranged in countries around the world. But nowhere was there more pride and excitement about the upcoming quincentenary than in Le Marche where celebrations at the achievements of its most famous native son were heralded as offering a beacon of light in the wake of the preceding four tortuous years.

In recognition of the importance of the upcoming anniversary the *New York Times* nominated Le Marche, and in particular Urbino, the northern *marchigiana* city where Raffaello Sanzio, Raphael, was born, as one of the most noteworthy places to visit in 2020, while *Lonely Planet* placed Le Marche on its list of the world's top ten destinations for travellers to discover, second only to the Central Asian Silk Road.

As the year got underway the vivid scarlet, indigo and golden robes of Raphael's masterpieces adorned posters on walls throughout Italy, including in the colonnade of Amandola's main square. Bursts of colour that brightened the winter gloom, rivalled only by the vibrant blaze with which Amandola sprang to life on the last Sunday before Lent in late February. Women in fluorescent pink and purple plumed head-dresses paraded through the streets. Children dressed as chicks with fluorescent orange beaks and yellow capes, others as exotic flowers and birds, followed in their wake. When the streets were filled with music and men and women wearing traditional *marchigiana* dress danced the boisterous *saltarello* behind a sign that read: '*Come una volta, tra natura e passione!*', Life as it was once lived, in nature and with passion!

This was *Carnevale* and the theme of the day was climate change and global warming. Michele from the hardware store was there dressed as a penguin, his friend Fabiano as an iceberg, another as a whale – all collapsing with great theatrics and flailing to squeals of laughter from the children watching. My kind *geometra* Gianni, who helped me so much when I first bought my house, was there dressed as the Pope, accompanied by a pizza-eating bishop, mitre askew, dispensing blessings from the flatbed of a lorry. There were whistles blaring, children eating ice cream and cheers from the crowd as the procession of trucks and tractors transformed into floats wound its way up the hill, one of them decorated as *Amandola-Amazzonia* festooned with paper palm trees and parrots. The piazza was packed and on the steps of the town hall a giant puppet of a clown with red striped trousers had been erected and was leering over the jostling, laughing throng.

Oreste was there with Manuela and their two young children, Luisa with Dom, along with Nicola Kardos, Luigi Bellesi and, in the middle of the throng, the mayor Adolfo Marinangeli. Luana, the owner of my favourite fruit shop, stood smiling, arms crossed, on the steps of the restaurant run by her son, the one that served my favourite *pizza bianca al tartufo*. Antonio was there with his grandsons Alessandro and Giorgio, Alessandro now grown taller than his *nonno*. We could barely hear each other above the commotion. But when I spotted Antonio's nephew Luigi, the road sweeper, on the edge of the crowd and tried to persuade him to break into song, he threw his head back and laughed '*La prossima volta*,' – next time.

It was the first time since the earthquakes that Amandola seemed alive with smiling faces and an atmosphere of fun. Though many in The Crater were still struggling, there was finally the beginning of a sense of hope and optimism in the air.

Within a few days all this evaporated.

Less than a fortnight after Amandola echoed with the music and laughter of its first exuberant carnival since the earthquakes, an eerie silence descended over the town. The stillness of the main square was broken only by the insistent flapping of a poster of Raphael's rare vision of beauty, torn loose by the wind. Four days after the once-in-a-lifetime exhibition of Raphael's work opened to great fanfare in Rome, the doors of the Scuderie palace were shut, the final painting in the exhibition – a self-portrait of the artist with calm but questioning eyes – plunged into the dark. Beyond the palace walls, the Piazza del Quirinale where the museum sits was all but deserted. As was the normally packed St Peter's Square in the Vatican City. As were streets and squares throughout Italy and, increasingly, elsewhere in the world.

More than seven hundred years after Amandola lost half of its population to the bubonic plague, and a century after millions perished worldwide from Spanish flu, the white horse of pestilence envisioned by John the Apostle in a bygone age once again set about trampling the earth. A virus first identified in China just two months earlier, which even the week before the carnival had not officially received the name by which it came to be known, novel coronavirus SARS CoV-19 or simply Covid-19, had begun silently stalking the global population. And, in Europe, Italy was the first country to feel the full brutal force of the oncoming viral storm.

In stark contrast to the aftermath of the earthquakes, when the people of Amandola and elsewhere in central Italy feared remaining in their houses as the ground shook, once Italy became the epicentre of the shifting global pandemic, all Italians were ordered to stay in their homes, with the threat of hefty fines if they did not. As virtually all flights in and out of Italy were cancelled, and those with any future travel plans were advised to leave, I flew back to London believing I would be back in my mountain home within a matter of months. No one at the time could conceive of the scale of the catastrophe that would unfold.

In contrast to the deafening noise that issued from deep beneath the earth in the central Italian mountains four years earlier, this latter-day plague led to a quietening of our entire planet. Aside from the incessant sound of sirens accompanying those rushed to hospital, and the tolling of bells for those who did not make it, the global din tied to human activity was temporarily silenced. Nature made a resurgence. Birdsong was heard more clearly. Dolphins patrolled docksides where boats bobbed, abandoned. Shoals of tiny fish repopulated Venice's empty canals. The word uncertainty was on everyone's lips. Suddenly everyone everywhere was thrown onto shifting terrain. And it seemed never-ending.

In those first weeks and months of the pandemic there was a profound realisation of individual frailty. Every one of us came to appreciate more deeply the most basic of things we take for granted: the ability to breathe deeply, gather with friends and loved ones, feel another's touch, walk freely in nature. A reminder, yet again, that what we hold dear can disappear in the blink of an eye: our health, our home, life itself.

Some spoke early on of the global seismic shock as an opening for change. An opportunity to reimagine and re-evaluate the way we live and to truly understand the fragility not only of our relationships with each other but with the natural world.

During the first lull in the Covid storm, when many believed, or at least hoped, the worst of the pandemic had passed, thousands of city dwellers confined for months in concrete-sprawl flocked to the countryside, including to the Sibillini mountains, gasping for fresh air and contact with nature. As remote working became the norm some speculated this could lead to a revival of Italy's semi-abandoned hill towns and villages. But just as suddenly as they came, the crowds dispersed. In The Crater, where so many were still sheltering in temporary homes, some spoke of the pandemic as a *colpo di grazia*, a *coup de grâce* for communities they feared might never revive.

In the earliest days of the pandemic, however, Amandola remained relatively unscathed. Tucked away in the mountains, in the first wave of what would become a rolling tempest, there were less than a handful of cases and all who fell ill recovered. But as the first summer of the pandemic turned to autumn then winter, successive waves of the virus began to take their toll. Three of my neighbours fell ill, two of them brothers, one of whom died of the disease. The two brothers were the sons of Delia, the old lady who I often greeted as she walked her little dog up the lane past my house. Two months earlier Delia had died too, though of an unrelated illness. Delia's surviving son Michele once boasted to me that his mother was 'the most photographed woman in the world, more photographed even than Michelle Pfeiffer'. This because, in the summer months, she used to sit by her open bedroom window, high up overlooking the main square, waving to passers-by and tourists who often took her picture.

Delia was nearly a hundred years old when she died, and when she was laid to rest, not far from Don Federico, the black and white photo on her grave showed her sitting in that same high window knitting, a gentle smile of her face. Due to Covid restrictions, none of the traditional funeral rites still common in small Italian communities could be observed – those where a procession of villagers or towns-people follows a hearse to the cemetery and shops lower their blinds as it passes out of respect. That winter all gatherings were forbidden and most shops were under government orders to remain closed.

As the pandemic ground on into its second and then third year, there was growing talk of the need for concerted global reflection. Many foresaw it shifting societies' tectonic plates. For just as fault lines, when they rupture, leave deep gashes in the landscape and expose bare rock, so this modern-day plague unmasked existing fractures in society, deep inequalities and profound injustice. Then, just as the global dread of the disease began to recede, humanity's tectonic plates once again shifted on a catastrophic scale. When the red horse of war, followed by those of hunger and death, once again stalked the continent of Europe in Ukraine, all the seeming certainties of the post-cold war world order stood on the verge of collapse. The aftershocks of which will be felt for generations to come.

Astronomers have termed the twenty-first century probably the most pivotal in human history. With the human species now so numerous and conflicted, and consuming nature's resources at such speed with so little regard for the consequences, some believe that, without radical action, our wounded planet could become virtually lifeless within a few generations.

Through the ages it is the unknown that has driven our thirst for knowledge. Uncertainty has fuelled the imagination, propelled discov-eries, opened up possibilities in ways that certainty could not. The speed with which new vaccines against Covid were developed by scientists collaborating around the world was proof that given global co-operation the seemingly impossible could be achieved. Some described the aspiration to vaccinate every person on earth against the disease as the immuno-logical equivalent of the moonshot. But while science has provided solutions to many catastrophes and led to countless discoveries that have improved our lives, there is much that remains beyond the understanding and control of man, and always will, and probably always should. For we are only a small part of nature and need look no further to understand this than the extraordinary inner workings of our planet.

In the quiet of the evening, when I was finally able to return to my Italian home, I stood looking out at the Sibillini mountains bathed in moonlight. On the wall behind me hung three photographs, all taken far out in space by the crew of *Apollo 15* and given to me by the crew's commander, David Scott. One of the photographs shows him walking on the surface of the Moon, to the west of the Sea of Serenity, *Mare Serenitatis*, so named by the Italian priest and astronomer Giovanni Baptista Riccioli, as were other lunar craters four centuries ago in recognition of mankind's varying states of mind. In the background, and reflected in the glass of Scott's visor, are the *Montes Apenninus*, the lunar Apennines, the Moon's highest mountains, named after their Italian counterpart over two hundred thousand miles away on the Earth below. The second photograph, captured with a Hasselblad on board the Apollo spacecraft, is an image of the Moon showing the Sea of Tranquillity, *Mare Tranquillitatis*, near the Sea of Crisis, *Mare Crisium*, clearly visible on its pockmarked surface.

The third photograph, taken by the crew thirty thousand or so miles from Earth, shows our blue marbled planet in its delicate moist membrane with the white swirl of a North Atlantic storm sweeping westwards from Greenland. Thirty years after he set foot on the surface of the Moon in 1971, one of only twelve men ever to have done so, Scott spoke to me of the moment he stood in the fine soot-like dust of the lunar surface looking back at our blue planet. And how, when he held up his stiff, gloved thumb, our shared terrestrial home disappeared entirely from view.

Of the many hours we spent talking together in a room over-looking the River Thames, and the many more I spent in Moscow's Star City speaking with the Russian cosmonaut Alexei Leonov when I collaborated on writing the two men's interwoven memoirs, it was Scott's fleeting description of the ease with which our own cherished planet could be obliterated, if only momentarily, that left the deepest impression on me. His conviction too, and that of many, that unless we humans protect and nurture our planet, everything with meaning – music, poetry, literature, art, science and history – will disappear in a relatively short period of time, just as our vibrant globe vanished with that one small twist of his thumb. After all, it is the perspective of such early space explorers witnessing Earth's full beauty from a distance that helped spark the global environmental movement and fuelled a growing awareness of the fragility of the planet we call home.

Thanks to the work of the Apollo moonwalkers, and that of many successive generations of scientists, we also now know it is not only our own planet that experiences seismic shifts. Moonquakes, starquakes, sunquakes and quakes on Venus and Mars have also been detected. Seismology is now an interplanetary science. As is geology, with rock samples brought back to Earth from space missions far beyond anything Don Federico might have dreamt possible as he stooped to collect samples for Amandola's children on his solitary walks through the Sibillini.

Sometimes, when not in Amandola and I look up at night, I think of the Moon casting her light on the cobbles of the main square. If I follow this light, and the shadows it creates, up the pedestrian lane to the front door of my house, I can step inside in my imagination and once again feel a sense of peace. I am thankful then for having been able to bring this long-abandoned home back from the brink of ruin, not once but twice, and to have done everything I can to make sure it is able to withstand the dancing of the earth beneath for years to come.

Whatever we do and wherever we live for any length of time, we all leave traces of our lives hidden in the stones. Few as mysterious as those left by Don Federico Bellesi. But we are all only ever temporary custodians of the places in which we live. So, long after my Italian home has passed into another's hands, the Moon will continue to illuminate its garden, planted differently no doubt, and move silently across the night sky, shining first through one window then another to inspire someone else's dreams.

As long as I live, however, the sights and sounds of Amandola and kindness of its people will always stay with me. The song of the blackbird in the pear tree at the end of my garden. The smell of bread baking in ovens close by and coffee brewing in the Gran Caffè Belli. The tolling of the bells of the church of Saint Augustine and the high-pitched chorus of swifts circling its campanile.

Swifts are restless birds and remain in flight for most of their lives. They rarely touch the ground and can, it is said, fly the equivalent of eight times to the Moon and back before they perish. There was a time when they were thought to hibernate in mud at the bottom of lakes and ponds when they disappeared in the autumn and winter months. This led some to call them Devil's Birds. Others saw them as symbols of the resurrection – beings that linked two worlds as they soared from beneath the earth towards the heavens. Scientists now believe swifts use the earth's magnetic field and the sun and stars as a compass to navigate their way from Africa where they winter to the sites in Europe where they nest every year. Moreover, it is known that successive generations return to these exact same sites, often nooks in church spires, perhaps over centuries.

There is no evidence I know of that speaks of humans possessing a similarly remarkable homing instinct. And yet, there are places that inexplicably pull at something deep inside so that, no matter how far we roam, we are drawn to return to them. For me, regardless or perhaps because of its fragile beauty, that place is Amandola. The Welsh have a word for this that has no direct English equivalent: *hiraeth*. Some translate it as homesickness. But *hiraeth* has a deeper meaning too. It conveys both a yearning and nostalgia, sometimes tinged with grief, for something that has been lost and is not necessarily a place. A feeling of longing, as one Welsh-born writer put it, 'for something greater than a spot on the map.'

I like to think that the swifts I see from my window in Amandola are descendants of those Don Federico would have seen and heard as he walked down the lane to the square of a morning or as he returned home from evening prayers.

As darkness falls, swifts are known to spiral up towards the stars. They sleep on the wing. I doubt they dream. Often, they keep one eye open. So, as I slip towards sleep, I think of them drifting high above, dark iridescent scimitar wings glistening in the moonlight, keeping watch on all below.

Acknowledgements

A heartfelt thank you to all of the following:

Firstly, to my agent Mark Lucas who took this story to his heart and has tirelessly championed, and gently guided it from the start. To Weidenfeld & Nicolson's former chairman and non-fiction publisher Alan Samson who did the same with great care and unstinting support as my first editor. And to Ellie Freedman, Lettice Franklin and all those at Orion whose dedication and enthusiasm carried it forward once the editorial baton was passed.

To my immensely supportive friends, family and early readers for their faith in me and this book and for keeping my spirits afloat through truly tumultuous times. Not least John Cornwell for his generous counsel and endless patience with my questions on matters ecclesiastical and so much more; Jonathan Margolis, for his keen insights, good humour and boundless encouragement; Ellen Hampton, Pauline Betts, Fiona Biggs, Nicola Webb, Susan White, David Williams and Emma Vickers who offered thoughtful suggestions and reflections as my writing progressed.

To the many endlessly kind Amandolesi who welcomed me to their mountain home and helped make it my own. Special thanks to the Bellesi family for sharing their memories and to Luisa Pieroni for helping to bring those memories and the mysterious history of my house to life. To all those in this book and the many others besides who took the time, amid their own troubles, to tell me their stories and help me stay balanced as the mountains danced. And in Sicily to those who helped me journey back in time to the island's tortured past, most notably Eleonora Iannelli and her family.

And finally, to my darling daughter Inés, always there with open arms, a warm heart and wisdom beyond her years, and Enrico, without whom this journey of love would never have begun.

Quoted Material

p.vii   Darwin, Charles. 1839. *Voyages of the Adventure and Beagle, Volume III – Journal and Remarks, 1832–1836.* London: Henry Colburn.

p.1   Erri De Luca. 2016. *'Naufragio in terra'.* Fondazion Erri De Luca: www.fondazionerrideluca.com/naufragio/.

p.5   C.S. Lewis. 1941. 'The Weight of Glory: A sermon given at Oxford University Church of St Mary the Virgin on June 8, 1941'. *Theology, November 1941.*

p.11   Leopardi, Giacomo. 1835. *'Le Ricordanze'. Canti.* Naples: Saverio Starita.

p.18   Massi, Francesco. *'Rinvenuta in una casa del centro storico una bomba razzo risalente alla seconda guerra mondiale pronta ad esplodere'. Corriere Adriatico.* 15 September 2004.

p.20   ibid.

p.34   Kreiner, Paul. *'Ein Totenanz von apoklayptischem Ausmaß'. Stuttgarter Zeitung.* 18 December 2008.

p.34   Casalini, Simona. Gagliardi, Giovanni. Matteucci, Piera. *'Terremoto di 6,5 tra Norcia e Preci. È il più forte in Italia dal 1980. "Si temeno 100mila sfollati"'. La Repubblica.* 30 October 2016.

p.46–7   *Il Resto del Carlino*. 13 December 2017.

p.54   Leopardi, Giacomo. 1835. *'Il tramonto della luna'. Canti*. Naples: Saverio Starita.

p.55   Leopardi, Giacomo. 1835. *'Canto notturno di un pastore errante dell'Asia'. Canti*. Naples: Saverio Starita.

p.55   D'Avenia, Alessandro. 2016. *L'Arte di essere fragili*. Milan: Mondadori.

p.56   Le Pichon, Xavier. 3 October 2017. Lecture from Session 1, William Smith Meeting 2017: Plate Tectonics at 50. London: The Geological Society.

p.60   Zagari, Guglielmo. 1910. *'L'Emigrazione'. Rivista Marchigiana Illustrata*.

p.68   Saviano, Roberto. *'Quando la terra trema, il cemeto uccide'. La Repubblica*. 14 April 2009.

p.85   Calvino, Italo. 1972. *Le città invisibili*. Turin: Giulio Einaudi Editore.

p.87   Yourcenar, Marguerite. 1951. *Mémoires d'Hadrien*. Paris: Librairie Plon; English language trans. Yourcenar, Marguerite. 1954. *Hadrian's Memoirs*. New York: Farrar, Straus and Giroux.

p.93   Hutton, Edward. 1913. *The Cities of Romagna and the Marches*. New York City: The Macmillan Company.

p.98   Ferrero, Augusto. *'Cavalcando'*.

p.98   Ferrero, Augusto. *'Perché?'*.

p.99   Mazzucchetti, Augusto. *'Rondinelle di Dogali'*.

p. 104   Guasco, Maurilio. 1971. *Fermenti nei seminari del primo
            '900*. Bologna: Edizioni Dehoniane.

p.106   ibid.

p.106   'La bancarotta del Darwinismo'. *La Voce*. 15 February
            1906.

p.107   Di Vito, Mario. 2019. *Dopo: Viaggio al termine del
            cratere*. Alberobello: Poiesis.

p. 119   Michels, Roberto. 1912. *I Limiti della morale sessuale*.
            Milano: Fratelli Bocca Editori.

p.133   Durrell, Lawrence. 1957. *Justine*. London: Faber and
            Faber.

p.151   Pascoli, Giovanni. 1914. *Pensieri e discorsi*. Bologna:
            Nicola Zanichelli Editore.

p.153   Special correspondent. 'Messina destroyed in twelve
            seconds'. *The New York Times*. 24 January 1909.

p.154   Douglas, Norman. 1915. *Old Calabria*. London: Martin
            Secker.

p.155   Special correspondent. 'One wild shriek and all was over'.
            The New York Times. 24 January 1909.

p.156   *Giornale di Sicilia*. 24 December 1908.

p.158   Dickie, John. Foot, John. Snowden, Frank. 2002. *Disastro!
            Disasters in Italy Since 1860*. New York: Palgrave
            Macmillan.

p.166   Campo, Saveria. 1997. 'Fragilità dell'Essere'. *Voli*. Messina:
            self-published.